THE LETTER OF THE LAW
IN J. E. CASELY HAYFORD'S WEST AFRICA

The Letter of the Law in J. E. Casely Hayford's West Africa

Jeanne-Marie Jackson

PRINCETON UNIVERSITY PRESS
PRINCETON & OXFORD

Copyright © 2026 by Princeton University Press

Princeton University Press is committed to the protection of copyright and the intellectual property our authors entrust to us. Copyright promotes the progress and integrity of knowledge created by humans. By engaging with an authorized copy of this work, you are supporting creators and the global exchange of ideas. As this work is protected by copyright, any reproduction or distribution of it in any form for any purpose requires permission; permission requests should be sent to permissions@press.princeton.edu. Ingestion of any IP for any AI purposes is strictly prohibited.

Published by Princeton University Press
41 William Street, Princeton, New Jersey 08540
99 Banbury Road, Oxford OX2 6JX

press.princeton.edu

GPSR Authorized Representative: Easy Access System Europe - Mustamäe tee 50, 10621 Tallinn, Estonia, gpsr.requests@easproject.com

All Rights Reserved

ISBN 9780691270999
ISBN (pbk.) 9780691271002
ISBN (e-book) 9780691271019

Library of Congress Control Number: 2025936706

British Library Cataloging-in-Publication Data is available
Editorial: Anne Savarese and Emma Wagh
Production Editorial: Sara Lerner
Cover Design: Katie Osborne
Production: Erin Suydam
Publicity: William Pagdatoon
Copyeditor: Melanie Mallon
Cover Credit: Ivan Vdovin / Alamy

This book has been composed in Miller

10 9 8 7 6 5 4 3 2 1

For Adwoa Opoku-Agyemang

Oguaanyi papaapa

CONTENTS

Acknowledgments · ix
Important Dates · xi

Introduction: The "How" Behind the
"Who" of Gold Coast Letters ... 1

CHAPTER 1 A Matter-of-Fact Kind of Man ... 30
The Gold Coast Intellectual Situation ... 31
Truth in Plain View ... 40
The "Educated Native" in Profile ... 56

CHAPTER 2 A Gold Coast Constitution ... 68
A Foundational Inheritance ... 70
The Novel and the Constitutionalist ... 82
Personality in the Balance ... 94
Constitutionalism's Spiritual Shadow ... 98

CHAPTER 3 The Jurisdiction of Morals ... 105
The Bond of 1844 as Jurisdictional Modernity ... 106
A Rightful Order ... 116
Citation's Moral Lines ... 130

Epilogue: Where in the World
Is J. E. Casely Hayford? ... 141

Notes · 149
Works Cited · 175
Index · 183

ACKNOWLEDGMENTS

THIS BOOK came to fruition during the busiest stretch so far of my adult life. I'd not have had it any other way, but it means I owe a truly immense debt of gratitude to the people and organizations who made researching and writing it possible. Thanks to a career-changing Andrew Carnegie Fellowship in 2021 and Johns Hopkins's generous leave policies, I was able to devote multiple full semesters across four years entirely to this project. Krieger School deans Chris Cannon and Chris Celenza offered essential support, as did Mark Thompson and Sally Hauf as (respectively) chair and administrative manager of the English Department. Jamison Murphy was a superb research assistant. At Princeton University Press, I am grateful to my editor, Anne Savarese, for shepherding this project to completion, as well as to the two anonymous readers who offered thoughtful and encouraging comments at both early and later stages of its development. Archive staff at PRAAD in Accra and Cape Coast, the British Library, SOAS special collections, and especially Celia Pilkington at the Inner Temple were a great and friendly help.

For organizing talks that helped me work through the book's finer points, I thank Bryan Wagner at UC Berkeley; Margaret Cohen at Stanford; Madhu Krishnan at the University of Bristol; Grace Musila at Wits; Chris Ouma at the University of Cape Town; Cajetan Iheka at Yale; John Hoffman at the University of Marburg; Elizabeth Anker at Cornell; Nasser Mufti at NAVSA; Patrick Fessenbecker at Bilkent; and Mukti Mangharam and Seth Koven at Rutgers. I also thank Kwabena Opoku-Agyemang for serving as a respondent for the Wits talk, as well as Imraan Coovadia at UCT and Grant Farred and Gautam Hans at Cornell for the same. Small parts of this book were first worked out in invited chapters published in the Bloomsbury edition *African Literatures as World Literatures*, edited by Alex Fyfe and Madhu Krishan, and in *The Cambridge History of the British Essay*, edited by Denise Gigante and Jason Childs.

I am consistently awed by the quality and range of my intellectual company. I love coming to work among both long-time and new faculty in the Johns Hopkins English Department: Sharon Achinstein, Mary Favret, Andrew Miller, Larry Jackson, Jared Hickman, Nadia Nurhussein, Jesse Rosenthal, Drew Daniel, Chris Cannon, Johaina Crisostomo, Doug Mao, Chris Nealon, Aamir Mufti, Nan Z. Da, Harris Feinsod, Chris Grobe, and Michaela Bronstein. Jesse is the best "work spouse" a workaholic like me could ask for, and the reunion of Yale's "three musketeers" feels like a dream. At Johns Hopkins beyond English, I'm grateful for drinks, conversations, and collaboration with Dora Malech, Yi-Ping Ong, Lucy Allais, Abe Stoll, Liz Thornberry, Minkah Makalani, Lester Spence, Bill Egginton, Francois Furstenberg, Alice Mandell, Dawn Teele, Paul Delnero, and Kofi Ofori, who is much missed. To Dora, Jesse, Harris, Yi-Ping, Chris, and Michaela: happy hours are never sad. Theresa and Tyran—the "Snark Club"—light up my texts with academic laughs. And away from the Homewood campus, I'm grateful for enduring intellectual friendships with Tsitsi Jaji, Maria Taroutina, Tendai Huchu, Imraan Coovadia, Cajetan Iheka, and Sangeeta Ray.

This book would not exist without the extended network of African and postcolonial humanists with whom I was in constant dialogue across the years of its taking shape. In one way or another, it has benefited from exchanges with Ato Quayson (*me nua* and mentor), Olufemi O. Taiwo, Ato Sekyi-Otu, Ebony Coletu, Chris Ouma, Madhu Krishnan, Abena Dove Osseo-Asare, Anakwa Dwamena, Kwasi Prempeh, Emmanuel Gyimah-Boadi, Jennifer Hart, Ankhi Mukherjee, Nana Osei Quarshie, Trevor Getz, Reginald Sekyi-Brown, Barima Peprah-Agyemang, Jeffrey Ahlman, Zeyad El Nabolsy, Mpush Ntabeni, Peter Kalliney, George Hull, Bruce Janz, Kwasi Konadu, Mary-Alice Daniel, Nathan Suhr-Sytsma, Kwabena Opoku-Agyemang, Matthew Taunton, Fui Can-Tamakloe, Ainehi Edoro, Adom Getachew, and Maria Casely-Hayford, as well as others whom I have no doubt neglected to mention. Adwoa Opoku-Agyemang occupies a special place in this book's life, intellectually and personally, and I cannot imagine it without her influence. I also owe a special kind of gratitude to Gus Casely-Hayford, who, as busy as he is, has been unfailingly generous with his time and insight into his grandfather's career.

Finally, I thank my family. My mother, Ellen, sister, Erin, and brother-in-law, Joe, keep me grounded even when times feel tough. My mother-in-law, Francesca, and Awotwi siblings-in-law—Effuah, Zatta, Maame Yahan, and Egyaiku—keep me fueled with new Fante vocabulary and Awotwi lore. I have hugely valued my work with Kweku Awotwi and the Elmina Heritage Foundation. Everything else I owe to my husband, Kwamina, and our son, Benji Eyiku, who together fill my life with daily meaning and joy. In so many ways, this book is an effort to make sense of the long history that extends through them.

IMPORTANT DATES

1866—Joseph Ephraim Casely Hayford born in Anomabu, Gold Coast
1896—Casely Hayford called to the bar at London's Inner Temple
1897—Co-founds the Aborigines' Rights Protection Society (ARPS)
1902—Co-founds the *Gold Coast Leader* and the Fante National Education Fund
1903—Publishes *Gold Coast Native Institutions*
1911—Publishes *Ethiopia Unbound*
1913—Publishes *The Truth about the West African Land Question*
1915—Publishes *William Waddy Harris, the West African Reformer: The Man and His Message*
1916—Joins the Gold Coast Legislative Council
1919—Co-founds the Gold Coast National Education Scheme for secular high schools and publishes *United West Africa*
1920—Hosts inaugural event, in Accra, as co-founder of the National Congress of British West Africa (NCBWA)
1927—Elected Municipal Member for Sekondi on the Legislative Council
1930—Casely Hayford dies in Accra, Gold Coast

THE LETTER OF THE LAW
IN J. E. CASELY HAYFORD'S WEST AFRICA

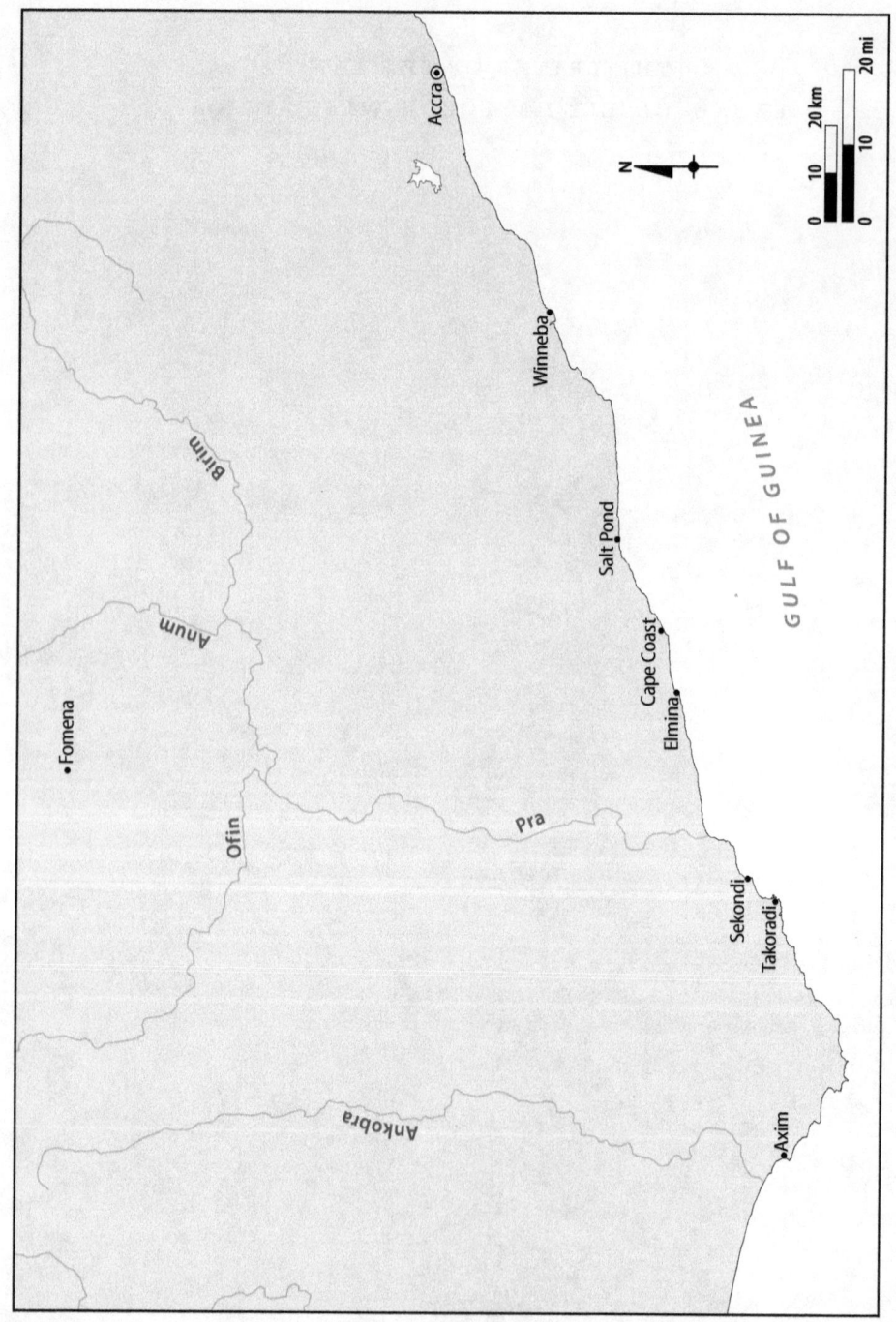

Map. J. E. Casely Hayford's Gold Coast. (Map created by Ron Draddy)

INTRODUCTION

The "How" Behind the "Who" of Gold Coast Letters

THIS IS A book about what it means to be a certain kind of person in a particular time and place. It is not, in other words, a biography but a study of writing as civic-minded self-orchestration: a process of moving elements of history, politics, culture, and ideas around on a page so that they add up to something recognizable, in public, as character. The person doing the "moving" here is J. E. Casely Hayford, the Gold Coast statesman, barrister, newspaper editor, and writer who led the charge to modernize British imperial West Africa in the early twentieth century by way of its indigenous legal and political traditions. In addition to his life's work as an intra-imperial power broker and institution builder, Casely Hayford was the first African to publish a novel in English—*Ethiopia Unbound*—in 1911. That book, his two major customary legal treatises, and a bevy of essays and speeches show collectively how legal concepts can be used to scaffold far-reaching questions of how to be. What sorts of intellectual temperament, habits of mind, and analytic propensities were befitting of a new kind of African leader, who was as much a scholar as a politician? Through what key terms could the shape of a text be made to align with the presentation of a self, at once distinctive enough to command transnational respect but general enough to be a local aspirational "type"? The well-tuned interplay such queries suggest of conceptual frameworks, individual aspirations, and social legibility, at a watershed moment in Africa's intellectual and political history, are best drawn out not by recounting the details of Casely Hayford's life, but by mapping the contours of his thought.

In the chapters that follow I aim to do just that, by pairing each of a series of legal-conceptual terms—facticity, constitutionalism, and jurisdiction—with a major text animated by local historical context. The book proceeds by way of these "lenses" because they can be flipped to magnify either epistemic paradigms or individual qualities, somewhere between which reside principles of textual organization. Casely Hayford's claims to be presenting historical facts, that is to say, also advance a vision of what it looks like to be an objective person, and his writing about constitutionalism foregrounds figures who embody its associated ideals of balance and restraint. Similarly, his interest in signal controversies around legal jurisdiction in the Gold Coast opens up into a multipronged concern with how an ability to make fine distinctions is a leadership credential. In each case, law does double duty as an immediate topic of concern and a conceptual substratum; it binds convention to creativity. To say that Casely Hayford had a "legal mind" is not simply to point to his training in the common law at Peterhouse, Cambridge, and the Inner Temple (one of London's four Inns of Court), or to his scrupulously researched account of indigenous Akan customs. It also invokes patterns of reasoning and composition, in which legal ideas act as levers to move between philosophies of governance and their ideal personification. Casely Hayford was a lawyer who wrote often about law. But what this background allowed him to do, as a writer, is more to this book's point, as it resituates the history of West Africa's intelligentsia within a deep-seated cultural predisposition to text. Law, in Casely Hayford's moment, was the dominant means of thinking through *writtenness* and its valorization as a force for both individual and ethnic cultivation.

J. E. Casely Hayford's body of work is arguably ground zero for studies of the African novel and West African legislative politics, to say nothing of so-called customary law. In addition to writing the first African novel in English, he stood at the helm of three major political organizations across his career: the Aborigines' Rights Protection Society (ARPS), which he co-founded in 1897 as part of an effort to thwart a British override of African systems of land tenure; the National Congress of British West Africa (NCBWA), which he co-founded in 1920 to promote regional institution building and national self-representation; and the Gold Coast Legislative Council, the colony's official law-making body, on which he served from 1916 until his death in 1930.[1] His major treatises on Akan laws and traditions, *Gold Coast Native Institutions* (1903) and *The Truth about the West African Land Question* (1913), are to this day cited as authoritative sources on their subject matter, albeit with little regard for their literary or curatorial dimensions. This does not mean that there were not significant written texts in West Africa before his, or that he is politically foundational in some solitary "Great Man" sense. Casely Hayford was acutely aware of the traditions within which he worked and, as the following chapters show, paid homage at every turn to his peers and predecessors.[2] It means, rather, that he was his era's most emblematic figure, in that he helped author a widely respected set of political ideals around African self-representation that he sought to advance by virtue of being himself. This was no delusion of ego: the Gold Coast newspapers of his day tracked Casely Hayford's comings and goings like a celebrity, with his eminence clearly fulfilling a social need.[3] Such prototypicality means that he is worthy of far more attention than he has received. But it also suggests the need for an approach that gets beyond the common goals, vis-à-vis marginalized intellectual traditions, of "championing" understudied thinkers' accomplishments or restoring them to broad visibility as ends in themselves.

Pre-independence African intellectuals deserve more than reverential recovery when they happen to fall in line with contemporary views; they deserve serious reckoning with their texts *as texts*, and with their ideas on their own terms. The fact that Casely Hayford is exemplary of a bygone moment and milieu—one that backed an elite-led, self-consciously erudite, and liberal-constitutionalist approach to African self-determination within the British Empire—means that his reputation has naturally waned with changing times. Though Ghana's more radical first president, Kwame Nkrumah, was openly indebted to the generation before his, scholars since then have more often picked up the thread of African anticolonial politics with Kwame Nkrumah.[4] Twenty-first-century critics and academics tend to valorize the opposite of many of Casely Hayford's identifying traits and beliefs. The most hard-hitting work on twentieth-century Black thinkers skews toward racial radicalism and global-systemic overhaul, an understandable response to the atavistic politics and rapacious capitalism plaguing even the world's most "developed" nations.[5] It is galvanizing—perhaps comforting—to uncover trajectories of political thought and organization that forestall perceptions of present circumstances' inevitability. And as Jonathon Earle observes in a useful overview of global intellectual history, the field is "increasingly interested in how Africans have shaped the intellectual history of the modern world, a topic that has been understudied."[6] I share an investment in filling in the details of Africans' robust participation in shaping our globalized political modernity; Casely Hayford's leadership of the NCBWA, in particular, is crucial to understanding the bureaucratic mobilization of Pan-Africanist ideals in the early twentieth century. But I am also attuned to how readily African ideas are cherry picked to support Africans' idealization as globally redemptive figures. The desire to recover Africans' prescient, alternative forms of globality and liberatory visions of the future is always fraught, and the work that results from it is often tendentious.

Mamadou Diouf and Jinny Prais, for example, count Casely Hayford alongside the African American intellectuals W.E.B. Du Bois and William Henry Ferris as one of "the first generation of thinkers to seek a more inclusive understanding of universal narratives of the human past and experience," a claim that forms part of a welcome effort to reintegrate Africa and Africans into the thriving field of Black Atlantic studies.[7] At the same time, they adapt the historical details of Casely Hayford's career—no doubt inadvertently—to bolster this project. Diouf and Prais report that the figures at the heart of their chapter crossed paths at "the various congresses such as the Pan-African conferences (1900, 1919, 1945) and the First Universal Race Congress (1911) in western Europe," where "the presence of participants like DuBois and Casely Hayford ... nurtured and strengthened the international connection and dialogue among black intellectuals and launched black global intellectual history." They are committed to the argument that "Black intellectuals traveled in the same black circuit that encompassed the Atlantic world," illustrated by the fact that "Casely Hayford and DuBois, along with other black intellectuals ... were present at the first Pan-African Congress in London in 1900."[8] In actuality, Casely Hayford attended none of these events. His first correspondence with Du Bois seems to have taken place in June 1904, when he sent the American a letter to praise *The Souls of Black Folk* and suggested that "if leading thinkers of the African race in America had the opportunity of exchanging thoughts with thinkers of the race in West Africa, this century would be likely to see the race problem solved."[9] They maintained a very occasional and mutually respectful correspondence until Casely Hayford's death in 1930, but he declined Du Bois's Congress invitations.[10] And while Casely Hayford's ideas were represented at Booker T. Washington's International Conference on the Negro at Tuskegee in April 1912, they seem to have been read there in his absence by his brother, the Methodist minister turned Baptist evangelist Mark C. Hayford.[11] Casely Hayford never traveled to the Americas, nor met W.E.B. Du Bois.

What are we to take from such a pronounced and yet, on the surface, wholly plausible miscasting of the historical record, in one of the few substantive efforts to give Casely Hayford his due as a thinker of global significance? It is certainly not cause to assert a crude juxtaposition between "racial" concerns and "African" ones, which he understood were largely one and the same. Casely Hayford held Du Bois's work at the *Crisis* in high regard and worked throughout his career to advance understanding and exchange between West African and African American intellectuals. He was also influenced by the St. Thomas–born Edward Wilmot Blyden's thinking on the "African Personality" during his time at Fourah Bay College in Sierra Leone, which was then known as "the Athens of Africa" because of its flourishing cultural life. The West Indian writer and diplomat had relocated there from his adopted neighboring homeland of Liberia after losing a bid for its presidency in 1885 and attracted a cohort of learned West African admirers. *Ethiopia Unbound*, in a fictional speech by its main character, grants Blyden a position of singular wisdom, opining, "The work of men like Booker T. Washington and W. E. Burghart Du Bois is exclusive and provincial. The work of Edward Wilmot Blyden is universal, covering the entire race and the entire race problem."[12] By no means, then, did Casely Hayford hold Africa at a distance from questions of Black oppression or advancement.

But his views later diverged from Blyden's, too. While both men believed the British Empire would rise to its greatest heights through African leadership and encouraged British "development of the natives along the lines of their own idiosyncrasies as revealed in their institutions," Casely Hayford grew to place a greater premium than his diasporic elder on the role of born and bred West Africans in shaping the region's political program.[13] In general, as his career in the Legislative Council progressed, his politics and self-location moved among three concrete geographies: London; British West Africa (the Gold Coast, Sierra Leone, the Gambia, and Nigeria); and the towns of what today is known as Ghana's Central Region (especially Cape Coast, Sekondi, and Axim). His foremost cultural concern through the early decades of the twentieth century was with cultivating a distinctive national character and political space for Fante—which, as the second largest group within West Africa's Akan meta-ethnicity, even today number only between two and three million people—whom he and his peers saw as equipped to steer not just the Gold Coast but all of British imperial civilization toward its spiritual zenith. Casely Hayford wrote amid what then was called the "Gone Fante Movement," described in the *Gold Coast Leader* on March 4, 1911, in a short piece called "The Atavistic Tendencies of the Age: A National Asset," as a return to a traditional habitus—but with modern embellishments. "To 'Go Fante' marks the mental terminus of the Gold Coast native and describes his ultimate Reversion to the primitive simplicity of his ancestors," the paper declared, "sobered and matured with all that is excellent in Western civilization and Religion." While literate Fante published public notices of reclamatory English to Akan name changes—"Hayford," in that vein, had once been "Afua," and Casely Hayford signed his books also as Ekra-Agyiman—he nurtured plans for formal African language education. These later came to fruition with the founding, in 1924, of the Gold Coast's first government-run co-educational boarding school, the renowned Achimota College, which he supported in his role on the Legislative Council and on whose first advisory board he sat.

While he no doubt "thought of the race," as his son Archie wrote, the more abstract circuits of the Atlantic world were at best a secondary concern in a day-to-day sense.[14] The takeaway, then, from the ease with which Casely Hayford can be affixed to "bigger" social and political stories is more about methodology than content. There is no transnational narrative into which he can or should be inserted to unlock his true significance; the Gold Coast, for him, was the fixed point of a moving compass. He stayed up to date on global intellectual developments from theosophy to poetry, to American philosophies of education and Meiji-era Japanese empire building, but he did not spend the heady years of the early twentieth century in the same rooms as America's Black vanguard. In fact, he developed his most grandiose political aims while chairing events and presenting papers on Gold Coast history in its small towns.[15] Correcting the record here does not contradict an understanding of Casely Hayford as one of Africa's earliest and most significant race thinkers, because he was. But this book digs into the ways in which his universalist racial ideals were moored to local movements and institutions, informed from afar but ultimately forged along the coast where he was born. His stature as a British imperial intellectual, less endearing a line of recovery though it may be, works according to a similar logic of wholes mediated by parts. For instance, he engaged with theosophy—the esoteric spiritualism that was all the rage in Victorian and Edwardian England—not mainly through its founder and figurehead, Helena Blavatsky, but through his close friendship with a Gold Coast teacher and follower of the movement, Kwao Brakatu Ateko.[16] This is not to argue that Casely Hayford should be read locally *instead* of globally, but to derive the terms for making sense of his intellectual dynamism and political priorities from his own life and work. Neither "nationalism" nor "cosmopolitanism," furthermore, captures how he exemplified both at different times, for different reasons. "Orchestration," or perhaps "choreography," best describes his powerful ability to bring changing sets of coordinates into strategic arrangement, in his style of reasoning as well as in his written self-presentation.

At the end of the day, Casely Hayford was a visionary but not especially imaginative writer. Even his one work of fiction is more combinatory than outright inventive, as it organizes real people, places, and textual influences to express the mind and bearing of an ideal Gold Coast intellectual leader and public servant. By assessing these moving parts instead of the success or failure of his work's anticolonial mission, *The Letter of the Law* asks readers to eschew a pervasive use of "contradiction" to characterize nineteenth- and twentieth-century African state builders. Whether in reference to African nationalists' imperial sympathies, or to perceived rifts between their national and Pan-African political ambitions, contradiction puts too neat a stamp of existential difficulty on complex or composite situations. A postcolonial lexicon steeped in paradox, tension, and tragedy quickly looks past African intellectual conditions in favor of African intellectuals' "condition," begging the question of ultimate alienation or defeat. And while contradiction hunting has yielded insights in a neoliberal and neocolonial frame, amid a protracted sense of liberal politics' exhaustion, it is ill-suited to grappling with minds poised at the zenith of progressive ideologies. Casely Hayford was a practical man, drawn to venues and projects where he thought some advancement was possible. David Scott, in his study of the Trinidadian intellectual C.L.R. James, elevates "moments when great historical forces were at irreconcilable odds with each other ... and in which new kinds of subjects ... were being thrown upon the historical stage [to embody] within their single selves the mighty conundrums and divisions of their age."[17] In contrast, this book finds in its subject a stolid will to external reconfiguration. Casely Hayford may have been wrong about plenty, but his view of the modern Gold Coast leader was not tragic—he did not "[suffer], like Hamlet, the modern fracturing of thought and action" so much as try to solve problems around it.[18] All the same, my metaphors of cohesion should not be taken to imply that his thinking always coheres. They suggest, rather, an approach to African text and character that maps elements' interaction in light of evolving goals, instead of prying self-division loose.[19]

Casely Hayford's prose has often been perceived as a high-flying jumble of interests and affinities, even an "infinitely expandable rag-bag," in Stephanie Newell's words.[20] But what can often feel like the patchwork nature of his writing, where appreciation for Japanese commercial expansion rubs elbows with dreams about an African Shakespeare (not an African equivalent of Shakespeare, mind you, but the man himself), gains in narrative purpose if seen through a legal-theoretical lens.[21] Law is a consummately worldly metaphysics, as typified by the pithy, well-known expression "the law is made for man, not man for law."²² It is essentially concerned with structuring high ideals in relation to actual human behavior. "If law . . . is a bridge from *reality* to a new world," Robert Cover wrote in his essay "The Folktales of Justice," then "there must be some constraints on its engineering."²³ Casely Hayford is more like an engineer, in this view, than a creator, working within the limits set by the worlds he knew. While some of his rhetorical high points channel a glimpse of the future—including *Ethiopia Unbound*'s final chapter, which is set fourteen years after its 1911 publication, in 1925—he expends the bulk of his written efforts on figuring out how to get there. As such, and for all its invocations of Christ, Akan cosmology, and a Fante prophetic spirit, his oeuvre rewards an approach that stresses ingenuity over rupture or rebirth. His work enfolds spirituality into a sturdy formal and conceptual grid and anticipates, in its archetype of the legal-minded leader, the philosopher Kwasi Wiredu's later argument that the supreme Akan deity (Nyame) should be understood as logical and orderly rather than miraculous.²⁴ Cover, here again, speaks to the larger point when he offers, "One of law's usual functions is to hold off the Messiah. Messianism implies upheaval and fairly total transformation. Law ordinarily requires a cautious discernment among commitments."²⁵

The law, in this understanding, becomes something like a *sensibility*, which is decidedly and yet—just as crucially—idiosyncratically elite in its nineteenth-century Fante expression. Casely Hayford's legal "self-fashioning," to use a term made famous by the Renaissance scholar Stephen Greenblatt, fused elements of high birth with those of hard-won intellectual meritocracy. He was a descendant of, through his mother, the prominent eighteenth-century Irish merchant and chief of Anomabu Richard Brew, and through his father, a line of Fante royals.²⁶ And yet "elite" status on the Fante coast had emerged from a complex history of relationships across trading and missionary communities (especially Methodist) as well as stool-holding families; it was not a "class" in a British sense, and it did not necessarily entail substantial inheritance of property or wealth.²⁷ Indeed, Casely Hayford's fastidious and often quite anxious attention to finances is a noteworthy part of this book's primary source archive. In a speech to the Legislative Council on June 19, 1930, he takes up the matter of African Civil Service salaries in detail, walking his colleagues through his own monthly expenses before leveling an accusation of colonial hypocrisy. "I say seriously, Sir, that you have made us what we are," he reflects. "[You] have created wants and aspirations in us, and I am asking in all seriousness if any thinks that the African will wear what you wear, drink what you drink, at £48 a year?"²⁸ His concern with and candor about money stand as testimony to the fact that the Fante intelligentsia were not clear-cut counterparts of the British elite alongside whom they were educated. By extension, it suggests the inadequacy of the "elite" label to sum up and then move past Casely Hayford's place in literary and intellectual history. Lawyering was the role by which he "artfully shaped" a family pride accrued across centuries into an income-generating force for dogged political progress.[29] To stick with Greenblatt's phrasing, legal training played an outsize role in "governing the passage from abstract potential to concrete historical embodiment," both in Casely Hayford's writing and in writing about him.[30]

The common law itself was in some ways beside the point. As Lauren Benton and Lisa Ford attest in *Rage for Order: The British Empire and the Origins of International Law, 1800–1850*, the first half of the British nineteenth century saw a strong but scattered effort to gather a "cacophony of law talk into a loosely unified but flexible framework for order," elevating law from a local procedural mechanism to one of sweeping global reorganization. "Law was everywhere," they continue. "It was the medium of multiple, parallel projects of imperial change, and it provided the text and subtext of numerous colonial controversies, including debates about colonial legislative powers and crown prerogative."[31] By the time of Casely Hayford's professional ascent in the century's last decade, law in the Gold Coast had clearly overtaken missionary Christianity as the venue par excellence of what we might call interpretive modernity, or one that staked its goals for civilizational advancement to the cultivation of self via engagement with a shared set of texts. "The lawyers," Kwaku Larbi Korang has summed up their standing, "would step forward as the defenders of a corporate native interest."[32] They did so through reading, reflection on reading, and mutual (and self-) citation, grabbing hold of ambient legal questions to craft an ideal of an intrinsically literary African cultural milieu. In this sense, as well as in terms of generational continuity in the tight-knit world of colonial Cape Coast, the historical progression from the Methodist ministry, for Casely Hayford's father, Joseph de Graft Hayford, to Casely Hayford's legislative activism was organic. As Gus Casely-Hayford rightly observes, the rise of the Fante legal intelligentsia in Casely Hayford's era was "tied tightly into the development of the stool," or a literal and symbolic seat of traditional Akan authority, which emphasized "emotional affiliations to the family" alongside civic duty and therefore encouraged overlap of "political, professional and personal hierarchies."[33]

The younger Casely-Hayford is also on sturdy ground in his contention elsewhere that efforts to narrate the history of the Gold Coast legal profession in isolation are wont to exaggerate the "alienation" of Casely Hayford's professional milieu from other, preexisting social and discursive forums.[34] To make this point he emphasizes Casely Hayford's (as well as his close peer John Mensah Sarbah's) upbringing in the households of well-known Fante *okyeames*, or court linguists—in Casely Hayford's case, that of his grandfather James Hayford, also known as Kwamina Afua.[35] The common translation of *okyeame*, who literally speaks for the chief, as "linguist" is a bit misleading, as others (including Casely Hayford) have long pointed out.[36] A fuller explanation of the role emphasizes its facility with language and on-the-fly public paraphrastic prowess, as well as a trained ability to move deftly between direct and metaphoric or circumlocutionary speech. Kwesi Yankah boldly describes its prominence in the first sentences of his definitive book on the topic, *Speaking for the Chief*: "okyeame, or its cognates, connotes rhetorical competence par excellence, the reason being that it designates the most crucial diplomatic and communicative position within traditional Ghanaian political hierarchies. The okyeame . . . is, among other things, the chief's diplomat and orator. In such areas as West Africa, where there is a great passion for persuasive public speech, any functionary whose discourse is regarded as the quintessence of rhetoric must be held in high esteem indeed."[37] And as Casely Hayford himself points out in *Gold Coast Native Institutions*, the okyeame also does specifically legal work, as the chief's "mouthpiece in every public function, as well as judicial proceedings."[38] To discount Casely Hayford's intimate exposure to this commanding position, which was traditionally passed down from father to son, is to prioritize wrongly his synchronic affiliations (to Cambridge and London) over his diachronic ones (to his Fante background) in the determination of his professional course.

A lot falls into place about Casely Hayford's career when these elements are brought together. A way with words was his inheritance, as well as his main professional tool, meaning that language for him was the key to both historical and networked ways of positioning himself in the world. His formal choices also hit differently with awareness of his Fante genealogy. Many critics, for instance, have homed in on the unwieldy eclecticism of *Ethiopia Unbound*, as it swerves between lessons, philosophical dialogues, and fictional vignettes, as evidence of its fragmentariness or even modernism. And so, in part, it may be. But Casely Hayford's way of making political points indirectly might also be understood as an okyeame-like demonstration of circumlocutionary skill. An okyeame, according to *Gold Coast Native Institutions*, cloaks chiefly decisions in "wit and humour," as he "[makes] use freely of parables to illustrate points in his speech."[39]

Likewise, the main character of Casely Hayford's novel teaches his son about imperial injustice through the Aesopian fable of the wolf and the lamb, couched within a playful paternal exchange.[40] More relevant still to this book's hybrid legal and characterological framework, Casely Hayford sees in the figure of the okyeame a certain replicable *style*, not just function, of person. He is "so cool, so collected, so self-complacent!," he exclaims. "He comes of a stock used to public speaking and public functions."[41] And in addition to this lineage, Casely Hayford was born into the *anona* (parrot) clan, or *ebusuakuw*, one of seven such affiliations with character traits designated by totems and myths of origin. The *anona* clan is named for a parrot who saved its founding ancestor from murder by echoing his words, which created the illusion of an ensuing crowd. It holds particular esteem among Fante even today, standing, as it does, for eloquence and the power of speech and intellect over might.[42] While it is easy to see Casely Hayford's legal cohort as having capitalized on the imposition of British institutional forms, there should also be room to imagine them, less cynically, as having "plugged in" such enduring character profiles and values to a new power structure that history just happened to hand them.

Whatever the intrinsic properties of their subject of expertise, then, Gold Coast lawyers represented the apotheosis of two kinds of elite in one social role: the first trafficked in good family names, and the second in rigorous education. Casely Hayford's status as a barrister comingled with his (imprecise) designation as a prince in the Gold Coast press, grafting his relatively marginal place in upper-crust London to his absolutely central one back home.[43] His own work often uses lawyers to summon Akan cultural insiderness and underscore the administrative importance of being sensitive to facts on the ground, as in his advice that British outsiders looking to mine Gold Coast lands consult "an experienced legal practitioner with a knowledge of the country."[44] An unsigned *Gold Coast Nation* editorial from June 6, 1912—"The Personnel of the Deputation to Downing Street, London"—captures lawyers' indispensable but not expressly legal role within the Gold Coast social order. "We can dispense with their services as Lawyers," it notes of a group of intelligentsia traveling to England, "but the Kings and Chiefs have commissioned them to go because apart from their professional position, they occupy niches in the structure of the Country which requires that their knowledge of local conditions and intelligent appreciation of the situation expressed and implied should be placed at the disposal of the race for the safety of the public." To use "elite" in a vacuum is meaningless. Law, in this context, channels a nascent civic mindedness trying to find its proper place among other forms of canny expression and esteem.

All the same, Casely Hayford is in many ways an unlikely subject for a new book-length study. Definitive work on colonial-era African intellectual history has long had a populist bent, in line with Nkrumah's professed desire to take African politics "to the people." An emphasis on everyday habits of reading and storytelling alternately upholds "print culture" or oral tradition in place of more rarefied literary forms, taking it as given that a vital cultural space, much as Nkrumah described the political one, is "doomed to failure" without mass participation.[45] Casely Hayford was many things, but he was neither a radical nor a populist. He did not seek social disruption or a break with the past or present; indeed, he did not even advocate for a break with the British Empire. I will leave a deeper exploration of the relationship between his imperial and anticolonial politics for the chapters to come, but it is worth noting here, given this book's literary orientation, that his incrementalism often found impressive rhetorical form. His taste for anaphora (the repetition of a word or phrase at the beginning of successive clauses or sentences) is on full display in a February 25, 1929, speech he delivered to the Legislative Council:

> When we speak of Nationhood, Sir, some of our friends may think that we are aiming at an immediate unofficial majority in this Council. It is no such thing. We know we have got to go slowly. We know that we have got our lessons to learn, and that we must learn them well; but we know also that sooner or later, having learnt our lessons, we shall arrive at the goal. We know that we must learn to shoulder our responsibilities, and when we have done this, then of course the privileges that come from responsibilities must also by right be ours to expect and to command. Furthermore we know that we must begin to help ourselves, and when we have done this, then of course the privileges that come from responsibilities must also by right be ours to expect and to commend. Furthermore we know that we must begin to help ourselves, and we mean to do so and intend to help ourselves; I for one have not the slightest fear that when the African has put up a well thought out plan and placed before government such processes by which he can help himself the sympathy of government will not be secured.[46]

The politics here is far from admirable from a radical nationalist perspective, appearing more aligned with imperial paternalism—Kipling's so-called white man's burden to "civilize" Britain's racialized colonial subjects—than with more renegade contemporaries like the Jamaican Pan-Africanist Marcus Garvey. I have no interest in "saving" Casely Hayford from present disapproval. But the elegant and cumulative structure of his phrasing, as he builds from repetition of "we know" to "furthermore we know," conveys a profoundly narrative and logical sense of African political advancement. His words do not storm any barricades, but they offer a deft and summary demonstration of cause and effect, with the process of African education hopefully configured as the veni, vidi, vici of intra-imperial cultural pluralism.

Casely Hayford was, furthermore, ambivalent about more firebrand figures now enjoying a resurgence of scholarly interest, with Garvey as a powerful example, and steadfast in his commitment to expertise as an essential component of African state administration. "To-day," he complained in a 1920 meeting in London, "what happens is that in various parts of British West Africa we have officials who, though not legal men, are placed in charge of legal work, to the grave detriment of the people."[47] He was open minded, though guarded, about African American repatriation to the Gold Coast, arguing in 1920 that were they to arrive there, members of Garvey's Universal Negro Improvement Association (UNIA) should be permitted to "try and make money as all others are doing" but with due respect for Akan propriety.[48] Casely Hayford's major works make scant reference to Garvey, and there is evidence that he eschewed their definitive public connection even as the UNIA cause later won his strategic support.[49] Archie Casely Hayford, in his unpublished manuscript, claims, "Marcus Garvey had a great admiration for Casely Hayford and though little known to anyone, when at the height of his activities during the Black Star Line Organization in America . . . conferred upon Casely Hayford a Knighthood of the Order of the Star of Ethiopia, the author of this work being the only person Casely Hayford ever told this to, or ever showed his signed commission so appointing him."[50] His second wife, Adelaide Casely Hayford, collaborated with the UNIA to raise funds for a school for girls in Sierra Leone, but only after separating from her husband in 1914. This partnership, too, was short-lived due to disputes over money's organizational flow. What I want to underscore is that Casely Hayford was more than a node: he is not compelling mainly on account of his place in a political or intellectual network, Black or otherwise. His work was his own, in searching conversation with but neither determined nor legitimized by his associations.

I do not, in this book, back away from Casely Hayford's social exemplarity to favor a narrative of his heroic "Big Man" exceptionalism, nor do I downplay parts of his worldview that make him a tricky candidate for absorption into a mostly diasporic understanding of African history, for example via what is often called the Black radical tradition. At the same time, he was far from a colonial stooge or bourgeois comprador. Kwame Arhin, as editor of *The Papers of George Ekem Ferguson: A Fante Official of the Government of the Gold Coast, 1890–1897*, upholds Casely Hayford as the counterexample to his own "extraordinary" but apolitical statesman subject. Ferguson, he notes, was "either too young or too busy to philosophize on the rightness or wrongness of colonial rule; nothing in his writings indicates that he, for example, faced the problem with which Casely Hayford later grappled [in 1903]."[51] Casely Hayford was intensely critical of the colonial order. And yet approached from one side of our scholarly moment, he looks like a contrarian addition to the current surge of interest in a more global kind of British imperial intellectual history. Beyond his faith in legislative (as opposed to popular) politics and his commitment to elevate reasoned argument over anger, he was a man who wrote precisely the sort of "systematic treatises" that Andrew Fitzmaurice describes the field as broadening beyond.[52] Like Fitzmaurice, however, I strive for an approach that goes "grubbing in the archives *and* [deals] with philosophical, and legal, treatises," building out the context of Casely Hayford's writing where and by whatever means necessary, across primary and secondary sources alike.[53] I see this as in keeping with Casely Hayford's written persona, which was not just wildly eclectic in its influences and references but concerned with expressing the impressive social density and "superior culture" of his local situation.[54]

Approached from a different angle, Casely Hayford is just as precisely the kind of prescient, pre-independence African race thinker that a broadened British intellectual history now wants to encircle, as do various branches of literary studies as they cultivate "decolonized" archives. For these traditionally "Western" fields, he makes an ideal long footnote or bonus chapter. Meanwhile, specialists in Ghanaian history and print culture often speak of the region's "coastal elite" as a dominant or default topic, from which they too now seek to move on to more urgent and inclusive concerns. In this way, Casely Hayford has fallen through the cracks of shifting disciplinary priorities. But it is difficult to imagine any other area of scholarly research that lacks even a single full-length book on one of its pioneering figures; the cart of field expansion has been placed before the horse of building out the things it takes for granted. Casely Hayford has been studied almost exclusively in profile, as one among a group of "early nationalists" whose historical niche is more notable than his actual work.[55] Even where some of that work *does* come up for closer examination, as in Kwaku Larbi Korang's important *Writing Ghana, Imagining Africa*, it is read through the lens of Casely Hayford's generational predicament: he stands in for the "alienated" condition of being not quite "African" and not quite "European," neither fully colonial nor fully sovereign. But Casely Hayford was an exceptional writer and thinker, not just a textual millwheel in the currents of his moment. It is high time for an effort to put the pieces of his life and work together in a systematic way. That said, and despite its relevance across fields and disciplines, this book will not move anyone's ideological needle very far. The banal truism "it's complicated" is true, and Casely Hayford's dedication to whatever he saw as being in the best interest of his people—as well as "the general good of the Gold Coast," irrespective of "African or European" considerations—did not conform to any political script, nor does it now.[56]

What did hold steady was his awareness of speaking as an "Educated African," and his belief that this role entailed a social leadership responsibility. Indeed, British efforts to discredit Casely Hayford's criticisms of their increasing oversight on account of his elite status are a recurring point of bitterness in his writing. In the same 1920 London meeting, he reminds his British interlocutors that "though we here happen to be dressed in your way, and happen to speak your language, it is not true or accurate to say that we are divorced from the institutions and customs of our people. An absolutely reverse statement should be made. I personally belong to an African community, an African family, so does my friend the Hon. T. Hutton Mills [the NCBWA's first president], and so do we all."[57] Similarly, in a different speech delivered in 1923, he identifies "the half-educated African ... rather than the thoroughly educated African" as the likelier kind of person to be "de-Africanised."[58] Casely Hayford, simply put, forcefully rebutted accusations of his cultural inauthenticity. Some of the motivation for this book derives from my own frustration with how a vague charge of elitism is still often leveled against Africans who break from one party line or another. Casely Hayford and his ilk believed in leadership by an educated minority, but their intense civic mindedness also made them a far cry from the class of self-enriching, apathetic postcolonial officials pilloried in Frantz Fanon's *The Wretched of the Earth* or Ayi Kwei Armah's *The Beautyful Ones Are Not Yet Born*. There is plenty of ground to lay claim to between mass uprising and rule by expensive suits sequestered in armored SUVs.

This is not to say that Casely Hayford's passion for representing the people he was from, if not quite of, resulted in a heightened rhetorical temperature. Whereas Nkrumah's Midnight Speech calls for the "TOTAL LIBERATION OF AFRICA," Casely Hayford studiously avoided all-or-nothing propositions. His speeches present even the most galvanizing causes as matters for deliberation. He peppered his 1925 Presidential Address at the NCBWA's third conference in Bathurst, Gambia, with "buts," "if/then" formulations, and "at the same time," phrases to link broad-minded goals with multifactorial consideration. This shape of argument can work both for and against cries for Pan-African unity. "To-day," Casely Hayford states at one point, "where two or three of our race are gathered together, the thought uppermost in their minds is how to attain African emancipation and redemption. At the same time it is true that we are all intensely attached to our several nationalities."[59] He then works through the competing forces of global racial alliance and local patriotic feeling to usher the speech toward another, structurally similar act of offsetting a goal with a challenge, this time directed to England. "At the same time it must be recognised that co-operation is the greatest word of the century," it reads. "With co-operation we can command peace, goodwill and concord. Without: chaos, confusion and ruin. But there can really be no effective co-operation between inferiors and superiors."[60] Casely Hayford remained measured even in the face of his stark recognition that "the African" was forced to be "the burden-bearer of the world," because he saw such level-headedness and willingness to negotiate with power as an obligation conferred by his privileged status.[61] His liberal proceduralism and his anticolonialism were both fully fledged, and he often staked the viability of Gold Coast self-determination to his and his peers' ability to prioritize sound process.

What Casely Hayford took from his legal training, then, beyond a technical vocabulary and a day-to-day livelihood, was the belief that the details of an argument really matter. As a writer he works things out patiently even when it lessens his rhetorical charisma, casting "the lawyer" as a paragon of slow reading. A 1922 speech in the Legislative Council, addressed to a British bill to regulate the authority of Gold Coast chiefs, puts this in bold relief. After reading aloud from John Mensah Sarbah's 1897 treatise *Fanti Customary Laws*, the precursor to Casely Hayford's *Gold Coast Native Institutions*, Casely Hayford twice repeats, for full effect, "That is the reason I read that paragraph."[62] A bit later, he piggybacks on a quotation from a British official that he again reads out loud to suggest that the bill in question "was hurriedly read [in the Legislative Council] and did not have that proper consideration it should have had."[63] A noteworthy merging of priorities is on display here, as Casely Hayford steers political speech to address practices of textual engagement. By insisting on careful reading as a bedrock of legitimate political process, he safeguards the role of formal education in cultivating a new class of Gold Coast leaders distinct from what were then called "natural rulers," or traditional kings and chiefs. But from another, livelier direction, he pries open hermetic processes of legal study and adjudication to shared interpretive debate. Jeremy Waldron's *The Dignity of Legislation* is useful here for pinpointing the significance of Casely Hayford's decades-long work on the Gold Coast Legislative Council to his overall worldview. In contrast to a legal outlook that centers an "idealized picture of judging," especially pronounced in the common law given its reliance on uncodified but binding judicial precedents, Waldron elevates "the process of legislation." He describes it, compellingly, "as something like the following: the representatives of the community come together to settle solemnly and explicitly on common schemes and measures that can stand in the name of them all, and they do so in a way that openly acknowledges and respects (rather than conceals) the inevitable differences of opinion and principle among them."[64] Casely Hayford would no doubt have assented to this vision of how law gains force in the world, by way of shared and adequate textual contention rather than judgments conferred from on high.

It is, moreover, far from an obvious political strategy to object to a piece of legislation on the basis of its having been hastily read. There is a long tradition of seeing lawyers as people who cheaply instrumentalize text; that is, as quasi-technocrats in whose hands the moral values of earlier kinds of textual training, philosophical and ecclesiastic, met their profitable and soulless demise. A huge part of law-and-humanities scholarship is devoted to "humanizing" law and legal study, salvaging it from disinterested scientific aspirations through an emphasis on its socially constructed nature. In wresting law away from its treatment as "a bundle of rules and social policies," for instance, Paul Gewirtz has spoken to a growing interest in "the ways law brings together story, form, and power."[65] And a persistent focus on law's "everyday" existence, both within and beyond the postcolony, pairs neatly with African literary studies' bent for breaking down social barriers and revealing unjust power arrangements.[66] But here again, Casely Hayford breaks with present-day decolonial form. His sense of his responsibility *as* a member of the educated elite urges him toward a humanistic understanding of legal practice. In his 1922 Legislative Council speech, he lays out the means by which law's Africanization, in his expert hands, is synonymous with its humanistic recapture. "I do not know how it is," he remarks, "but I have always heard it said that the lawyers of this country fleece people. We have been reminded here by Counsel that the lawyers out here are both conveyancers and counsel, they are solicitors and they are advocates. . . . In England, when you go to a solicitor for an interview, he charges you for it. He charges for every letter he writes. Here once retained, always retained." He then offers a colorful account of the "African" demands of his livelihood, with "persistent" clients dropping in to visit, greet, and make idle chitchat every day.[67]

Gold Coast lawyers, as opposed to their English counterparts, had to be intrinsically and at all times attuned to their clients' social needs, rather than just commissioned to perform set transactions. And this understanding of legal practice there, in metonymic relation to the "new" educated elite, seems to have been widespread. A short and anonymously authored column, "In Praise of Cape Coast Barristers," from the April 4, 1912, edition of the *Gold Coast Nation* is worth including in full because it so powerfully captures this localized twist on law's professional ascent and situates Casely Hayford within the milieu whose archetype he becomes:

> Ever since the late Hon'ble J. Mensah Sarbah, C.M.G., set the bright example of serving the Country free of all charges by returning his retainer of 400 Guineas in connection with the late Governor Maxwell's Lands Bill, Cape Coast Barristers have been trying to follow in his steps. Whenever there has been cause for so doing, the majority of them have been found ready and willing to place their valuable services at the disposal of the Country without hope of recompense or reward. When journalists are passing through purgatorial fires and are within an ace of the Prison Cell, the Lawyers have come to the rescue; when the town needed help of any kind, they have not, as a body, been loth to essay what they are best able to do. We are therefore pleased to learn that at the recent Conference our Natural Rulers extended warmest thanks to Messrs Hayford and Brown for the good work they were doing for the Gold Coast. We pray that such kindly expressions of appreciation and goodwill may inspire these gentlemen to live for the motherland without detriment to themselves or their connections.

It is not enough to read this as one among many culturally specific expressions of a pervasive nineteenth-century nationalism, though on the surface it is certainly that. Law, in a deeper sense, is where traditional kinds of virtue and social obligation meet the modern political sensibility of what Waldron (following John Robert Seeley) calls the legislative state, "a form of state devoted to the business of making continual improvements in the life of the community by means of explicit legal innovations."[68] This meeting is personified by the accord the *Nation* notes between Casely Hayford and traditional chiefs, whose relationship was a steady source of political tension in the decades after formal British colonization of the Gold Coast in 1874. But it is also legible in Casely Hayford and the *Nation*'s shared conception of Gold Coast lawyering, in which a kind of noblesse oblige is soldered to liberal civic duty by the force of close textual engagement, what Casely Hayford refers to as "a lot of hard office work."[69]

Though it is far flung in a historical and geographical sense, John Pocock's essay on "Virtues, Rights, and Manners" can shed light on the conceptual architecture within which I see the Gold Coast legal intelligentsia as having worked. This is because, in a much later period, Casely Hayford's writing walks a fine line between liberal and aristocratic conceptions of the individual's role in politics—in a way that resonates beyond his family or Fante cultural particulars. In Pocock's discussion of early modern political thought, he *counterposes* "jurisdictional and jurisprudential terms" with "terms arising from a humanist vocabulary of *vita activa* [the active, as opposed to contemplative life] and *vivere civile* [civilized living]."[70] He does not, contrary to common historical understanding, see a "law-centered paradigm" for political organization as fundamentally a liberal one, because the latter values exchange over conduct in its ideal of citizenship.[71] Needless to say, this has particular contours and implications in the context of Roman civil law and early Italian republics that are well outside the bounds of relevance here. What Pocock offers that is transportable, however, is an analysis of virtue as mismatched with "the vocabulary of jurisprudence," which, from Locke onward, has been preoccupied with possession and with "that which can be distributed, with things and rights."[72] The upshot is that in defining "the individual as rightbearer and proprietor," liberal jurisprudence skirts the question of what kind of *"personality* [is] adequate to participation in self-rule."[73] It therefore privileges the rise of a bourgeoisie, or possessive class, rather than of *vivere civile*, commonly translated as "decency" but in academic discussions of its Machiavellian origins meaning something like free and equal political participation by those who demonstrate the capacity for it. And for Casely Hayford, personal bearing holds a lot of weight.

Pocock ultimately sees virtue as having been redefined by and reincorporated into liberal jurisprudential society as "the practice and refinement of manners" in the eighteenth century, through an emphasis on increasingly complex and numerous social relationships.[74] (These were brought about mainly through the emergence of new and discrete spheres of existence, for instance, those of commerce and leisure, access to which was mediated by specialists.) Self-expansion as its own end, facilitated by mannered social interaction, took the place of the more substantive political participation that virtue had once abetted. Virtuous people led, whereas their mannered successors merely developed. As Pocock, finally, puts it: "if [the individual] could no longer engage directly in the activity and equality of ruling and being ruled, but had to depute his government and defense to specialized and professional representatives, he was more than compensated for his loss of antique virtue by an indefinite and perhaps infinite enrichment of his personality."[75] I cannot evaluate the specifics of this argument as it concerns the Italian Renaissance and its European afterlives. What I can assert is that this way of naming the changing relationship between personal qualities and systems of political organization is of great use for teasing out the different kinds of ultimate credential of personhood—moral versus socioeconomic—that converge in Casely Hayford's self-conception as a Gold Coast lawyer and intellectual. His position therefore defies ready periodization along European lines. He *is* one of the "specialized and professional representatives" amid whose rise virtue gives way to manneredness in Pocock's account, as it anticipates the history of widespread professionalization and bureaucratic expansion in nineteenth-century Europe. As I have said, Casely Hayford embraces the role of lawyers as essential experts.[76] But he also adheres, in his vigorous participation in the Legislative Council and his account there of what makes his legal practice "African," to what is more easily seen as an earlier ideal of virtue. How he acts and who he is, not what he has (be it rights, property, or training), undergirds his claim to political leadership.

A joining of nobility and political labor—that "hard office work"—drives Casely Hayford's understanding of his position in other ways, too. This book's second chapter on his novel *Ethiopia Unbound* includes discussion of one of its most important sections, "A Similitude: The Greek and the Fante." In it, Casely Hayford suggests that Homer's *Odyssey* "reflected the everyday life of [his] own people," the Fante, because of how even "the highest in birth preserved native simplicity" by doing their own laundry in a nearby brook. While he acknowledges that this is no longer the case among Gold Coasters of his own status—who lived in "extra-civilized days" with servants to do their dirty work—he yearns for the cultural reclamation of such ennobling hands-on exertion.[77] His vision of African leadership, then, entails an assiduous work ethic, not just even-keeled erudition. Even his descriptions of purely intellectual work are often couched in the language of toil, such as when he refers to political criticism, in *Gold Coast Native Institutions*, as a "thankless task," which had nonetheless to be undertaken "no matter ... the personal inconvenience" to himself.[78] In general terms this is not surprising, since the early twentieth century marks the pinnacle of "muscular Christianity" and an intense focus on discipline in the British

Empire as a whole. But the implications for how best to conceive of Casely Hayford's overarching intellectual sensibility are significant.

As I have described his politics up to this point, it is perhaps most readily comparable with W.E.B. Du Bois's ideas about the "talented tenth," also the title of the famous 1903 essay in which he argued for the advancement of a Black American elite through selective access to an expansive liberal arts education. Its first and last sentence—"The Negro race, like all other races, is going to be saved by its exceptional men"—may very well have directly inspired Casely Hayford's reference, in *Ethiopia Unbound*, to "men of light and leading in Fante-land," in whose view "the salvation of the people depended on education."79 Though Du Bois granted the importance of industrial education and "the paramount necessity of teaching the Negro to work, and to work steadily and skillfully," at this stage of his career he prioritized the development of what he went so far as to call an "aristocracy of talent and character."80 Conventionally (albeit not always with nuance), these views are juxtaposed with those of his historical archrival, Booker T. Washington, whose Tuskegee Institute, founded in 1881, emphasized farming, trade, and other practical pursuits. But Casely Hayford valorized both approaches to racial advancement, even referencing Du Bois and Washington in succession as "sons of God."81 And rather than seeing intellectual distinction and industrial know-how as orientations meant to work in complement across different social echelons, he synthesized them into the figure of an African nobleman, of sorts, who was acutely attuned to the nuts and bolts of state development.

This flickering between the loftiest reaches of literacy and the literal mechanics of day-to-day leadership is one of the most characteristic and remarkable aspects of Casely Hayford's writing. His intellectual creativity was always bound to matters of unglamorous practicality, as he saw beyond competing African and British value systems into the decisive nitty-gritty of what made a modern state tick. His speeches to the Legislative Council buttress goals like fair and elective African representation with interest in the literal routes of Africans' political journey, both by road and rail.82 This was true to the spirit of the public sphere he helped shape—most prominently as owner and editor of the *Gold Coast Leader* newspaper, as well as working under S.R.B. Attoh Ahuma's editorship at the *Gold Coast* [originally *Western*] *Echo*—in which one was as likely to encounter an opinion on sanitation as on the cultivation of national character. A representative Editorial Notes section from the February 24, 1912, edition of the *Leader* glides from the topic of dustbin maintenance to that of building roads in a scientifically informed way, landing finally at a short paragraph about the Ado Literary Club. Here still, the attention to detail is impressive. The author of the notes, quite possibly Casely Hayford, takes the club's president to task for sending correspondence on "unbecoming" paper, as well as failing to repay the government for his postage. An interest in town infrastructure and its functional minutiae were by no means confined to the journalistic arena, either. It is captured pointedly in the main character of *Ethiopia Unbound*, whose ambitious political career and consummately rational demeanor are plainly modeled on Casely Hayford. When he travels in a dream to the afterlife to see his late wife and child, he comments at length on its built design, a practical penchant his beloved shares with him even in death. She sends him back to earth because the building in which he is meant to spend eternity is not ready: while it appears symmetrical, a close inspection reveals "a seam here, a fissure there, unevenness in places where there should be uniformity."[83]

One way to contextualize Casely Hayford's melding, in this idealized fictional self-portrait, of high-minded constitutionalist activism and an appreciation for the finer points of urban engineering is by looking to his legal education. The Inner Temple, where he matriculated on January 25, 1894, and was called to the bar in the Michaelmas term of 1896, was, needless to say, hardly the Tuskegee Institute.[84] Its curriculum offered what one might expect of a high imperial education, despite slow movement in the direction of cultural pluralism; at the time of Casely Hayford's attendance, it covered a wide range of traditional British legal subjects.[85] Notably, in the context of Casely Hayford's efforts to co-navigate his nationalist and imperialist affinities, an effort was made in 1893 to "institute, by way of experiment, a course of lectures on Hindu and Mahommedan Law, and another course of lectures on Roman Dutch Law." Unfortunately and to the "[great] regret" of the Council of Legal Education, too few students enrolled to sustain them. The Inns of Casely Hayford's day were also bastions of social elitism and imperial masculinity, with nearly all of those called to the bar alongside him hailing from Oxford and Cambridge, and real deliberative energies devoted to questions of food and libation.[86] This privileged fraternalism is not, however, the whole picture. In its emphasis on members' day-to-day self-regulation, the Inner Temple also no doubt helped instill a contextually transposable cultivation of practical attentiveness. Despite the Inns' barring admission to anyone who was otherwise employed, its list of member committees and tasks looks almost like a trade school of its own. The Electric Lighting Committee, a noteworthy case in point, at its meeting on May 6, 1892, saw debate about the merits of installing a gas versus a steam engine.[87]

All the same, the Inner Temple is only one small piece of Casely Hayford's intellectual formation. There is no reason to think that it influenced him any more or less than various other West African forces and factors. The important point to register through this description of its mundane organizational aspects is that Casely Hayford was accustomed, even in the most elite enclaves of his education, to thinking in terms of institutional function and continuity. Korang grants as much when he labels Casely Hayford a "pragmatic modernist," who believed that "good modernity, materially speaking, could in theory be separated from bad," allowing him to focus without contradiction on the "promise of material amelioration of Africa's comparative backwardness in the matter of infrastructure, social amenities, scientific agriculture, and industrial forces."[88] His political goals were unified by their concreteness—both in a literal sense (fixing roads and improving sanitation), and in terms of spearheading new bodies, such as a House of Assembly, proposed in 1920, to give elected African officials financial oversight of the Gold Coast colony. This means that despite his extensive learning and frequent emphasis on careful study and argument, his ideas do not always add up to philosophical precision.

They were not meant to. It is common these days in academic treatments of so-called Global South traditions to say something along the lines of "But what about non-Western *theorists*?," as opposed to their long-standing relegation to the status of those to whom "theories" originating elsewhere are applied. (I too have made a version of this argument at length.) In Casely Hayford's case, such restoration of his rightful status as an "ideas man" needs to be accompanied by reflection on the brass tacks mindset that he proudly broadcasted. Robert Higney's work on what he calls "institutional character," in his book by that name, points to a more fitting conception of selfhood figured out across work. "The term," he specifies, "denotes the variety of ways that modernists imagined character as inhering in the workings of institutions rather than in the development of the singular individual—even as character in the novel necessarily finds expression in and through individuals."[89] It is not of great interest to me whether or how Casely Hayford is a "modernist" writer—or a Victorian one, for that matter, though his work bears imprints of both. But it is impossible to disentangle his sense of who he was from what he built, and what he built (or intended to) is a central preoccupation of what he wrote. Higney places his work within a "broad rethinking of [character]" that shifts away from psychological depth, within whose ambit he argues, "Rules, actions, habits, and values, more than deep interiority, are the bases of institutional character, and the individual emerges through the repetition and accumulation of these elements in narrative."[90] I do not want to go so far as to suggest that Casely Hayford did not have an internal life, because he surely did, in all his triumphs and griefs. But though he marks space for solitary reflection in his novel and legal treatises, by describing his reading and research processes and their crucial importance, he does not actually delve into its psychological content. Character, in that view, is something that he *plots* rather than describes or embodies.

I end this main part of the introduction in that spirit of mapping the repetition and interaction of elements in Casely Hayford's work, thereby summoning the qualities that make up the kind of person it inscribed on history. He published his last book, *United West Africa*, in 1919, a year that also gathers the threads of his career into a portrait of sorts. Its personal and political milestones mark a rich constellation of local institution building and global racial zeitgeist, of literary personhood and generational movement: his father's lonely death in a London hostel; the installation of the liberal-reformist Gordon Guggisberg as governor of the Gold Coast colony; Guggisberg's appointment of Casely Hayford as an MBE (Member of the British Empire); and the first Pan-African Congress in Paris. Casely Hayford, at age fifty-three, turned to full-time political and civic work, which does not seem to have entailed any real slowing down. Achimota College opened in 1927, and the fourth NCBWA Congress took place in Lagos in 1929, just a year before he died in Accra.

But *United West Africa*, despite its galvanizing intentions, does have a slightly weary undertone and serves better as a distillation of previous works' strongest elements than as a capstone text in its own right. It is structured as an exceptionally clear explanatory note, which prizes a "temper of mind" open to "fair constructive criticism of Government policy," followed by three longer sections.[91] The first two are speeches previously delivered to secondary school students in Lagos (in absentia) and the members of the Cape Coast Literary and Social Club. The third part, by far the most memorable, is titled "To A Young Friend" and presented as a letter to Casely Hayford's twenty-year-old son that can speak to his whole generation of rising West African leaders. It is loving and a bit pedantic, open to God's grace and fusty in its Methodist insistence on hard work as the path to its revelation. For my purposes here, it also offers an ideal encapsulation of how law—as a conceptually dense but worldly ordering system—held steady as a low hum beneath Casely Hayford's intellectual life. It represented a nexus of verbal precision, big picture thinking, and the trained dedication of self to the (textual) task at hand, all tangled up with Fante lineage and the institutional as well as literal infrastructure of British imperialism.

The addressee of "To A Young Friend," we learn, was born with a temperament well suited to a life of professional service to his home continent, which Casely Hayford saw as his birth obligation. This epistolary section of *United West Africa* offers advice on marriage and friendship, urging vigilance around matters of health so that the next generation may "yield service unto God"—in Archie Casely Hayford's case, also through a career as a barrister.[92] But it contains moments of real poignancy for thinking about the human habits moving the Gold Coast forward in the name of its past. In one of its more arresting transitions, Casely Hayford follows his staid marital wisdom ("In no step in life, therefore, is greater circumspection desirable" than in the selection of a spouse) with a paragraph's worth of insight into his own balancing act between writing and other kinds of work. "Since writing the above," he admits, "I have been interrupted by constant travelling and pressing engagements. And that brings me to a question you asked me in one of our recent letters, How I find time for journalistic work amid the numerous other calls upon my time, political, literary and professional?" Casely Hayford's answer does not hinge on a political mission, or patriotism, or even on God, but on how he *organizes* his life and thoughts at the macro level. "Well, I can answer in one word," he replies: "system." Another new paragraph then adds, "To the systematic man all things are possible. It is the only fulcrum to great achievements."[93] Finally, a page later, studied systematicity reaps its true reward, which is no less than inner peace. "Indeed," Casely Hayford tells his son, "there is need to cultivate calmness of temperament, if it is not natural to one. It is an indispensable atmosphere for great work, work that is abiding and useful. Besides, it is a condition of the soul to be envied. It implies one being at peace within himself and outside himself. In such a condition our own emotions trouble you not, and the world around cannot ruffle you."[94] With words come order, and with order, release. And it is beautiful.

Chapter Summaries

The best description of *The Letter of the Law*'s approach to Casely Hayford's work might be "conceptual history," albeit of a more porous sort than the version made famous in English by the likes of John Pocock and Quentin Skinner, who were stricter about delimiting period and tradition. The general idea, as Andrew Fitzmaurice puts it succinctly, is that "in order to understand what a person meant by a particular action, we need to understand the broader range of discourses which could inform that action."[95] By invoking it, I mean that the book works from the lynchpin vocabularies of a set of written texts—augmented by substantial archival research—to capture an overarching sense of their purpose and mechanics. This obviously entails focused intertextual engagement with Casely Hayford's Gold Coast peers and predecessors, as well as with much of the specialized research on their (pre-)colonial period. But unlike a "proper" conceptual history, and its project of reconstructing past horizons of meaning, this book also gathers into itself the full range of material that the daunting scope of Casely Hayford's erudition demands. It strives thereby to honor him, even if not indiscriminately to sing his praises. In each of the main chapters, as I have here, I work freely with legal and political theory as well as literary and philosophical scholarship, so long as it abuts the relevant subjects of objectivity, constitutionalism, and jurisdiction. My hope is that Casely Hayford emerges, ultimately, as not just important but *interesting*, worthy of as serious and protean a textual engagement across present-day disciplines as those many he entertained.

CHAPTER 1. A MATTER-OF-FACT KIND OF MAN

Each of *The Letter of the Law*'s three main chapters takes shape around a key legal-analytic concept, and the chapters are ordered chronologically by publication date of Casely Hayford's major works. The first, on "Objectivity," shows how the leadership profile represented by the new Gold Coast legal milieu cohered around the epistemic ideal of factuality. Who, they asked, had the capacity to see the whole truth of the British Empire, thereby making good on its broken promises? At the center of the chapter is Casely Hayford's 1903 legal-humanistic treatise *Gold Coast Native Institutions*, which intersperses detailed descriptions of Akan (Fante and Asante) customs across domains including marriage, succession, and property distribution with commentary on Gold Coast history and cultural character. Far from being merely a dry recitation of customary precedents, *Gold Coast Native Institutions* argues outright for their timely political as well as characterological salience. At the level of form, this means that readings of Gold Coast court cases are interspersed with character sketches and frequent morally charged invocations of facticity as the "missing piece" of British imperial leadership. The chapter thus elaborates a milieu-specific politics that was simultaneously anticolonial and pro-imperial, showing in detail how the Fante legal intelligentsia around the turn of the twentieth century sought to *redeem* the empire through their own project of self-standardization, based on what they saw as their unique ability to apprehend colonial reality and so rectify its errors of strategy and understanding. The treatise form worked well to solder the contemplation of character to the valorization of facts, furthering an ideal of objectivity that was not a "view from nowhere," per Thomas Nagel's famous formulation, but a view specifically from the Gold Coast in 1903.

CHAPTER 2. A GOLD COAST CONSTITUTION

The second chapter of *The Letter of the Law* presents Casely Hayford's 1911 novel *Ethiopia Unbound* as a constitutional document. It does so by casting Gold Coast intellectual life not only as foundational to twentieth-century traditions of African literature and politics, but as open-endedly engaged with the enduring challenges *of* legal and philosophical foundationalism. In drawing out the implications of Casely Hayford's novelistic practice for thinking about constitutionalism as such, a formative text for African literary history emerges as the progenitor of anticolonial legal thought. Furthering this book's diachronic rather than global "network" emphasis, constitutionalism is also a concept whereby Casely Hayford cultivates a modern Fante genealogy—in short, one of intrinsic predisposition to textuality—that he overlays on his family genealogy as such, looking to his cultural and actual ancestors during the Fante Confederation era (1868–74). Weaving *Ethiopia Unbound* with Casely Hayford's speeches on the topic of constitutionalism, as well as constitutional theory ranging from Aristotle to recent postcolonial critiques, the chapter shows how character here too is a unifying preoccupation. In the novel form and its emphasis on the representation of the individual, Casely Hayford finds a means of fleshing out the relationship between constitutional*ism* and constitutional*ists*. Ultimately, however, the chapter argues that he is not able to represent persuasively the movement from charismatic would-be constitutionalist leader to systemically entrenched constitutional ethos. As such, his writing on character looks elsewhere: to the exploration of charismatic Christian leadership in his long, path-breaking essay *William Waddy Harris, the West African Reformer: The Man and His Message*, published in 1915.

CHAPTER 3. THE JURISDICTION OF MORALS

The last of the three chapters that make up the body of *The Letter of the Law* takes up the concept of jurisdiction as a driving force in the development of Gold Coast textual consciousness. It takes off from a pivotal document called the Bond of 1844, an agreement made that year between British officials and a small group of Fante chiefs that extended the range of British jurisdiction in the Gold Coast. As far as the chiefs were concerned, however, the extension was of only criminal and not civil authority. By foregrounding Casely Hayford's explicit engagement with Fante-British divisions over how to read this event, the chapter argues for fine distinction making rather than unity as the guiding tenet of West African textual modernity. Its backward historical leap from the independence era to the mid nineteenth century is also valuable because it bypasses the corrective role to which postcolonial Africa is often confined—that is, the taking up of a continent full of every imaginable development and position because it "troubles" Western politics or aesthetic history. More substantively, the chapter shows how the drawing of boundaries, both legally and to mark moral lines in the sand, can be a self-enfranchising act. The chapter focuses on Casely Hayford's 1913 treatise *The Truth about the West African Land Question*, in which he argues for the preservation of Akan systems of land tenure within a modern legislative state, to elaborate "jurisdiction" as a formal operation that aids in moral discernment. In this way, it brings work on legal pluralism into dialogue with work on textual design and citational practice, showing how *getting small things right* is both a political imperative and a stylistic hallmark.

EPILOGUE: WHERE IN THE WORLD IS J. E. CASELY HAYFORD?

This book's epilogue considers the resonance of Casely Hayford's career and persona long after his death, both within and beyond present-day Ghana. What, the epilogue asks, is Casely Hayford's legacy today? This question has many answers, and that is the point. Whereas Casely Hayford's persona merged political institution building, cultural nationalism, educational activism, the building of civic and literary institutions, and the public cultivation of day-to-day aesthetic refinement, these pursuits each now occupy a different social niche. The epilogue is shaped as a reflection on how the public image of an ideal jack-of-all-trades leader in the colonial Gold Coast has been "shattered" into many parts through Ghana's social and economic upheaval in the twentieth and early twenty-first centuries, as well as by the dissolution of the British Empire. It surveys some of the foremost Ghanaian political, cultural, and educational settings where Casely Hayford might now be "found," none of which include the country's real seats of power, before concluding with a move to London. I suggest that Casely Hayford's temperamental legacy, at least, may be most palpable in the

Casely-Hayford fashion design house, founded there by his late grandson (and namesake) Joe Casely-Hayford in 2009 with strong awareness of the family line. In addition to being an interesting story that brings *The Letter of the Law* into decisive contact with the present, it enables the epilogue to consider whether and how it is still possible to harmonize African political substance and aesthetic style.

Finally, two short notes about this book's composition. While *The Letter of the Law in J. E. Casely Hayford's West Africa* is best read from start to finish, each chapter should also make sense on its own. This means that there are occasional repetitions of historical details from one chapter to another, which I hope will not prove too distracting to readers of the whole. Like all writers who work across disciplines, I harbor ambitions that the book will be of interest both to readers from nonliterary and non-Africanist fields, as well as to those working directly in the intellectual history of Ghana. To ease reading for nonspecialists, I have standardized all alternate spellings of "Fanti" and "Fantee" to the current spelling of "Fante." References and extended historiographic notes are at the end of the book, except for references to Gold Coast newspapers. Accessed at the British Library, those are cited in text by date and title.

CHAPTER ONE

A Matter-of-Fact Kind of Man

FROM 1868 TO 1874, self-determination in Cape Coast got ahead of Africa's standard anticolonial timeline, which locates the advent of viable nation building in the middle of the twentieth century. What had been a loosely allied group of Fante kingdoms evolved in the 1860s toward the new administrative form of the Fante Confederation, what Kwaku Larbi Korang calls a "protonationalist" state, which possessed a constitution, judiciary, and the capacity to wage war and collect taxes.[1] Though short-lived in its efforts to thwart the consolidation of British rule, the following generation of Fante leaders—with Casely Hayford most prominent among them—built a powerful intelligentsia in its image. A small but formidable canon of legal-humanistic essays and treatises by Casely Hayford as well as by John Mensah Sarbah (1864–1910) and S.R.B. Attoh Ahuma (1863–1921) sought to define Fante intellectual character through its personification as the "Educated Native," who was typically, though not always, a lawyer. This figure's distinguishing trait was an ability to perceive facts where the British could not, especially when it came to Gold Coasters' role in advancing imperial history. He embodied objectivity as a situated rather than "placeless" intellectual ideal and claimed it as a distinctly African virtue.

Gold Coast intellectual life around the turn of the twentieth century is, therefore, an important but largely overlooked coordinate in the literary history of objectivity. What kind of person could see the whole truth of the British imperial condition, Casely Hayford asked in his 1903 treatise *Gold Coast Native Institutions*, and thereby make good on the empire's broken promises? In tethering Fante objectivity to the empire's redemption, he occupied what David Scott has memorably called a "problem space" that is in this case both pro-imperial and anticolonial, eschewing the familiar opposition of empire and self-rule to apprehend an "ongoing moral argument" over the most righteous synthesis of available positions and ideals.[2] The collectively authored figure of the Educated Native, or African, advanced a cool-headed standardization of indigenous knowledge alongside a passionate claim to cultural messianism. The first promoted a posture of neutrality vis-à-vis facts, and the second saw the capacity to *see* facts as the product of a specific and redemptive historical position. Rather than just moving between the metropole and colony as a translator or mediator, Casely Hayford's character type positioned "character" as a homegrown but universalizing moral epistemology. While he did not see Victorian ideals of objectivity as on their face misguided, he believed that only the so-called Educated Native could see them through. Fante self-explication thus aimed to one-up the British late nineteenth-century confluence of facts and fate, scientific "rigor" and foreordained progress. By pinpointing what London failed to see about its colonies, Gold Coast intellectuals sought to fulfill their proclaimed destiny of situating the view from nowhere as uniquely theirs.

The Gold Coast Intellectual Situation

As Casely Hayford's first major work, and the one in which he most fully fleshes out the Fante elite's self-conception at the turn of the twentieth century, *Gold Coast Native Institutions* (hereafter, *Native Institutions*) is at the heart of this chapter. I also contextualize its standardization of Akan culture through the exposition of an "objective" character with reference to a few other Gold Coast treatises and essays, all of which balance customary legal expertise with an interest in the figure of the African legal statesman. *Fanti Customary Laws* by John Mensah Sarbah (1904) and *The Gold Coast Nation and National Consciousness* by S.R.B. Attoh Ahuma (1911), as well as various newspaper editorials, together fill in the bigger picture of Casely Hayford's milieu. The formation of an official Fante Confederation in 1868, led by a group of kings, chiefs, and merchants, including the famous Krio intellectual and surgeon Africanus Horton, was central to its sense of historical possibility. Reflecting on the political fervor around the so-called Lands Bill of 1897, a British effort to misappropriate Gold Coast property that I treat in more depth in chapter 3, Casely Hayford looks back to his father's Confederation generation. "But how came this sudden outburst of patriotism and political spirit ... at a critical juncture in the history of the country?," he wonders out loud. To which he then responds, "If you wish to understand the political movement of 1897 and 1898, you must at the least go back twenty-seven years in the political history of the Gold Coast."[3]

As is true for each of this book's chapters, this is also a well-timed invitation to provide some essential historical and historiographic background to a more conceptual argument, in this case regarding the Gold Coast rhetoric of facticity. Twenty-seven years before 1897 or 1898 lands Casely Hayford's reader in the early 1870s, the moment to which he dates the formation of the Confederation, adding that it was spurred by a "patriotic impulse."[4] His timeline is not necessarily mistaken, even as it diverges slightly from historians' more common starting point of 1868. On the contrary, such inconsistencies demonstrate just how "live" a documentary project African history was at the time of *Gold Coast Native Institutions*' publication. Relations between African and European factions on the Gold Coast—mainly though not exclusively the British and Dutch—were fluid and contingent, often appearing in clear chronology only in retrospect. Following Lennart Limberg and Dennis Laumann in their work on, respectively, the Confederation's economics and historiography, its immediate cause in 1868 was a Dutch-British agreement to swap several forts, expanding the British presence in Fante-led areas.[5] This, in turn, threatened to upset the Fantes' role in negotiating between the inland Asante and the Europeans. Other milestones might nonetheless seem plausible as founding events for the Confederation. Its first official president, Robert Johnson Ghartey, was chosen in 1869, and what Limberg describes as its "impressive, complicated, and massive constitution" was drafted only in 1871.[6] Though Francis Agbodeka broadly assents to a starting year of 1868, he maintains that the African-led founding in 1863, and subsequent banning by the British in 1865, of a group called the Gold Coast Rifle Volunteer Corps is what really set the stage for focused state-building action.[7] Laumann suggests that Casely Hayford later exaggerates the Confederation's nationalist motivations, as opposed to Fantes' having joined forces to maintain a profitable balance of power. For my purposes here, it does not matter much whether this criticism holds; I am concerned with the Confederation's role in the self-authorship of the Gold Coast legal class.

This class has not always fared well in its critical treatment, in part because of its members' pride in their British legal credentials. Ghanaian political scientist F. K. Drah, in his 1971 introduction to the second edition of J. W. De Graft Johnson's essay collection *Towards Nationhood in West Africa*, berates "accusations, often made with an inflated sense of self-importance by some latter-day nationalists against the earlier generations of western-educated West African leaders . . . that nearly all the pre–World War II educated leaders were 'colonial stooges' who did not want self-rule for Africans."[8] When Korang turns to Casely Hayford's nonfiction writing in English, he describes Fantes' mediating role as that which "bears the uneasy symbolism of fatal compromise."[9] The notion that Casely Hayford and his ilk were at once European and African—in its generous version, a way to praise their cosmopolitanism—can easily be inverted, a both/and cultural situation cast pejoratively as neither/nor.[10] By now, this rush within later African decolonial movements to condemn forebearers' insufficiently radical politics has received nuanced historical attention. Philip S. Zachernuk's 2000 study of the southern Nigerian colonial intelligentsia, *Colonial Subjects*, arrives, for example, at a notably similar formulation to Scott's "problem space" in describing the Saro (Creole) population: "The educated community was not moving from the African to the European," Zachernuk writes, "but rather was seeking to define itself within an emergent Nigerian society. This was not an unstable transitional society waiting to find order by absorbing Western norms but an admittedly changeable society engaged in an ongoing—and unending—process of living through problems as it met them."[11] Such thinking rightly suggests that understanding the "successful" national independence movements of the mid twentieth century should entail reckoning with earlier frameworks on their own terms.

As Drah offers, the salient question in addressing the turn-of-the-century Gold Coast intelligentsia is how an ideal of self-determination worked within the perceived constraints of its moment. "They were constrained to be reformist in outlook and conduct," he reasons, "partly because they were confronted by adamant, technologically superior alien rulers," and, as Korang notes, also partly because the group "had an interest in maintaining and preserving the hegemony of the modern in the particularly British [liberal-constitutionalist] institutional form—albeit not its specific colonial political form—that it had come to the Gold Coast."[12] While Korang's attribution of liberal-constitutionalism to Britain alone is limiting (a point I take up in depth in the following chapter), it is certainly true that Casely Hayford et al. saw Britain at its best as a paragon of constitutional rule. The Fante Confederation, however, introduces a second, local reference point for an intellectual position geared toward the preservation of previously existing "modern" governmental forms. To reduce it to having been simply a pale copy of a British original reinforces the primacy of British influence where it was not always present; the intellectual leaders of Casely Hayford's era strategically navigated among institutional precursors that were themselves synthetic.

Even a brief glimpse at the historical background guiding Drah's remarks reveals just how fluid the relationship was between "self-determination" as an overarching goal and the particular political alliances of a career like Casely Hayford's. From the earliest days of the Aborigines' Rights Protection Society (ARPS), formed in Cape Coast in 1897 to oppose the Lands Bill, the educated Fante leadership was beset by internal disagreement over their place in working toward self-governance versus that of the traditional rulers or chiefs. That these two factions worked together at all was a major credit to the organization, as well as a testament to the close-knit nature of the region. "Not only was the close co-operation between the educated and traditional elites during the early years of the Aborigines Society due to a common interest in opposition to an alien government," S. Tenkorang writes, "but also it was due to the blood relationship between them."[13] The ARPS was further held together by a shared interest in global affairs, and in increased transnational organizing around racial solidarity.[14] Eventually, however, the position of the legal elite fractured, catalyzed in part by the amplification of indirect rule in 1912 and Britain's elevation of traditional leaders to do its bidding. Casely Hayford was staunchly opposed to this turn, but he also parted ways with the society's more radical members. When dispatched to London in 1926 under the auspices of the ARPS, he came around to supporting Governor Gordon Guggisberg's proposed Provincial Council of Chiefs, which would grant six total chiefs drawn from three provinces a place on the Gold Coast Legislative Council. This compromise secured increased African representation in the colony's government, but Africans continued to be excluded from its Executive Council. Where Casely Hayford imagined himself as pragmatic, some of the younger ARPS membership—including well-known writer Kobina Sekyi—saw him as a sellout.

Though there is more to this history of Gold Coast political institutions, this chapter's goal is ultimately to come to grips with Casely Hayford's *Gold Coast Native Institutions*, and with the conceptual and characterological work of the legal-humanistic treatise in his intellectual tradition. My intention here is to recapture some of its context's open-endedness, amid debates over what might now seem like fine points of an inevitable movement toward Ghana's birth as a nation-state in 1957. These debates surrounded, for example, the question of the Gold Coast's status *as* a colony rather than a protectorate, and the thin line between British partnership and paternalism. Such consequential determinations were, in Casely Hayford's view, often made more or less haphazardly. He writes in *Native Institutions*, "We somehow, either through lack of intelligent appreciation of the fact, or through the peculiar conditions of scattered interests in political matters in the country, acquiesced in a sense to be called a colony, where we should have made a firm stand against the applicability of the misnomer."[15] Casely Hayford's use of "scattered" invokes the many moving parts and uncertain political status of the geographical terrain now known as Ghana, reminding his reader that weighty outcomes are not always the result of careful deliberation. "What gets lost in narrating history as the triumph of freedom . . . is a sense of *process*," Frederick Cooper has fittingly observed, whereas the historian's aim should be to reinhabit "moments of divergent possibilities, or different configurations of power, that open up and shut down."[16] When this attunement to process is brought to bear on Gold Coast intellectual history, anticolonial and pro-imperial politics do not seem so intuitively opposed. As Cooper notes of a slightly later period, "our gaze backward from the era of independence fails to appreciate—or belittles— . . . another form of politics in Africa in the 1940s and 1950s: an effort not to escape empire, but to transform it."[17]

This is truer still of Casely Hayford's moment, occurring, as it does, on the heels of the Fante Confederation experiment in actual, intra-imperial African self-rule. To see themselves as real partners in advancing what Attoh Ahuma in 1911 refers to as the British imperial cause of "justice, freedom, and fairplay" in "the bond of peace [under] one paramount emperor" may not have been quite as naive as it rings to a twenty-first-century ear.[18] On September 30, 1897, around the time of the ARPS's founding, the editors of the *Gold Coast Methodist Times* declared, "We most emphatically protest against the principles which underlie the [Lands] Ordinance. No legislation founded upon absurd dogmas and strange theories can be tolerated in the Protectorate; and if the Honourable Members of council have, one and all, any real and genuine respect, reverence and love for the Queen, they will make it their duty to lay the sword of justice unto the root of the unprincipled Bill." This quotation conveys the local intelligentsia's understanding of imperialism as entailing a responsibility to be educated about and do right by the empire's constituent nations, odd as it may seem now to see shared reverence for a European monarch in this light. But a sense of allegiance to a set of imperial values that transcended imperial politics was the lifeblood of Gold Coast nationalist ferment. Even in 1911, as Casely Hayford railed against the British program of indirect rule and its increasing segregation and paternalism, he describes Queen Victoria's "halo of womanly virtues" as "the kind of thing before which, in all ages and in all climes, the heart of universal man bows low in reverential homage and respect."[19]

A number of postcolonial scholars have sought to explain this curious conjunction of imperial pride and African self-determination. Simon

Gikandi acknowledged in *Maps of Englishness* that even for later, more firebrand nationalist intellectuals, "this was not a contradiction: the reason they were fighting colonial rule was not because they wanted to return to a precolonial past (in spite of the nationalist rhetoric gesturing that way) but because they wanted access to the privileges of colonial culture to be spread more equitably, without regard to race and creed."[20] In the colonial period, as opposed to the transitional and independence periods, this also bears a specific Victorian imprint. Victoria J. Collis-Buthelezi, for instance, in her work on Cape Town as a site of Black Victorian modernity, finds the history of radical mid-twentieth-century African social movements in a (lost) faith in earlier liberal imperial reforms. "Many leading figures on both sides of the Atlantic saw the vote and education as the way into freedom for the black race," she reminds the reader steeped in postcolonial expectations. "Black victorians did not envision independent nation-states; instead many hoped for the end of racial and colonial oppression through *empire*."[21] Similarly, Adom Getachew's response to Chris Taylor's book *Empire of Neglect*, about Caribbean imperial liberalism, invokes the common occlusions of a broader British postimperial framework. "It is tempting to narrate . . . declarations of imperial fidelity and fraternity by figures so deeply associated with the age of decolonization as mere preludes to the triumphal rise of an anticolonial nationalism that birthed the postcolonial nation-state," she writes in reference to C.L.R. James. "In doing so, we rehearse a familiar story in which the counterpoint to empire is necessarily sovereign statehood."[22] For Casely Hayford writing in 1903, the preferable option to the existing British Empire was to nurture a set of sovereign states *within* it, a counterpoint in the true musical sense of harmonic interdependence.

Part of the difficulty of finding an apt critical language to describe Casely Hayford's historical understanding is a widespread emphasis on imagination and futurity in relation to Black self-determination. The Black past as it actually existed is often viewed as quicksand rather than steady ground, and with good reason. Yogita Goyal's deft introduction to a 2014 special issue of *Research in African Literatures*, "Africa and the Black Atlantic," captures the dominant tenor of that field in phrases like "the struggle to find a useable past" and, following Paul Gilroy, a desire to get beyond cultural nationalisms' "romantic narratives" of a pure African past.[23] But the mere fact of the Fante Confederation's existence in the 1860s and '70s means that Fante intellectual leaders of Casely Hayford's generation were not just "imagining" ways to make the round peg of self-determination fit through the square hole of empire; they were also *remembering* having done so.

Its leaders were still fully "real" to the Gold Coast intelligentsia working and writing around the time of the Lands Bill and the founding of the ARPS, who tallied their forebearers' practical achievements in public view. After an announcement of the Fante Confederation president King Ghartey IV's death—followed by a detailed description of his funeral and a brief farewell letter calling on younger leaders to continue his work—the September 15, 1897, issue of the *Gold Coast Methodist Times* includes a "Brief Sketch" of Ghartey's life by his son. It is notable for how little it offers by way of evocative or even descriptive language, aside from its mentioning that Ghartey was known by "the local Government as loyal, faithful, trust-worthy, and a reliable authority on native affairs." Instead, it consists of a list of his milestones and achievements, from introducing a Temperance Society, to pioneering a new system for timber flotation, to writing his *Guide to Coomassie*, the first travel book published on the Asante region. Ghartey's "character" is assembled from his organizational paper trail, in a testament to the enduring *material* legacy of his nous.

In contrast, for example, to Chris Taylor's account of West Indian imperial attachments as an expression of desire, reliant on fiction—he describes them as "a fantasy that madly conjures a responsible empire that never in fact had a presence"—Casely Hayford thus had what he took to be hard evidence for his view that a reciprocity of African self-governance and imperial common cause was possible.[24] In the first chapter of *Native Institutions*, in which he censures the British for what is "in some cases, an insane thirst for territorial acquisition," he also upholds that "the Aborigines of the Gold Coast triumph in the wave of imperialism which at present sways the public sentiment of Great Britain."[25] Later, in offering a detailed criticism of the Gold Coast's governance structure and the insufficient number of African members—just two out of five—among its Legislative Council's unofficial (i.e., mainly advisory) membership, he admits that he "can understand why, for example, you will rightly or wrongly refuse full representative government, say, to Jamaica or Trinidad" on account of their not having "an indigenous people" with a history of representative institutions.[26] Casely Hayford views his own milieu as offering a *true* possibility for cross-racial cooperation in the name of civilizational advancement. With their demonstrated indigenous capacity for representative government, he writes, "the Gold Coast is perfectly unique among all the other so-called Dependencies of Great Britain."[27]

I am not suggesting that Casely Hayford and his milieu actually *were*, retrospectively, on equal political or economic footing with London; Casely Hayford grows more scathing in his structural economic critique later in his career. What I *am* arguing is that they had no bones about presenting themselves in writing at least as equals, and often as superiors to their British counterparts in government. In an unsigned *Gold Coast Echo* editorial from August 10, 1888, the occasion of John Mensah Sarbah's appointment to the Gold Coast Legislative Council prompts reflection on what is expected of someone in his position. "The man who is called upon to discharge the duties arising from such a station must, in our opinion, be an individual of great independence of mind," it reads, "besides being bold and fearless. He must be prepared at any time to incur the displeasure of the Governor when he finds himself obliged to thwart his schemes." The Fante Confederation—having from this viewpoint been full of such fearless men—stands as a key point of evidence for what Casely Hayford sees as the right and, ultimately, reclaimable course of imperial affairs provided that such duties continue to be fulfilled. Approaching the turn of the twentieth century, Fante intellectuals' typical reaction to their "demotion" by the British is one of forthright scorn and derision, not vulnerability or fear. Another editorial in the *Echo*, this one from September 25, 1888, declares Governor William Brandford Griffith's intention to eliminate "all natives from their [official] appointments" as "[bearing] upon the very face of it the impress of absurdity." The British, in this light, have not forsaken a romantic past horizon of mutuality so much as they have foolishly deviated from a practical arrangement that served all parties well.

At this point in Gold Coast history, the Fante Confederation represents an entirely real and therefore realistic African political and technical modernity that was advanced in full view of British imperial leadership. It lends confidence to Gold Coast writers and state builders in the decades following its demise, rebuffing crisis-inflected approaches to literature's postmissionary significance in other parts of the African continent. Jennifer Wenzel, for example, has discussed South African author Thomas Mofolo's novels, written in Sesotho as early as 1905, as having been shaped in part by "the horrors of the pre-colonial displacement" of the Basotho people and the "looming threat of subjugation through incorporation into the Union of South Africa" in 1910.[28] In other words, pinning the origins of long-form African prose to South Africa tends to emphasize imagination as compensation for African civilizations' destruction or denial. Wenzel follows Fanon, to this end, in dialogue with Bakhtin, joining the former's focus on "national liberation as not-yet determinate" to the latter's theorization of "historic and generic instabilities [that are] bound up with ontological instabilities."[29] Shifting to the Gold Coast as the ground of the novel's eventual emergence from the customary legal treatise, in Casely Hayford's career, urges the discussion toward more sure-footed terrain. As Olufemi Taiwo has noted in relation to S.R.B. Attoh Ahuma, born just three years before Casely Hayford, in 1863, "Ahuma and his contemporaries felt that Africa could not afford to waste any more time in the race for progress and enlightenment given that there were people like them who already were the harbingers of the brave new future that modernity represented."[30] The transition from African kingdom to African republic on the Fante coast was not an imaginative prospect but a practical template.

Directing his British readers to the Confederation's constitution (also called the Mankessim Constitution), Casely Hayford concludes that it is "harmful" and "useless . . . for a Government to attempt to set back the onward tide in the progress of a nation under its protection."[31] The momentum this warning describes is not just a generic recourse to some kind of Hegelian historical rationality, though various and sometimes contradictory notions of national teleology no doubt influenced Casely Hayford's thinking. It is, in fact, a forceful contextualization of the Fante Confederation at the intersection of two specific national timelines. *Native Institutions* understands the Confederation not only as a defensive response to British disruption of the Fante economic position regarding the Asante, after the fort swap with the Dutch, but as a natural next step in the evolution of Akan political institutions irrespective of British involvement. The origins of the modern Fante state, in other words, predate and place limits on the influence of the British Empire, even as the empire becomes its enabling condition. In the stream of a detailed explanation of the Gold Coast's federal states—which he lists as "Fante, Ahanta, Insima, Ga, Wassa, and others"—Casely Hayford sets out to "usefully trace the beginnings of the Native State from the hamlet to its highest development, a union of Native States under one King or President."[32] The upshot is that Akan have deep roots in a form of governance that fuses monarchy and republicanism, with an elected king exercising total and lifelong rule but nonetheless deferring in most cases to the provincial chiefs who sit beneath him. "Thus, with a strong central government, directed by a strong personality," Casely Hayford writes, "the Native State has all the elements of progress, liberty, and enlightened good government in its composition."[33]

Far from waxing poetic on this point in *Native Institutions* on a shared imperial bond, he proves it by extolling the Confederation's logistical foresight. He cites its constitution article by article, homing in on the parts of it geared to building in a literal sense. "Fancy the Aborigines of the Gold Coast, thirty-two years ago, thinking of the necessity of good roads, fifteen feet wide, connecting the principal producing districts with the sea coast!," he muses.[34] Rhetoric is one thing, and governance another; Casely Hayford has inherited from his father's generation an interest in the dirty details of state expansion. And whereas the Fante Confederation set itself to concrete kinds of progress, British leadership in the decades that followed is mired in "stupid officialism and red tape."[35] The Confederation's plans for education, likewise, had been foiled by British refusal to grant it formal recognition. In its "special provision for female education, and provision for meeting the expense of school building, and ensuring the attendance of all children between the ages of eight and fourteen," fulfilling it would, in Casely Hayford's view, have meant "the emergence of the country in two or three generations from a lower to a higher order of civilization."[36] All of this practical ground will now have to be recovered, when it had been in line with the supposed goals of British imperial modernity all along.

Truth in Plain View

If there is one epistemological motif that captures Casely Hayford's confidence in the Fante past as he marshals it to direct the future, it is that of the fact. *Native Institutions* opens by stating its intentions to get the British Empire back on course in terms that grant "facts" much the same kind of muscle that it later grants national progress. "I consider that there can be no greater safeguard to British administration on the Gold Coast than in the free dissemination of the historical facts embodied in this book," Casely Hayford declares on its first page.[37] He regularly sanctifies the self-announcing form of the fact, along with its close cousin evidence, since he believes that they will guide colonial administrators in the process of refinding the Fante Confederation's path. A couple of pages later, when revisiting the ARPS victory in defeating the Lands Bill of 1897, he notes, "The Colonial Office yielded to the logic of facts," and in the book's first chapter, he opines, "Science will tell you that there can be no healthy growth except from within; and the history of the Gold Coast will disclose to you the facts and circumstances which must guide such internal growth."[38] *Native Institution*'s recourse to the vague instructive force of "history" and "science" is broadly characteristic of nineteenth-century European positivism, which, in the figure of the Sierra Leonean surgeon and researcher Africanus Horton, had a pioneering emissary within the Fante Confederation (who will re-appear in this chapter's next section).[39] The text is replete with references to history as the domain of facts unmarred by any particular historical misprision, including that of British colonial ethnography.

History is determined for Casely Hayford before the historian arrives on the scene, and one can only be counted as a historian by accepting this order of things. "The reader must be prepared to disabuse his mind of all prejudice in this matter," he advises. "If you once start with the premises that the Ashantis are a barbarous, bloodthirsty people . . . you naturally take a different standpoint from the historian, whose object is the ascertainment of truth from facts as they are, and not as they are supposed or wished to be for purposes of argument or invective."[40] In *Native Institutions*' chapter "The Conflict of Systems," which elaborates a long tradition of representative government among the Akan, he again clears space to assert the Gold Coast's *verifiably* unique role in the British Empire, the details of which have now "passed from the province of controversy to that of history."[41] Importantly, however, facts evolve toward self-revelation at the site of their emergence, not by being "processed," as it were, in a different and bigger one. Anticipating "the criticism that self-government is reserved by Great Britain for those English-speaking Colonies whose populations are nearly or wholly white," Casely Hayford thus offers an alternative standard of competency to a racial one, which is at once more universal and less generalizable from place to place. "I am inclined to think that it is not so much a question of the particular people inhabiting a particular Dependency," he writes, "as yielding to the logic of facts in the given circumstances."[42] The facts of the Gold Coast's uniqueness are observed by Gold Coasters *because they are facts*, not because they are being observed by Gold Coasters. In British philosopher Thomas Nagel's classic work *The View from Nowhere*, he writes, "The aim of objectivity would be to reach a conception of the world, including oneself, which involved one's own point of view not essentially, but only instrumentally, so to speak: so that the form of our understanding would be specific to ourselves, but its content would not be."[43] Casely Hayford essentially sees himself as having inherited a situation that grants him a leg up in being able to hold such a view, and so accepts this ideal of a self-inclusive objective viewpoint quite unproblematically. Facts for him are born, not made.

This does not, however, mean that facts bear no relation to the formation of character. For the Fante intelligentsia, facts do not just reveal an objective historical reality, but index an unevenly distributed ability to *see* that reality that contradicts the political hierarchy in which it is enmeshed. The "real" essence of history, in other words, exists apart from the history that shapes even the impulse to get it on record. Another way of putting this is that Casely Hayford, in *Native Institutions*, calls on the self-evident nature of facts in order to make Akan traditions *into* facts in the act of their written systematization. He sees history as dynamic but not fundamentally shapeable and therefore can position himself both as its proud product and its neutral print conduit. He shares this goal and posture with John Mensah Sarbah, the Gold Coast's first barrister and co-founder of the ARPS, as well as the author of *Fanti Customary Laws* (first published by William Clowes and Sons in London, 1897), the closest precursor and intertext to *Gold Coast Native Institutions*. In each case, an air of unassailable neutrality surrounds the demonstration of individual good sense that they nonetheless mark as an act of curation. In Sarbah's preface, addressed to family friend and senior Gold Coast jurist George Eminsang—who facilitated the Dutch-British fort swap around the Fante Confederation's founding—he confesses that this is his "first attempt in the thorny paths of literature."[44] While he clearly intends "literature" here to refer to written texts as such, the description nonetheless foregrounds the literary attributes of Sarbah's work in a stricter sense.

On the one hand, Sarbah's reference to a "thorny path" invokes the messiness and variability of the Akan lived experiences from which *Fanti Customary Laws* draws by way of Gold Coast court cases. On the other hand, he is guided by a standard of accuracy—rather than just aptitude—in their print rendition. "I know that you have often given the first *correct* idea on Customary Laws to newly arrived European officials," he praises Eminsang, and later remarks on the failure of his own text "to test [Customary Laws'] accuracy by comparison with similar cases in other districts affecting the same class of persons."[45] The "literary" work, then, done by both *Fanti Customary Laws* and *Gold Coast Native Institutions* is in their dual claim to creation (as they bring an archive of customs and traditions into "official" existence) and to be recording merely what is already true. They harness a virtuosic cultural vision to a more prosaic kind of documentary responsibility. Extrapolating from this description to provisionally define the literary as a category in and for this milieu, Sarbah's thorniness suggests that literary authorship is marked by a sheer will to disciplined observation—staying *out* of the thorns, so to speak. Along these lines, Casely Hayford announces *and* effaces his own presence in *Native Institutions*, narrating his planning process as a step toward affirming his commitment to speak through evidence. The variation between the two facets of the work is evident even in its syntactic rhythms. Casely Hayford's self-narration across two full paragraphs reads like a parade of clauses: "It occurred to me, in the course of my critical examination of the issues raised and the evidence necessary to throw light upon them, that ample data existed, if only one would search for them," and so forth.[46] A paragraph right after attests to the book's extensive work with legal sources and contains only a single comma. Such a performance of laboring toward ideological *suspension* in the name of political self-rule diverges from the long-standing critical tendency to identify African literature (usually for the better) with its ideological credentials, based on later struggles that reverberate more strongly in today's political battles.

To some degree, this stitching together of narrative sensibility and value-neutral external sources recalls the central argument of Mary Poovey's monumental *A History of the Modern Fact*, which charts the means by which the fact, over the British eighteenth and early nineteenth centuries, came to "[sustain] the illusion that numbers are somehow *epistemologically* different from figurative language, that the former are somehow value-free whereas the excesses of the latter disqualify it from all but the most recreational or idealist knowledge-producing projects."[47] Numbers as such are not really at issue here, but Casely Hayford imbues history with something like this same neutral valence. The fact that the Fante Confederation existed is imagined to provide clear-cut insight into Fante cultural uniqueness, which in turn bolsters Fantes' claim to intra-imperial leadership. As Poovey summarizes in her introductory discussion of historical epistemology (that is, the history of the terms and categories by which knowledge is organized), "facts seem (and can be said) to exist as identifiable units only when they constitute evidence for some theory—only, that is, when there is a theoretical reason to notice these particulars and name them as facts."[48] The literary, in Sarbah and Casely Hayford's terms, might thus also be said to consist in how they perform this act of "notice," in service of the idea that the Fante past provides evidence for the British Empire's best line of advancement. As Casely Hayford puts it in *Native Institutions*, Akan self-governance is a matter of "ordinary common sense," and observing the legitimacy of Gold Coast political traditions one of "practical statesmanship."[49] They nonetheless demand hundreds of pages of skilled explanation.

Neither *Native Institutions* nor Sarbah's *Fanti Customary Laws* makes for gripping reading on the order of well-plotted fiction, but they both derive theories of personal and social character from their analyses of court cases and forms of government. Sarbah's introduction lays out a "vain dream to hope a time is coming when the several [Akan] nationalities, united under a beneficent and enlightened Government, will develop and foster the clan feeling and instincts, which in times past have been as free from the impulses, which have degraded the African nature, as great in the qualities, which have ever graced manhood in all ages and under all climes."⁵⁰ In addition to once more upholding an evidentiary, historical basis for Akan leadership ("in times past"), which Casely Hayford praises in his own work, Sarbah looks to the promise of Fante personhood in his turn to "nature" and "qualities."⁵¹ In this light, it becomes possible to read these treatises and, by extension, their intellectual context through a claim to objectivity as what I have called a distinctly African virtue. Casely Hayford takes this a step further in *Native Institutions* when he analyzes Asante civilization, closely related to but still distinct from his Fante perspective. "Cautious, slow, and diplomatic," he observes, "the Gold Coast man is sometimes by the ignorant foreigner labeled 'stupid,' but when this stupid piece of human mechanism is examined with a calm and impartial judgment, it is found to possess those high qualities which make it easily, in the race for existence amidst its own environment, the survival of the fittest."⁵²

Through what now registers as a cultural essentialism about Asante, Casely Hayford offers a striking, double-layered characterization of objectivity and rational calculation as homegrown African traits. Cautious, diplomatic Asante stand in implicit contrast to impractical and arrogant British officials, all presented by a calm and impartial Fante barrister. But how can one possibly see clearly one's own clear-eyedness? This question haunts nineteenth-century British intellectual life. As Amanda Anderson explains in *The Powers of Distance*, "The cultivation of distance informed many intellectual and aesthetic practices in the Victorian era, including ethnography, sociology, and novelistic discourse, to name some of the most prominent."⁵³ Many Victorian writers, however, greeted this development with ambivalence, fearful that detachment could evacuate claims to knowledge of essential details derived from lived experience as well as moral conscience. George Eliot, Anderson writes, "[showed] how the stance of detached analysis undermines the individual's moral character and responsiveness, and also produces false forms of knowledge."⁵⁴ At the same time, following Anderson, Eliot appeals to "specific forms of distanced understanding" such as psychology and irony in her writing. To the extent that a solution exists, Eliot's is to endorse the "participant-observer" model of knowledge acquisition that she finds in the work of German ethnographer Wilhelm Riehl.⁵⁵ Sarbah and Casely Hayford engage with similar challenges around how to square a pursuit of unbiased truth with respect for the moral demands that only attachment can exert. But instead of an abstract intellectual model, they offer up *themselves* as the resolution, finding both objective understanding and moral direction in their intimate knowledge of Gold Coast life.

This insertion of the attached self as an objective guide also shifts the weight of their argument from the status of objectivity as such—in Poovey's rendition, the evolution of the fact from the Enlightenment to the nineteenth century—to its embodiment in a particular Fante character type. Anderson's turn to Eliot to defend nuanced forms of Victorian detachment points to an ideal bridge here with Casely Hayford's milieu, and with its understanding of intellectual distance as a benchmark of *political* character specifically. The bridge, in a name, is S.R.B. Attoh Ahuma, for whom Eliot's work is a repeated point of reference. Casely Hayford worked closely with him, as a fellow Gold Coast editor, and greatly admired his journalistic ethos at the *Gold Coast Methodist Times*; large parts of their literary background and sensibility were shared. Attoh Ahuma's major work, aside from his essays and editorials collected in 1911 in *The Gold Coast Nation and National Consciousness*, is a book called *Memoirs of West African Celebrities: Europe & c., 1700–1850, With Special Reference to the Gold Coast* (hereafter *Memoirs*), which was published in 1905.[56] Composed as a series of nineteen biographical sketches of regional intellectuals, including William Amo, Ottobah Cugoano, and Phillis Wheatley, Attoh Ahuma intends the book as proof of "the moral, intellectual and religious capabilities" of Africans.[57] It also includes reviews of Sarbah's *Fanti Customary Laws* and Casely Hayford's *Gold Coast Native Institutions* as appendixes, naming both writers as "men of mark," along with some Fante Confederation and ARPS-related correspondence.[58] But one of its first epigraphs, as well as its last word, is given to George Eliot. In the first instance, Attoh Ahuma includes a substantial excerpt from Eliot's 1876 novel *Daniel Deronda*, her final long prose work and the only one to be set in her present day. On the very last page, *Memoirs* includes a stanza from Eliot's 1867 poem "The Choir Invisible." Though the book is full of references and quotations, she has a certain pride of place in its proud catalog of African intellectual achievement.

Attoh Ahuma's choice of Eliot excerpts zeroes in on the relationship between intellectual ambition and self-betterment, as it shades into self-transcendence. Her words also channel his desire to find pride in the Gold Coast past through its rigorous scholarly evaluation: he dedicates *Memoirs* to "the serious study of the rising generation, who, ignorant of the intellectual traditions and prestige of our beloved country, have not seen the footprints of our great men on the sands of time." The *Daniel Deronda* quote is taken from a heated conversation about Zionism in the novel, where the main character, the searching and motherless Daniel, is brought around to understanding the pull of heritage and belonging on present-day politics.

"The life of a people grows," it begins, "it is knit together and yet expanded, in joy and sorrow, in thought and action; it absorbs the thought of other nations into its own forms, and gives back the thought as new wealth to the world; it is a power and an organ in the great body of the nations."[59] A character named Mordecai speaks these lines, which, restored to their original context, nest nationalist feeling within its robust contestation. What Eliot goes on to describe as Mordecai's "spiritual fullness" is juxtaposed with the views of a third party named Gideon, who claims, "I'm a rational Jew, myself" as he advocates for ethnic and religious intermarriage, followed by further inquiry into the nature of rationalism.[60] The closing poetry stanza Attoh Ahuma selects likewise shows Eliot marrying spiritual and intellectual edification and is worth including in full: "O may I join the choir invisible / Of those immortal dead who live again/ In minds made better by their presence: live / In pulses stirred to generosity, / In deeds of daring rectitude; in scorn / For miserable aims that end with self / In thoughts sublime that pierce the night like stars, / And with their mild persistence urge man's search / To vaster issues."

One easy way to read this connection between Attoh Ahuma and George Eliot would be to take Attoh Ahuma as identifying with the Zionist character Mordecai, and, in his use of "The Choir Invisible," with a quest for the spiritual sublimity of national commitment. Given the plethora of other references (the final Eliot stanza is preceded by a more straightforwardly Christian one by Adelaide Anne Proctor, for example), one could also choose to overlook them altogether. Attoh Ahuma and Casely Hayford's commentary on one another belies this option. When he describes Casely Hayford's accomplishments in *Memoirs*, Attoh Ahuma captures the same essential collision between seeing truth individually from without and feeling it collectively from within that he seems to take Eliot's work to exemplify. "The more soundly and liberally the sons of the soil are educated the more readily do they acknowledge the wisdom of the fathers," he writes in his review of *Native Institutions*, before praising Casely Hayford's "genius for discrimination and accurate statement of facts."[61] Casely Hayford, meanwhile, remarks in *Native Institutions* on Attoh Ahuma's willingness to prioritize debate over religious obedience. Though Attoh Ahuma as an "able young man" was a Methodist minister, as the "intrepid editor" of the *Gold Coast Methodist Times*, "he saw no reason why the grievances of the people should not be ventilated, and their temporal amelioration advanced in as far as it lay within the power of that spiritual organ."[62] In Casely Hayford's telling, Attoh Ahuma worked to facilitate precisely the sort of testing of deeply felt beliefs that the scene he quotes from in *Daniel Deronda* depicts. Because the elevation of Fante civilization is, for them, evidence-based, it does not just withstand but demands interrogation to become a potent political force.

The Gold Coasters who undertook this interrogation almost uniformly had legal training; Attoh Ahuma is something of an exception in this regard. In the next and final section of this chapter, I elaborate further on the implications of this professional profile. First, however, I want to turn briefly to another Victorian critical touchstone to help clarify the significance of Gold Coast intellectual history to broader questions around colonial-era African writing: George Levine's *Dying to Know*, which likewise takes up objectivity as a moral quest and an epistemological commitment. In an effort to salvage objectivity from its sundry uses by false universalisms, and subsequent critical efforts to "reveal" the dishonesty of the paradigm, Levine revisits as flawed but noble the turn in nineteenth-century England to "moralized objectivity" as expressed in philosophy and scientific thought by "a surrender of the self to the thing studied."[63] His use of the word "disinterest" dovetails neatly with Anderson's close look at "detachment" in *The Powers of Distance*, as he shows how Victorian thinkers found their footing amid the rise of a "scientific model ... built on faith in the possibility of secular disinterest and in the uniformity of nature."[64] As the force of religious belief wanes, this story goes, a faith in science and method comes to fill the historical and moral void. Instead of a self that faces God, the self is suppressed or transcended in order to seek what Richard Rorty once referred to as an intrinsically flawed "Gods-eye view."[65] Levine also follows historians of science Lorraine Daston and Peter Galison in linking nineteenth-century objectivity not to callousness and indifference, but to a desire for social improvement. "In late nineteenth-century statistics," they write, "objectivity also took on a moral tinge," as its practitioners "called on enlightened citizens of modern polities to set aside their 'own feelings and emotions' for the common good."[66]

Casely Hayford and his peers in many ways plug easily into this broad mid-nineteenth-century paradigm shift from enlightenment to knowledge.[67] When Daston and Galison describe the fear among "men of science" of the time that "the subjective self was prone to prettify, idealize, and, in the worst case, regularize observations to fit theoretical expectations: to see what it hoped to see," it is hard not to see an anticipation of Casely Hayford's frustration with British ethnography, which minimized Akan sophistication to aid in the justification of indirect rule.[68] (This book's third chapter on jurisdiction treats this subject at length.) As far as most British colonial apparatchiks were concerned, objectivity and the "rhetoric of mechanical rule-following" that accompanied the expansion of the imperial bureaucracy *was* a ruse for a highly subjective understanding of African cultures.[69] But a historical explanation for the Gold Coast objective posture that is rooted in secularization falls short, for the simple reason that the intellectuals in question are enthusiastic, messianic Christians. This is not just a matter of Attoh Ahuma being a Methodist minister, as were his and Casely Hayford's fathers, or even of a residual missionary vocabulary. Their religiosity was dramatic and trended upward. Unlike many of their British journalistic and essayistic counterparts, Gold Coast intelligentsia writers expressed no sense of tension between the language of God and the language of self *or* state.[70] On the contrary, they typically moved between detailed, even dry documentation of Akan customs and practices and the mystical registers of a fervent, place-specific Christianity.

The Fante intelligentsia placed a heavy emphasis on political commentary in their manufacturing of an innovative, flourishing press, thereby re-creating the conditions usually associated with a distinct kind of secular-political discourse. But they then sanctified their efforts. As one case in point, Casely Hayford in *Native Institutions* segues quickly from a characteristic assertion that Akan have "organised government of a high order" to an unequivocal pronouncement of their chosen status. He writes, "If you believe me that the Gold Coast and Ashanti will lead the way in what will prove the grandest conception of the twentieth century—grandest because Ethiopia will have at length raised up her hand unto God,—allow me to indicate what sort of an empire this shall be, and on what lines it shall work."[71] Though he uses "Ethiopia," an expansive term, and then adds that "the black man shall have his day," he is clear that his own people will be at the vanguard of the coming God-ordained achievement of "fraternity without hypocrisy" across races.[72] This chosen status also applies to efforts to achieve social equality elsewhere, which he feels are forced and overdone in comparison with the social equilibrium ensured by Akan laws of inheritance and family relation. "While there prevails this equality," Casely Hayford notes to this effect, "there is yet scope for individual effort, success, and distinction. We have, in the family system of the Fantes and Ashantis, the panacea for all the ills of the socialism of the present day."[73] There is no doubt that Casely Hayford felt a sense of solidarity with Black people elsewhere and admired strong racial leadership. But at this stage of his career, his advocacy had a hierarchical core.

By observing the sophistication of Fante history as fact, anchored by the Fante Confederation and the British strategic error of hastening its demise, Casely Hayford and Attoh Ahuma offer a route to repurposing their history as prophecy. A brief section of "Editorial Notes" published in Casely Hayford's newspaper the *Gold Coast Leader* on February 25, 1911, begins, "The Fantes have always been remarkable in forecasting the future. Intuitively they have either approved or condemned proposals which the passage of years has invariably endorsed," before proclaiming outright, "The Gold Coast is a land of Prophets and Prognosticators." Casting Africa in this light was not unique to Gold Coast writers. Mamadou Diouf and Jinny Prais rightly observe that "in their quest to relocate Africa in world history and reaffirm Africa's presence on the world stage, many black thinkers [at the turn of the twentieth century] attributed to Africa the role of guide and savior and produced a form of intellectual history that effectively recomposed universal history."[74] Diouf and Prais link Casely Hayford to W.E.B. Du Bois and William Henry Ferris, a fellow scholar and editor, in their "adaptations of and engagements with universal narratives of history" as they moved beyond nineteenth-century African American conceptions of Africa as a heathen or savage space.[75] With Casely Hayford looking outward from Africa and Du Bois peering in, they stood face to face for a common cause.

But such positioning also entails the risk of looking past one another, and the comparison between Casely Hayford and Du Bois is interesting as much for their consequential differences as for their (literal and figurative) correspondence. Some of these differences are obvious given their respective geographical starting points. Du Bois, for one, is less celebratory of the past than Casely Hayford, whose vision of progress is rooted in a studious reclamation of precolonial Akan institutions. In the same year that Casely Hayford published *Native Institutions* to promote the viability of long-standing Fante and Asante political systems, Du Bois, in *The Souls of Black Folk*, tackled history's sober place in educating Black Americans for the future. "The history of the American Negro is the history of this strife,— this longing to attain self-conscious manhood, to merge his double self into a better and truer self," he famously wrote there, invoking his major philosophical concept of double-consciousness. "In this merging he wishes neither of the older selves to be lost. He would not Africanize America, for America has too much to teach the world and Africa."[76] While Du Bois was eager to collaborate with African intellectuals, his sense of history's direction and redemptive possibilities, at least in 1903, favored his own country. He invokes the Gold Coast in a diametrically opposed fashion to Casely Hayford, writing, for example, that "answers to such questions [of race and metaphysics] can come only from a study of Negro religion as a development, through its gradual changes from the heathenism of the Gold Coast to the institutional Negro church of Chicago."[77]

Without straying into the voluminous body of scholarship on Du Bois, including sundry and often conflicting explorations of his Afrocentrism, it will suffice here to remark that he understood the relationship between history and prophecy as interlinking but not overlapping. As such, his views offer a revealing point of contrast with his Gold Coast counterparts' agenda. Casely Hayford, Attoh Ahuma, and their ilk viewed *themselves* as the cool-headed protagonists of a prophetic story, in no uncertain terms. They narrated Fante's historical "chosenness" as a matter of factual observation and research, rather than mainly of spiritual intuition. Du Bois, meanwhile, assigns a prophetic role only to others, and with more self-evidently rhetorical intentions. In a moving recollection in *The Souls of Black Folk* of his infant son's death, he refers to a parental love that felt like a "revelation of the divine." And in reference to his meeting with African American minister and missionary Alexander Crummell, he recalls that he "bowed before this man, as one bows before the prophets of the world."[78] By the time of *Black Reconstruction*'s publication in 1935, Du Bois had made explicit his understanding of how historical objectivity informs—but does not in itself constitute—prophetic leadership. Its final chapter, "The Propaganda of History," takes both southern and northern American historians to task for failing to accurately portray the post–Civil War era of Reconstruction in the 1860s and '70s, insisting after a long review of the historiographical literature that "we have got clearly to distinguish between fact and desire."[79] The historian, in other words, must work in service of truth as a value unto itself, unhindered by social biases or narrative sensibility in order to let people's complex humanity shine through. "What we have got to know, so far as possible, are the things that actually happened in the world," Du Bois affirms. With this much, the pragmatic and fact-seeking Casely Hayford would surely have agreed.

How he might have felt about the division of labor that Du Bois thinks this more honest model of doing history entails is a stickier question. Du Bois's chapter continues, "Then with that much clear and open to every reader, the philosopher and prophet has a chance to interpret these facts; but the historian has no right, posing as a scientist, to conceal or distort facts; and until we distinguish between these two functions of the chronicler of human action, we are going to render it easy for a muddled world out of sheer ignorance to make the same mistake ten times over."[80] The philosopher and prophet are distinct from the historian, in this formulation, and the historian's work is essential to but uncoupled from the task of offering moral or spiritual guidance. An objective account of historical facts clears a path to social redemption but does not traverse it. The discursive environment within which Casely Hayford builds his career, however, often conflates Du Bois's "two functions." A representative essay in the *Gold Coast Methodist Times*, "Africa for Christ," published on October 30, 1897, enjoins, "If we divest our minds from all ideas of poetic license and base our faith upon the Impregnable Rock of Holy Scripture, we cannot help anticipating . . . that Africa For Christ is a glorious possibility." Facts here are *akin* to prophecy, not the preconditions of its emergence. This conjoining of predestined Fante leadership and nose-to-the-ground state building extends across outlets and across decades around the turn of the twentieth century, plainly influencing Casely Hayford. "Remember, after all, that the Aborigines of the Gold Coast and of Ashanti, as Tennyson has it, are the 'heirs of the ages,'" he addresses British readers in *Native Institutions*, "and who knows but there may be higher things destined for their achievement than you can conceive of?"[81] As I demonstrate in this book's next chapter, Casely Hayford was also transfixed by new forms of charismatic Christianity that were already on the rise in West Africa in his lifetime.

Even aside from this important historical difference in religious trajectory, however, George Levine's vision of the pursuit of objectivity as a force for shaping narrative has points of both relevance to and illuminating divergence from the post-Confederation Fante context. In the first category, Levine links science to Victorian literature by means of "the language of impartiality" and a "determination to thwart desire and preconceptions" in pursuit of truth.[82] On this score, at least, *Gold Coast Native Institutions* does indeed share a self-transcending moral vocabulary with a canonical nineteenth-century British writer like George Eliot. But *Dying to Know* steps back from the widespread critical view that "the self-abnegation that is part of the history of scientific epistemology must disguise some kind of interest"—Levine, that is, entertains the idea of a sincere commitment to seeing the world from outside one's own situation.[83] Casely Hayford and Sarbah, on the other hand, make no attempt to conceal their profound personal investment in the facts they present about the Gold Coast. Their critique of the British is that they are less objective about the Fante than are educated Fante; British politics, much like Du Bois's southern historians of American Reconstruction, makes them blind to the writing on their own imperial walls.

But nor is this a situation of colonized peoples seeing and "exposing" what the decolonial theorist par excellence Walter Mignolo calls "the darker side of modernity," thereby requiring that the colonized "de-link" themselves from their former Western oppressors.[84] Casely Hayford recites the cold, hard truths of the British Empire to British readers because he wants to help it help itself. Part of the difference between these two approaches to granting epistemic privilege to the colonized is what we might call temperamental. None of the Fante intelligentsia writing in the Gold Coast press really expresses a sense of having been oppressed or subjugated; Casely Hayford's complaint is rather that his "type" has been indefensibly disrespected and suspected of being anti-British. An editorial published under the pseudonym Africanus in the June 8, 1912, issue of the *Gold Coast Leader* scoffs at the "absurdity" and "unthinkableness" of the idea that "the Educated Native is seeking ... to over-throw the British connection," and then counters "without fear of contradiction that the Educated African prides himself on being more truly loyal to the person and throne of the monarch of the British Empire (knowing what the King and Empire really represent) than some Britishers one meets with out here." Surely you can't be serious?, such Fante intellectuals ask incredulously; have you seen who you are dealing with here? Levine contends persuasively that "the critique of an objectivity that turns out in fact to be a disguise of interest undercuts its own objectives if after the exposure of particular interests, it goes on to argue—or imply—that the very act of seeking objectivity is invalid."[85] This is a useful formulation because it clarifies how the Fante writers in question here do precisely the reverse: they *claim* their "particular interests" as a means of advancing their claim to objectivity, in the name of shared imperial goals.

Turning back to *Gold Coast Native Institutions* in this light reveals a more explicit connection between emplaced sensibility and place-transcendent perspective. A section called "The People" (which contains the description of Asante as cautious and diplomatic) upholds the "Gold Coast man" as intrinsically equipped with "the force of a logic which no decent British Cabinet can withstand" and free to adopt "European comforts and amenities" without assimilationist peril because of "the resourcefulness, tact, and practical common sense of his nature."[86] Later, in the section "The Fetish System," Casely Hayford flips the script on British condescension to native spirituality to make *theirs* seem like the unsubstantiated view. While certain forms of direct spirit-communion might "to the unscientific mind seem barbarous," he rejoins that "when critically examined, [they] cover a mine of truth and inspiration."[87] The English espouse objectivity but fall short of achieving it, so that their haughty affect is out of sync with Casely Hayford's "evidence" and thus ill-suited to imperial flourishing. "Your matter-of-fact Englishman is too prosaic for the average native intelligence," he writes bluntly.[88] From this view, the myopia of the Gold Coast governor is not helped by his being in service to "an over-taxed official [the colonial secretary], some 3,000 miles away, who may or may not be a capable man, and who gleans his information as to the local conditions from his obedient servant, the Governor!"[89] The tactical concern here is obvious: a closed informational loop of British leadership that excludes Gold Coast leaders from influence acts "against true imperialism and the expansion of British influence and prestige."[90] But on a conceptual level, this is a point on which Casely Hayford epitomizes the connection between analytic distance and cultural and geographical attachment. Levine, in *Dying to Know*, wonders poignantly whether "the insistence on the primary values of localism and particularism [has] done what good work [it] can, and are now ... playing into the obsessive individualism of contemporary social and economic structures."[91] In contrast, the Fante intelligentsia declare that only by seeing from within can one productively labor toward glimpsing truth from without.

To be sure, much of what these Fante intellectuals espouse is absorbed from different and overlapping strains of discourse from Victorian London; as Collis-Buthelezi's essay on nineteenth-century Cape Town makes evident, liberalism is "in the air" all over the British Empire. Lauren Goodlad pinpoints a shift from an early and mid-Victorian emphasis on "prescriptive character" to a late Victorian narrowing to "descriptive character," with the first valuing "the elasticity of character" in a way that "gave rise to ambitious schemes of moral perfectability."[92] Leaning heavily on John Stuart Mill, Goodlad argues that a prescriptive emphasis on character building is ultimately about the second part of that term; its precise contents are "infinitely plastic," configured and reconfigured to abet an engaged citizenry and institutions meant to link individual growth to "a holist social ontology."[93] In this way, the dominant Victorian notion of character might be seen as both liberal and collectivist, a pairing that also aptly describes Casely Hayford's post-Confederation Fante intellectual individualism as it is wielded for the larger project of Fante, Akan, and ultimately West African uplift at whose helm he stands. He envisions the Fante as "the predominant partner in the coming Imperial West Africa" largely because they have been most demonstrably concerned with education.[94] Dropping in references to Tennyson and the influence of Greece and Rome, Casely Hayford reminds British readers that they too have been a work in progress. "It is a matter of history that, at the beginning of the Christian era, you were worse off than we are today," he asserts, "greater darkness brooded over your intellectual horizon." No nation, and no person, can grow into the best version of itself without "that educational element which will draw out all the best [innate] qualities ... preparing and making him ready to contribute to life's work."[95] Character building on this model is a scalable and tailorable enterprise, valuable for its ability to plug developing human parts into a developmentally minded institutional grid.

By the dawn of the twentieth century, Goodlad and others suggest, a more punitive notion of character came to the fore. "Fueled by the globalization of capital, the quest for dominion over world markets, and the growing competition among European powers for far-flung empires," she writes, "these social and geopolitical factors were integral to the increasing rejection of an Enlightenment discourse that held human character to be fundamentally equal and perfectible across geographic, racial, and cultural boundaries."[96] Accompanied by the consolidation of racial pseudoscience beginning in the 1880s, in all its profane confusion of biological and social factors, "colonized people were conceived at best to be lagging in a temporal cultural trajectory that would eventually resemble England's, and at worst to differ incorrigibly from the normative qualities of Anglo-Saxon character."[97] This baseless version of the link between character and objectivity is the one Casely Hayford rejects; looking back to the Fante Confederation thus neatly overlaps for him and his peers with recapturing and grounding a more open-ended notion of character from Victorian intellectual life. To try to pinpoint specific sources for Casely Hayford's terminology is beside the point; it is equally as easy to find traces of Kantian empiricism in his work as it is to find Hegelian historical destiny. All of it is multiply refracted and digested, and all of it is molded to accommodate the Gold Coast's leadership ambitions. At the same time, he is not incoherently parroting British appropriations of European philosophical terms when he conflates science and history, or spirit and evidence, but attempting to restore them to some kind of tangible meaning. And the Fante Confederation is the *specific* history required to anchor History as such to a concept of development, even after British ideas have turned in more noxious directions.

Perhaps the most salient broad trend in Victorian ideas about character, however, in terms of how they permeated Gold Coast thought, is an emphasis on the moral value of *constraint*. As Stefan Collini has noted, "the blurring of the distinction between [explanatory and evaluative senses of character] was facilitated by the assumption that the possession of settled dispositions indicated a certain habit of restraining one's impulses. The contrast was with behaviour which was random, impulsive, feckless; and where the impulses were identified ... with the 'lower self' ... then a positive connotation was conferred on the habit of restraint itself."[98] This summary has explanatory force for how the Fante intelligentsia saw the relationship between moral standing and a capacity to be objective—to see "just the facts," even where one's own culture and self-interest are concerned. But it is also helpful for understanding their valorization of their decidedly *un*-representative milieu. The pro-imperial but anticolonial project of Gold Coast self-determination was as much about understanding the limits of epistemic agency as it was about having more political control. Collini's assessment that mid-nineteenth-century English liberalism was motivated less by the commonly cited priorities of liberty or individual rights and more by a "fundamental emotional dynamic" that he describes as "hostility to unreflective and unjustified privilege and a related hatred of being patronized" also rings true in this context.[99] From the perspective of Casely Hayford, Attoh Ahuma, or Sarbah, British imperialists erred by overstepping the *bounds* of their knowledge, rather than by fundamentally misunderstanding what knowledge is. Imperial flourishing from the Gold Coast perspective was best imagined not as top-down epistemological diffusion, but as a collation of different scales of self-representation in pursuit of a common truth. Facts could be brought into view by the part, for the whole; marking clear limits as to who knew what permitted those limits' transcendence.

Though it is far afield from the Gold Coast situation, Kunal Parker's work on the transformation of the common law in nineteenth-century American law offers a revealing discussion of how an ideal of constraint bridges moral, characterological, and political registers. As such, it makes for a fitting transition to this chapter's next section on the character profile that brings these realms together in Casely Hayford's setting. In Parker's telling, American legal-historical scholarship, beginning in the mid to late twentieth century, has taken an antifoundationalist view of history—a view, that is, that "Law's foundations may be dismantled in the name of history" so as to "[reveal] law to be a kind of politics."[100] He instead thinks back to a time when neither law *nor* history was imagined as contingent. "The ideational world of the nineteenth century was a world in which the notion of *given* constraints was very real indeed," Parker writes. "In other words, this was not a world in which the subject—whether an individual, a group, or a society—ordinarily deemed itself free to act entirely as it pleased, to reimagine the world in a thoroughgoing way."[101] The broad shape of this argument can be usefully overlaid on Casely Hayford's intellectual world, which also confounds now-prevalent ideas that law and history are "constructed" and thus open to radical intervention. Parker's interest in "the kinds of limits that were imagined, and the ways in which those limits were made to interact with each other" yields dividends when transposed to a text like *Native Institutions*, in which facts and political structures somehow *just are*, despite the presence of a self-aware and creative narrator.[102] If the British Empire is envisioned as bearing some intrinsic relation to the highest ideals of civilizational advancement, then African self-determination becomes a matter of internal reconfiguration within a predetermined shape.

For this reason, too, the intra-imperial independence of the Fante Confederation proves a generative reference point. Attoh Ahuma, for example, refers to an arrangement of *"imperium in imperio,"* or a state within a state, as "the highest organized form of government in creation."[103] Imperial symbols in this vision serve as the "true" form of what is to some degree historically variable content. "We are being welded together under one umbrageous Flag," he continues, "a Flag that is the symbol of justice, freedom, and fairplay; . . . The Gold Coast under the *aegis* of the Union Jack is the unanswerable argument to all who may incontinently withhold from us the common rights, privileges, and status of nationality."[104] The political constraint of empire here expresses the ultimate constraint of values that are imagined, as Parker notes, to be "given" and immutable, a way of seeing the world as derived from first principles that predates more recent understandings of it as "the product of nothing but history, as one historically locatable phenomenon giving way to another."[105] Like the American nineteenth-century legal theorists whose perspective Parker recovers, the Gold Coast intellectuals on view here see politics as a means to a historical end that is already known. "In other words," Parker writes, "political decision making, which took place in historical time, was constrained by a law that unfolded outside historical time. To many, this was not the contradiction that it appears to be to us."[106] We might ask in response how what now appears as a contradiction may have appeared to *them*. In Casely Hayford's world, the short and quite literal answer is: as a certain kind of man.

The "Educated Native" in Profile

The "Educated Native," or sometimes "Educated African," was a Gold Coast character type collectively authored by Casely Hayford, Attoh Ahuma, Sarbah (to a lesser degree), and any number of anonymous writers of their generation and milieu. They, in turn, looked to the Fante Confederation generation before them to ground their sense of how this figure could be most effective in the world, specifically in advancing the cause of an intra-imperial federation of independent West African states. Exactly who this man was—how he looked, spent his time, and imagined himself—was also a contentious subject of African and British exchange. In this way, the Educated Native was a participant in *and* the content of Gold Coast intellectual culture as it rose to meet the twentieth century; he was a catalyst for and an embodiment of historically mindful change. This figure was not representative, but he was exemplary. And, as I have shown, he claimed to have an objective view of his own anointed status.

When Sarbah invokes him in *Fanti Customary Laws*, calling customary law "a field of investigation which should engage the close and studious attention of every educated native," "educated" could easily be mistaken as a simple synonym for "literate."[107] And obviously, the ability to read and write was an important part of attaining "educated" status. As Stephanie Newell has richly demonstrated, English book culture in the late nineteenth and early twentieth-century Gold Coast—as the successor to a missionary print culture built around devotional literature, including scripture translated into local languages—facilitated the emergence of "a coherent set of African aesthetic values" that emphasized status and edification.[108] But literacy as such is not enough to fill out Casely Hayford's character profile, which emphasized a stricter and more curated set of traits, including self-discipline, observational rigor, and a kind of studied earthiness or inclination to "get one's hands dirty" while maintaining elegant composure. The subjects of Newell's work compose a "neglected, low-rank class of African reader in Ghana" mainly in the 1920s and '30s, who sought to "gain prestige in local (rather than imperial) systems," even as they focused on mastering the English language and acquired European home decor.[109] One of the most compelling parts of her analysis homes in on young, aspirational Gold Coast readers' propensity to use English often perceived by British speakers as "bombastic" or pompous, because "to substitute simple for complex words would have been to compromise the expression of mental culture and 'civilisation.'"[110] Casely Hayford is too British *and* too Fante a figure to fit in among this group, who were striving where he was slick.

The Educated Native of and for whom his writing speaks makes defter cultural transitions. One bit of Casely Hayford lore illustrates this trait with precision: "My grandfather wore Kente cloth to study at Cambridge, and Savile Row to visit family in Ghana," the late British-Ghanaian fashion designer Joe Casely-Hayford has recounted.[111] What might appear as hypocrisy in a still frame—such as when a newspaper photo of Casely Hayford "dressed in accordance with the best European style of the day" was accompanied by a note that "he was particularly critical of Africans wearing European dress"—looks in motion more like alertness to the need for frequent adjustment.[112] This attention to the external metrics of bicultural life also extended to his concern with language. Unlike the young Gold Coast scholars' efforts to speak a maximally "civilized" English, Casely Hayford worried about maintaining proper Fante. His second wife, the upper-crust Sierra Leonean woman Adelaide Smith, suggests as much in her letters to him from England, reporting that their daughter, Gladys, "has got a wonderful grasp of English already, but I am sorry to say is fast forgetting her Fante. Archie too is hardly able to converse with her now and finds great difficulty in expressing himself in Fante but I tell him he must try and talk to Baby or else you will be so dreadfully disappointed when you see them."[113]

In a straightforward and not especially interesting sense, Casely Hayford's close attention to his manner and appearance bespeaks his elite status and cosmopolitan formation. It is easy to see why members of his Fante milieu have so often been described as middlemen, with little ensuing effort to map the intellectual substance of that role. But the story of Casely Hayford's switching it up between Kente cloth and tailored English suits as he moved between social worlds is more than a fun family anecdote: it has a part to play in developing the kind of "emplaced objectivity" his work espoused. There is real effort involved in this kind of attention to the details of self-presentation, and it operates, at the level of action, along similar lines to those along which his writing upholds Akan political history as imperial prophecy. Both cases cast the Fante as a people who can watch themselves without affective interference, reacting to what they observe in deliberate ways. This is the essence of the Educated Native, at least for Casely Hayford. When he ponders the coming together of Fante and Asante in the name of larger political goals, and who should facilitate this "long-wished-for union," he concludes that "the foreign intermeddler is an utterly hopeless individual for this task. He has neither the requisite knowledge, nor the patience and coolness necessary for the great consummation. It must be the work of the educated Native, if the British Government will trust him to do it." This figure, unlike an outsider, can be relied on to maintain intellectual distance from his lived expertise. Casely Hayford vows, "He will take the Native State System as he finds it, and develop and improve it on aboriginal lines, and on scientific principles."[114] Intimacy breeds not contempt, but diplomatic acumen.

A similar dynamic defined the local journalistic arena in the first decades of the twentieth century. The hyperfocus on the Educated African among the uppermost Gold Coast intellectual stratum might now ring as a bit self-absorbed, akin to the *New York Times*'s inordinate twenty-first-century coverage of internal Ivy League university politics. At Booker T. Washington's International Conference on the Negro in Tuskegee in April 1912, which Casely Hayford did not end up attending in person, his was the only paper slated to focus on a kind of *person* rather than a broadly framed political, social, or pedagogical issue. The second presentation listed in the May 9, 1912, issue of the *Gold Coast Nation*, it was titled, "Progress of the Gold Coast Native." The papers before and after give some idea of the more typical format: the first listed in the *Nation*'s Tuskegee lineup was "Africa To-day—A Survey of Present Conditions," by American Cornelius H. Patton, and the second was "Educational Conditions on the Gold Coast," by Casely Hayford's brother, the Methodist minister Mark C. Hayford. In the context of his work back home, however, Casely Hayford's targeted sense of how best to characterize—quite literally—his concerns was part of a shared discursive agenda. As it happens, one of the other Tuskegee presenters listed was E. D. Morel, the influential editor of the Liverpool-based newspaper the *African Mail*, against whom the *Gold Coast Leader* (almost certainly Casely Hayford) had an ongoing polemic related to Casely Hayford's topic. A March 16, 1912, essay titled simply "The Educated Native" takes Morel to task for his reporting on the Forest Bill, in which he was accused of "[chiming] in with the general, but erroneous and impolitic opinion that the educated native is a danger to his Fatherland." The Englishman, the *Leader* contended, fundamentally misunderstood his Gold Coast counterparts through the warmth of his paternalistic glow. The piece continues, "Why has [the educated native] been such a bugbear to a certain class of Europeans . . . ? Of course Governments have invariably considered him a dangerous character, and have always more or less sought to separate him from his poor illiterate brother." Either the Educated Native must do the bidding of the British in misappropriating African resources under cover of management, or he is labeled "disloyal and a scoundrel." An African was welcome to *appear* educated, but not to be a serious interlocutor.

And to be a serious interlocutor, in the *Leader*'s view, again comes back to exhibiting the trait of self-encompassing and thereby self-enabling objectivity. Time and again, members of the Fante intelligentsia invited British journalists and officials to meet them in their efforts to get things straight, even when it entailed taking a critical view of themselves. Were the Gold Coast Africans *not* willing and able to do so, they would have abandoned the performance of self-objectification on which their claim to ascendency rested. When the author of "The Educated Native" remarks on his and his peers' previous high regard for Morel as someone who "stood up for [their] Race," he does not ask for praise but for clear-eyed respect. "We certainly do not say because he has made himself our champion, he should connive at our faults and mistakes," the essay clarifies, because "in that case he would not have been a true lover of our Race." Casely Hayford's *Leader* was nothing if not consistent in this position. The same March 16, 1912, issue reaffirms its universal commitment to telling it like it is, in the face of ARPS objections to being criticized where anyone might see. "Because we are all blacks, we must not criticize ourselves publicly," the *Leader* summarized that position, because "if we do this we give away ourselves to the [colonial] Government and ruin our case." Casely Hayford's (likely) response was unflinching, as he countered, "A journal is a journal and it has duties to perform irrespective of colour." The Educated Native, in this context, is a minority within a minority, holding his ground even where it was cause for his "becoming suspicious to his people." Facts were facts, and right was right, regardless of the social groups in question.

There was, however, an important caveat. The essay anchors its willingness to accept fair criticism across the bounds of race by reasserting the standard to which members of both races must be held: that of "unprejudiced and unbiased" writing, deemed as such by reading "soberly and discreetly." Reading, writing, and character analysis were meant to facilitate more than a deeper understanding of the self or even the world, which might then become "political" in an indirect way by cultivating engaged and questioning citizens. Literary faculties here *are* politics and indeed are outright existential. For E. D. Morel, as the leading British liberal voice on African cultural affairs, to propagate a misreading of the Educated Native threatened the historical outcome to which Casely Hayford had already staked his reading of the Fante Confederation past. For the signal role of the Educated Native to *be* true, in the sense of having the power to shape policies and institutions, the deeper truth of his character had first to be recognized as a matter of factual agreement. The ongoing controversy around how to read the Educated Native figure was a means of moving the dial on what was taken for granted about the Gold Coast by all parties, even where disagreement was otherwise encouraged.

For the Educated Native to participate in such debates about his own role meant letting himself be misleadingly objectified in the name of encouraging objective political discussion, as another, unusually long editorial in the March 30, 1912, issue of the *Leader*—"The Educated Native: As We See Ourselves"—remarked. An anonymous author, who, again, was probably Casely Hayford, wrote there, "Let us admit that with our training and present condition of things, with the present times, to serve one's country as his time and opportunities may let him means exposing one's self to every shade of misinterpretation." I do not want to make too much of how a single line is laid out, but "one's self" suggests a relation to a separable, external thing. To attain objectivity vis-à-vis "one's self," as it is actively molded into an ideal Fante character type, is much like learning to read for fixed truth and not only variable meaning. "Let the educated native divest himself of all prejudice and in his calmer moments think on these things," the essay's final paragraph advises. "It may be we have put them too crudely, but are they true?" An assumption of separable selfhood is also granted, collectively, to the British, albeit in the form of a warning about that self's neglect. Yet another relevant *Leader* editorial written under the pseudonym Africanus, "E.D.M. and the Educated African," printed on June 8, 1912, advises "John Bull," "You must strive to maintain yourself and your dignity; and send all those who would drag your fair fame in the mud about their business."[115] The British "self," however, is addressed as a popular national character, while the Educated African in its Fante incarnation is meant to embody their nation's best rather than most typical traits.

Studying, refining, and defending one's own social significance—an exposure to petty criticism made tolerable by the absolute assuredness of self-worth—was work intensive. It meant hours upon hours of focused reading, writing, and editing, in addition to practicing law, in Sarbah and Casely Hayford's cases. But it also meant "work" of a more abstract sort: that of constant self-examination and self-discipline, triangulating one's position as if from outside it. This laborious pursuit of the self-as-object was nonetheless a far cry from the pathos of Du Bois's influential concept of double-consciousness, which articulates the rending experience of internalizing the self-minimizing gaze of people with social and political power.[116] At base level, this is because Casely Hayford, departing from Edward Blyden's defense of African American leadership on the African continent, sought to "shift the orientation of 'natural' Pan-African leadership from African America to West Africa."[117] But there are also fundamental epistemological differences between Du Bois and Casely Hayford, in addition to those inscribed by geography. Double-consciousness is ultimately concerned with the *composition* of racialized subjectivity, and oppression's disruption of the holistic development of the self. The Educated African's view of the self as fact, as typified by Casely Hayford's writing, is more about what a subject does. The labor is in looking, not being.

This does not mean that Casely Hayford was right where Du Bois was wrong, or vice versa; who is to have the last word on what it is "really" like living under racial colonialism, from one place to another? It does mean taking at face value Casely Hayford's nonconstructivist understanding of the Educated Native or African, as developed in the *Leader* and elsewhere; he is engaged, that is, not in a dialogic process of self-making, but in a stalwart routine of self-honing. This is a figure who *already is*, who sees himself clearly and wants others to see him clearly too. Contra Korang's description of Casely Hayford as "investing 'Africa' and 'the African' in a fictive objectivity," which he sees as a tactical move against a false British colonial objectivity that evacuates Africans of full humanity, I see the promulgation of the Educated Native as an earnest effort at mimetic representation.[118] For him to be who he said he was meant there was hope for teaching colonial administrators to see the truth, in the era of their amped-up incursion. The guiding idea was that for John Bull to become objective would correct his tendency to the wrongful objectification of African people. But how, exactly, to do this? In what kind of conduct does objectivity obtain? Korang's language of Casely Hayford's Faustian deal and "impossible situation" locates the thrust of his intellectual work at the historical macro level, in the creation of a new kind of paradoxical Euro-African self.[119] Here it will be useful instead to consider Casely Hayford's performance of actual habits and exertions.

Returning to Daston and Galison's work on the consolidation of objectivity as an epistemic ideal in the nineteenth century offers a link, here, between the big picture of African modernity and a more mundane and habitual, less historically anguished version of Educated African selfhood. Their immediate focus is on changing forms of scientific observation, which they chronicle through the "nitty-gritty visual practices" recorded in scientific atlases (e.g., engraving, illustrations, and photographs).[120] But Daston and Galison also bring to the fore a salutary emphasis on distinguishing objectivity from mathematization as such. In the provocative formulation "To embrace objectivity . . . was not only to practice a science but also to pattern a self," they suggest that to think of oneself as objective entails certain *actions*, or codes of individual behavior.[121] More to the point, they argue that the pursuit of objectivity has always been an arduous endeavor, a self-conscious and exacting undertaking rather than merely a set of behaviors that a historian might observe after the fact. "But if actions are substituted for concepts and practices for meanings, the focus on the nebulous notion of objectivity sharpens," they write, and "resolves into the gestures, techniques, habits, and temperament ingrained by training and daily repetition."[122] They call this approach "objectivity in shirtsleeves," which dovetails perfectly with Casely Hayford's sense of himself as a practical man—including, for that matter, in his strategic use of clothing.[123] It also provides a critical language for how he operationalizes facticity more broadly in *Native Institutions*, by tethering his ability to read people correctly to an assiduous Fante work ethic. "The careless foreign critic puts down the nonchalance of the Native to ingrained laziness," he complains. He then continues, "Whenever I come across such critics I smile at their simplicity. As a matter of fact, the 'lazy Fante' is capable of putting forth effort amidst his own surroundings which men of no other race on earth can."[124]

A clear, if circular, set of relationships emerges by overlaying Daston and Galison's work atop Casely Hayford's, and it looks something like this: the Educated African's labor of maintaining an objective view of himself also allows him to see how other Fante make objective (because effective) real-life calculations. "Objectivity," in this way, can come for Casely Hayford to seem like a distinctive Gold Coast trait. Where foreigners misperceive a reticent, locally calibrated temperament as "lazy," he sees the character profile that has facilitated the rise of the Gold Coast's gold, mahogany, and rubber industries.[125] Objectivity is as objectivity does, and what one *does* also drives his understanding of character. In effect, then, objectivity becomes a character trait. The terms of Casely Hayford's praise for others reinforce this tight association between steady work habits, unbiased perception, and admirable kinds of personhood, especially where writing is concerned. In his brief history of Gold Coast journalism, he extols Charles Bannerman—founding editor of West Africa's first newspaper, the *West African Herald*, in the late 1850s as well as a "lawyer, wit, and publicist"—for his "extraordinary pains" in copying out issues by hand.[126] He offers similarly workmanly accolades to Bannerman's peers and close successors, calling them "able," "humbler" than others he knew, and, in the case of the *Western Echo*'s editor Prince Brew (also known in print as The Owl), describing his painstaking editorial process and openness to criticism.[127] There is a striking overlap between legal training and journalistic credibility in Casely Hayford's chronology of Gold Coast intellectual achievement, obviously in a biographical sense but also in terms of an idealized relationship between gritty, grubby intimacy with text and analytic distance. Working hard with words is what separates mere intuition from an evidence-based understanding of the Gold Coast's imperial exceptionalism.

In this way, Casely Hayford's Educated Native anticipates Daston and Galison's scientific observer in shirtsleeves. Both have their nose to the proverbial grindstone and their eye on representational truth. And following Rohit De's call to study "the labor and practice of lawyering, as opposed to merely . . . the declaratory acts of legislation and judgments" driving anticolonial histories (in De's work, later ones), Casely Hayford's professional identity fits neatly with an emphasis on small practices that support paradigmatic change.[128] There is, however, also a crucial and clarifying difference lurking here. Daston and Galison locate the objectivity paradigm's consolidation among nineteenth-century "men of science" in a new concern with self-discipline, as they now "insisted . . . on the importance of effacing their own personalities and developed techniques that left as little as possible to the discretion of either artist or scientist."[129] The ideal of objectivity, in other words, entailed the suppression of the self to maintain an open field for the object being studied. But this is not quite what Casely Hayford attempts, in that he is not trying just to record but to *distill* the reality of Gold Coast customary norms and political structures. A scientific rendering of a snowflake, to take one of Daston and Galison's examples, is a one-to-one correspondence even across changing understandings of what that means ("typical" vs. "accurate," etc.). The selection and synthesis of details from Gold Coast court cases, legal committee proceedings, and textual precursors like Sarbah's *Fanti Customary Laws*, meanwhile—the forging of salient facts from abundant information—is necessarily reductive.[130] To perform this reduction persuasively and advance his political goals, Casely Hayford's objectivity had to be a public performance. He rendered his labors of intellectual self-suppression self-expressively.

All told, this is *Native Institutions*'s most arresting feature: it is an "objective" customary legal treatise that is also a declaration of self. And because it is a lengthy exercise in *textual* collation and analysis, rather than an ethnography based on field observation, the relationship on which Casely Hayford's claim to objectivity and thus selfhood rests is between not author and world, but author and archive. Some of his methods for cultivating his reader's trust are straightforward, such as when he invites and then moves to dispel skepticism of his authority in the book's preface. "Now, the sources of information in regard to the Gold Coast are so meagre and, in parts, so unreliable, that the intelligent reader may justifiably enquire how I have come by the facts recorded in this book," he writes there. "I shall satisfy that curiosity; and I do so the more willingly, as I am desirous that the reader should have the opportunity of testing the truths herein stated for himself."[131] At this point, he describes the research process and materials—including "tomes of official reports and Government Blue Books"—that led him ultimately to his "correct" conclusions.[132] Like any good academic researcher, Casely Hayford also signposts his arguments to keep readers on track with the accumulation of evidence. Phrases like "as I have shown" (in his profile of the indigenous Gold Coast judicial system), and "Let it be distinctly understood" (in reference to slowed trade between Fante and Asante after 1830) continually assert his command of the text, and by extension, of general principles of textual organization.[133] Not surprisingly, such efforts to mark the objectivity of his authorial manner are most prominent when he performs his lawyerliness. He opens a section on "The King's Paramountcy" by reaching out to fellow legal minds, assuring them that he will clear up their understandable confusion on the topic. "To the student of jurisprudence, fresh from the law schools of Great Britain, the doctrines of Paramountcy in the Customary Law must be bewildering and difficult of comprehension," he concedes.[134] Casely Hayford's ideal of writing is not creative but collational; he has the way with words to make facts make sense.

In general, his written performance of legal reasoning outside the strict confines of the law becomes a template for how he presents his views as objective in other, nontextual domains. His process of clarification— "[ridding] our minds of misconceptions"—tends to proceed along some version of the following: a broad general statement of a practice or norm; a detailed but still general breakdown of how that practice or norm works; a specific example to illustrate the truth of the general statement; a summing-up of the evidence for, and reformulation of, the broad statement as (legally) actionable rules or principles.[135] This unfolds across pages, not paragraphs. A glimpse of one strong example of how such reasoning works, however, should suffice to take stock of Casely Hayford's movement between legal and nonlegal topics, as his legal credibility echoes through the text to drive the appearance of a broader objective viewpoint. Taking off from the general statement that "in the Customary law, we find no trace of individual ownership," he then explains the correspondence between different rungs of chiefly authority and different kinds of offering (i.e., tribute versus allegiance). Whereas that part of the argument uses examples labeled "A" or "B"—at first read, likely still to be a bit confusing to a cultural outsider—he then presents a pair of clearer, more vivid hypothetical case studies based on plausible real-life scenarios.[136] After *that*, he works at length through legal precedents for his reading of how Akan chieftaincies work, before ending the section with a numbered list of "simple rules" for keeping the concepts of ownership and paramountcy straight.[137] Casely Hayford's case feels airtight, less an "argument" than a patient untangling of what should already have been clear.

Outside the immediate legal realm, his techniques for demonstrating objectivity are less blunt and more narratively compelling. Casely Hayford "proves" general statements with his own stories when they present an ideal balance between his lived understanding of Gold Coast social life and his remove from its most representative subjects. By writing himself "reading" others who anyone else might have encountered, but of course did not, he makes his first-person accounts appear almost verifiable. Read what I've read, he ventures, and see what I've seen. One notable anecdote appears in the section on "The Fetish System" in the book's second chapter, also called "Native Institutions" and structured as a series of short profiles of foundational elements of Gold Coast life and rule. In terms of rhetorical formula, it takes the place of the hypothetical case studies in the earlier explanation of chieftaincy structures, appearing after the statement of a norm and the impersonal account of its mechanics. "The Native of the Gold Coast profoundly believes in the world of spirits," Casely Hayford declares on the first page of "The Fetish System." "He believes that the spirit in man never dies. So vivid is his faith that he holds open and direct communion with his dead friends, not through a medium, but, as it were, face to face."[138] (This is the general statement.) From this broad summation of an indigenous spiritual practice, he then invites his British readers into its world by switching to a second-person form of address. "You should watch him as he takes offerings of food and drink to the grave-side," he remarks, replicating the verification he invites in the book's preface, but now in relation to a living archive.[139] Finally, after describing the religious feelings of a typical Native whom he names only "He"—filling the role of the illustrative subjects "A" and "B" in his explanation of chieftaincies and offerings—Casely Hayford presents a set of personal recollections. "I shall not soon forget a scene I witnessed in the grave-yard of the Gold Coast not long ago," he writes, replacing a hypothetical set of scenarios with twinned memories of flesh-and-blood encounters.[140]

These encounters are memorable indeed. In the first, he describes watching a widow place the customary food and drink on her son's grave, to which she then adds—"gently"—a bouquet of flowers that she felt he would enjoy.[141] In recounting this detail, Casely Hayford compensates for the less-verifiable nature of the first-person "evidence" for his statement about indigenous religion with what feels like a *truer* case in point. It is standard practice topped up with warm idiosyncrasy, the letter of the customary law he has spelled out bulwarked by a poignant expression of its spirit. The second encounter links Casely Hayford's loss—that of his cherished first wife, Beatrice Pinnock—to the popular Akan belief system he is explaining. Standing in the same cemetery, he is greeted by a woman who then also casually greets his late beloved. "So fervent is their belief in the hereafter," he affirms on this basis. "To them man never dies."[142] At once tender and rhetorically efficient, these memories suture Casely Hayford's legal-analytic habits to his intuitive understanding of how character can convince. As the quintessential Educated Native, he showcases the textual virtuosity behind his objectivity to enhance rather than undermine its claims. It is not enough, therefore, to label Casely Hayford a cultural go-between when he is also a moving cultural exegete. His writing marks the meeting point of portrait and explanation, drawing out the richness of his world for all to observe.

CHAPTER TWO

A Gold Coast Constitution

IN MARCH 1920, J. E. Casely Hayford helped convene a landmark event in Accra called the First Conference of Africans of British West Africa. Hosted by the newly consecrated National Congress of British West Africa (NCBWA), the conference gathered a handful of delegates from Nigeria and Sierra Leone, and one from the Gambia, alongside their more numerous Gold Coast colleagues. Its remit was broad but clear: to chart a course toward African legal and political self-representation within the British Empire. As a regional successor organization to the Gold Coast–focused Aborigines' Rights Protection Society, the NCBWA sought to do this mainly by transforming the West African colonies' Legislative Councils—to which Africans could be appointed only as "unofficial" members—into bodies of elected representatives with real teeth in local affairs. Casely Hayford served as the NCBWA's first vice president under fellow barrister Thomas Hutton-Mills and in that role delivered a characteristically silver-tongued speech. Its high note resounded across more than two decades of Gold Coast history, as Casely Hayford recalled the intelligence and resolve of Fante Confederation leader King Ghartey's dying words in 1897: "Be constitutional." As Ghartey's unofficial heir, Casely Hayford now sounded this same call to his coastal compatriots. "We must be firm, we must be outspoken[,] we must avoid subterranean grumblings," he urged, "but in everything that we do, in the name of Heaven, let us be constitutional."[1]

His cri de coeur seems to have struck a chord with the lawyers and ministers, along with a few professors and editors, gathered in that Accra room: the conference transcript notes that Casely Hayford's speech was met with "loud applause which continued in a crescendo."[2] But what did it actually mean to "be constitutional" in this context, with no official Gold Coast founding document to uphold? The adjectival form of the injunction suggests that something more than a form of government was at stake; it invokes personal principles more than a clear set of political practices. To *be* a certain way entails a subject, linking a sense of self to a way of life. Linda Colley, in her magisterial study *The Gun, the Ship, and the Pen*, holds that "a constitution, after all, like a novel, invents and tells the story of a place and a people. These documents were—and are—always more than themselves, and more too than a matter of law and politics."[3] Casely Hayford's pronouncement of his constitutionalist politics in the NCBWA setting thus provides an entry point to working through its intricate choreography across his career, but especially in his 1911 novel *Ethiopia Unbound*. Simply put, novels have characters, and so it is this form in which the so-called Uncrowned King of West Africa found the readiest means of fleshing out the relationship between constitutional*ism* and constitutional*ists*. By creating a human figure to solder founding principles to founding acts, Casely Hayford advanced a set of values that are both governmental and temperamental: restraint, balance, and an abiding regard for text. In seeking to standardize constitutionalist values *and* the type of leader he associated with constitutionalism, however, he found himself in the odd position of relying on his luminary status to entrench a vision of the Gold Coast that downplays the significance of luminaries. Casely Hayford could not quite get out of his own way.

Jumping back just short of a decade from this speech and the groundwork it lays out for considering Casely Hayford, the main objective of this chapter is to present *Ethiopia Unbound* as a founding document. By this I do not just mean that it inaugurates the tradition of the African novel in English, though it indeed does that, and far earlier than most literary critics' starting point of Africa's national independence era, around 1960. Nor am I invoking a commonplace "nation and narration" paradigm, which tends to emphasize the mythic or inadvertent dimensions of forging a shared identity. I mean, rather, that *Ethiopia Unbound* carries the full weight of a Gold Coast constitution in a more specific and robust understanding of that word. It seeks to enshrine as text the guiding principles of a nation (the Fante) and a region (West Africa) by at once aggrandizing and restraining the figure it depicts as an ideal constitutionalist leader of both: Casely Hayford's fictional avatar is distinguished by his cool-headed moderation. Per Olufemi Taiwo's trenchant account of nineteenth-century West Africa's modernizing impulses, Casely Hayford's novel is attuned to the fact that "modern law is built on the metaphysical template of the self and the necessity to protect it from the predation of other selves," including autocrats or dominant groups of any stripe.[4] But *Ethiopia Unbound* is, crucially, a narrative: it is about one prominent "self" who is integral to building a political order that safeguards selfhood. Marking where and how founding figures give way to the systems they found is a tricky matter, which the novel with its vast representational toolkit is uniquely equipped to address. As a broad constitutionalist framework sheds new light on Casely Hayford's situation, his work in turn opens new vistas for considering the deep structures of constitutional thought in African and colonial contexts.

A Foundational Inheritance

Before he repeated King Ghartey's last words toward the end of his 1920 conference speech, Casely Hayford had already invoked within it two guiding frameworks for imagining a Gold Coast constitutionalist endeavor. One sought to elevate a certain kind of political system, and one to entrench certain standards of personal conduct. On the first count, his speech takes the Fante Confederation as a practical touchstone: a real, past African constitutional state that lends credence to his vision for those to come. Quoting Nana Amonoo V of Anomabo (a prominent chief at the time), Casely Hayford credited the Confederation with being proof of "strength . . . in unity" in its administrative merging of the key towns of Mankessim and Cape Coast.[5] This echoed the goals that Hutton-Mills had just voiced in his inaugural address. "We know that India has been recognised and given a constitution which to a large extent will meet some of their most crying wants," the latter remarked. "Egypt is also about to receive a constitution, and Malta has already been accorded self-government. Is it too much to ask and to expect that British West Africa should also receive due consideration?"[6] To be constitutional in this sense is straightforward: it means enshrining bedrock principles of self-governance in a shared document.

The second sense of constitutionalism in Casely Hayford's speech is more elusive. He links it to a particular social profile—namely, his own. The "we" of the illustrious NCBWA delegates stands in for the "we" of the Gold Coast, and constitutional values grow right from its earth. After encouraging fellow West African delegates to look kindly on African American hopes of returning to the continent to make money, he nonetheless confesses reservations about Marcus Garvey's Universal Negro Improvement Association by reinvoking King Ghartey's last words. This part of Casely Hayford's speech foregrounds this chapter's main themes, and so it bears quoting at length:

> [Returnees] have no idea of our laws and institutions, nor as to our rights of property, and they may seek to get into touch with us by some

channels that are not the right ones. Therefore I appeal to you young gentlemen, leaders of thought in West Africa, particularly to you, the Delegates of this Conference, that you should so steer our men and so influence them in constitutional methods that they may know that although they went from this country, we who remained on this soil have known better and understand the relations that exist between the Government and the governed, so that if they desire to come back and enjoy the milk and honey of their native land they may do so in a right and constitutional manner.[7]

Twice, in this brief segment, Casely Hayford asserts constitutionalism as a source of African well-being. He describes it as a method and a manner; as a tool for maintaining a strong polity, that is, and as the correct way of wielding that tool. To "be constitutional" thus appears as the means *and* end of West African self-representation, connoting a character prototype meant to enforce a new kind of government as much as it names allegiance to one that already exists.

Before wading further into the particulars of Casely Hayford's contribution to a nascent Gold Coast constitutional tradition, I want to pause and offer some lay of the constitutionalist land in the broadest sense. Constitutionalism defies reduction to a pithy explanation, but zeroing in on its essential ingredients of writtenness and normativity is a good start. British judge and barrister Stephen Sedley defined it recently as "the set of rules delineating and governing the exercise of state power," while the constitutional scholar Martin Loughlin offers the shorthand of "a theory concerning the role, standing, form, and telos of a modern invention, the written constitution."[8] Even here, things start to get dicey. The United Kingdom, for example, does not have one unified constitutional document, despite being often upheld (including by Casely Hayford and peers) as a model constitutional state. And more recently, scholars of marginalized political traditions have begun to think about what kinds of texts might be considered as foundational beyond constitutions named as such. Heidi Kiiwetinepinesiik Stark, as one compelling case in point, has turned to treaty speeches, creation stories, songs, birch-bark scrolls, and rock paintings as an archive of Anishinaabe sovereignty, bound to questions of origin and "the critical values and philosophies that . . . undergird many, if not all, aspects of indigenous governance."[9] Such texts' deliberateness in setting forth first social and political principles is key to understanding their constitutional resonance, and that of *Ethiopia Unbound*.[10]

In part because constitutionalism is so simple to define minimally and so hard to reckon with substantially, it has spawned a voluminous scholarly literature. Many of its weightiest entries concern the development of constitutionalism over the *longue durée*. In Charles McIlwain's classic guide to the subject, *Constitutionalism: Ancient and Modern*, he defines a modern constitution as "the conscious formulation by a people of its fundamental law," which he opposes to an "older, traditional view in which the word was applied only to the substantive principles to be deduced from a nation's actual institutions and their development."[11] McIlwain's formulation sets the stage for a long critical practice of negotiating between description and prescription in thinking about constitutions' essential function. Or, as James Tully elaborates in somewhat bolder terms, between a modern constitution viewed as "an act whereby a people frees itself . . . from custom and imposes a new form of association on itself" and an ancient one that functions as "the recognition of how the people are already constituted by their assemblage of fundamental laws, institutions and customs."[12] (Tully's terms for what I am calling the descriptive and prescriptive dimensions of constitutionalism are "recognition" and "imposition," but the general idea is the same.) Most often, the conceptual poles in play are Aristotle's theory of *politeia*, as the archetypal, mainly descriptive premodern version of constitutionalism, and the United States of America's founding moment as the modern, more aspirational one. Whereas Aristotle characterizes and evaluates different kinds of systems of government—six of them, to be precise—the United States' constitution in this schema represents a more proactive kind of foundationalism.[13] "Ancient" constitutionalism thus appears inferential and taxonomic, and "modern" constitutionalism more deliberate, even revolutionary.[14]

This is schematic, of course, but it offers some guiding precepts that can help flesh out the stakes of Casely Hayford's constitutional ambitions for the Gold Coast. To start with, we might ask whether the constitutionalism he imagined was an ancient or modern one. He was, in fact, influenced by both typologies, making it hard to pin down the relationship between hallowing the Akan past and building a West African future in his thought and world. While Casely Hayford did deduce fundamental cultural traits from the real development of Akan institutions—as this book's previous chapter on factuality and Gold Coast imperial leadership makes clear—he also did so with an eye to their textual consecration and future enforcement. As Taiwo remarks, he was part of a longer process of "[establishing] governance on new principles that combined the best of the old with the best of the new."[15] Casely Hayford's work is backward looking in its fidelity to long-standing Akan values and political structures, but zealously modern in its idealization of text as a liberatory self-representational mechanism. "You all know to-day in the history of nations that the written work goes farther than the spoken word," he proclaimed in his 1920 conference speech. "Truly has it been said, that in the rule of men, entirely great, the pen is mightier than the sword."[16] His trust in the inaugural value of writing offered an awkward complement to the cultural selfhood it was meant to advance, which in his view had been ordained long ago.

Casely Hayford worked at the same time with two different conceptions of history and of his role in it. In one, the "Gold Coast man of letters" serves at history's behest as a humble preserver of the Akan past. This outlook is perhaps best captured in *Ethiopia Unbound*'s penultimate chapter, "A Similitude: The Greek and the Fante," in which a main character (and Casely Hayford's clear stand-in) named Kwamankra concludes that "the Ethiopian ... gains vastly more in self-respect by intimate acquaintance with the ancient Greek than with the modern Saxon."[17] The Fante are imagined as the Greeks' successors, possessed of a similar earthy simplicity among even the highest born as well as a penchant for deliberation among rulers. To go by this strain of the novel's reasoning, Fantes' "ancientness" is their modern cultural imprimatur. But in the novel's other main self-exegetical line, Kwamankra and Casely Hayford are part of a rising transnational Black elite building a new identity through the power of print and emergent political bureaucracies. *Ethiopia Unbound*'s first chapter, "An Ethiopian Conservative," announces this right off the bat. "And there were sons of God among them, men whom the Gods visited as of yore," Casely Hayford as narrator states, "for even now three continents were ringing with the names of men like Du Bois, Booker T. Washington, Blyden, Dunbar, Coleridge Taylor and others—men who had distinguished themselves in the fields of activity and intellectuality."[18] In one breath Casely Hayford's cultural prestige is attributed to steadfast Akan attributes, and in another, to his imbrication in a tricontinental vanguard. As his grandson and Akan art historian Gus Casely-Hayford explains, what might seem like confusion here is better attributed to the social threshold atop which Casely Hayford rests. "Although Casely-Hayford may have been a 'lover of ancient institutions,'" the younger Casely-Hayford writes, "his generation had witnessed a gradual decay of the extended Cape Coast family system," from which they nonetheless continued to derive much of their local prestige.[19]

The tie that binds Homer's Greece to Du Bois's America in *Ethiopia Unbound* is a premium on specifically *textual* accomplishment. On this score Casely Hayford exemplified the tenor of Gold Coast public discussion in his era, which for decades stressed the overdetermined place of the Fante print intelligentsia in a long developmental trajectory. An unsigned editorial in the July 31, 1897, edition of the *Gold Coast Methodist Times*, for example—then edited by S.R.B. Attoh Ahuma—binds knowledge derived from books to essential self-understanding. "To the Intelligent Young Men of this Protectorate," it reads, "we would urge that no books are more worth reading at this stage of our political evolution than such as would impart a knowledge of themselves, their mother-land and laws by which they sought to be governed." More relevant to my focus in this chapter, the piece also includes a list of specific titles about constitutional law that were available for purchase in Cape Coast at that time. It then praises "the great principles of the British Constitution" and proclaims that no "power in England can dare dream of stopping that great Atlantic tide."[20] In short, prominent members of Casely Hayford's milieu saw textuality as such and constitutionalism in particular as intimately conjoined in a large-scale reconfiguration of imperial leadership.

The *letteredness* of constitutionalism, for them, spoke to something fundamental about Gold Coast civilization, and constitutionalism in turn was a means of working through the value of textuality in the public sphere. As Colley attests, discussion and drafting of constitutions gave "peoples outside the West . . . a chance to proclaim on paper and publicise that they were viable and modern, and therefore not fit targets for imperial takeover."[21] Casely Hayford's overarching aim as a writer was to get the facts of long-standing Fante social and political norms on record, thereby creating the basis for a "new" kind of text-based regional government that was rooted, in theory at least, in preliterate local practices and institutions. This tension, too, between the welcome strictures of heritage and the valorization of freedom has a storied place in constitutional thought, as well as in thinking about customary law.[22] Casely Hayford is perhaps best aligned with what McIlwain describes as "liberal conservatism," after a reading of eighteenth-century British politician and philosopher Henry St. John Bolingbroke. "A constitutional state was one that had preserved an inheritance of free institutions," he summarizes that worldview. "Precedent was the very life of these institutions as it was of all law."[23] The liberal conservative label fits Casely Hayford's career in several ways, not least of which is the fact that a textual record allows precedents to circulate and scale beyond their point of origin.

Such impetus to conservation worked in forward and backward historical directions, as he solidified Fantes' understanding of their recent past to announce their role in future imperial glory. As far as he was concerned, the constitutional outlook of the NCBWA was a continuation of the Fante Confederation project begun (and ended) a generation before. This is important because it means that his constitutional activism at the scale of "West Africa" was also a specifically Gold Coast textual response; it is "foundational" in its citation of an earlier and more local foundation—one with some dings but still intact. The 1871 preamble to the Fante Confederation constitution, which lays out a political modus operandi of Gold Coasters making good on London's failed promises, also works as a worthy introduction to Casely Hayford's career. It reads: "In the Constitution it will be observed that we contemplate means for the social improvement of our subjects and people, the growth of education and industrial pursuits, and, in short, every good which British philanthropy may have designed for the good of the Gold Coast, but which we think it impossible for it at present to do for the country at large." What's more, the fact that Casely Hayford's distance from this signal reference point can be measured in generational rather than epochal time marks a divergence from both English and other anticolonial constitutionalisms. A more abstract sense of "ancientness" is at the heart of the English common law's authority: the common law's cumulative formation, epitomized by the principle of stare decisis (literally, "to stand by things decided") is often imagined to extend all the way back to medieval writs and the thirteenth-century Magna Carta.[24] Similarly, in their work on nineteenth-century self-rule movements in Ireland and India, T. T. Arvind and Daithí Mac Síthigh recover efforts to "try to discover an ancient constitution," for example, a "separate Irish Magna Carta" or Bengali "ancient legends" suggesting "something akin to a separation of powers."[25] The Gold Coast constitutional timeline is self-consciously compressed.

Nor is Casely Hayford's positioning of himself within a constitutional lineage in the NCBWA speech just a rhetorical move. His affinity for King Ghartey is a matter of family inheritance: his father, the Methodist minister Joseph de Graft Hayford, was one of the founders of the Confederation, at one point arrested by British Gold Coast administrators when he refused to accept its formal dissolution. J. E. Casely Hayford's older cousin on his maternal side, James Hutton Brew, wrote the first draft of the Fante Confederation constitution, which Casely Hayford then published in full as an appendix to *Gold Coast Native Institutions* in 1903. Talk of constitutions was in the air, and in his blood. To this can be added the fact that Brew's Confederation constitution then served as a template for the constitution of the Aborigines' Rights Protection Society, as Gus Casely-Hayford notes.[26] We might even say that this textual genealogy comes to stand in for what had been the all-important role of family lineage in determining structures of Gold Coast authority. A 1920 memorandum prepared by the NCBWA for King George V all but states this outright. Its signatories, including Casely Hayford, attest that West Africans' "demand for a franchise" honors local and not foreign models. They write, specifically, that "it is important to notice that the principle of electing representatives to local councils and bodies is inherent in all the systems of British West Africa. According to African institutions every member of a community belongs to a given family with its duly accredited head, who represents that family in the village councils, naturally composed of the heads of several families."[27] Casely Hayford's family tree dovetails with an inherited understanding of family as an explicit guarantor of political standing. In some sense, he was born to represent.

The NCBWA's framing nonetheless fails to acknowledge obvious differences in the two kinds of political systems they analogize here: one that centers rule by consent, and one whose democratic practices take place within a larger hereditary schema. The memo signatories' claim to be advancing a long West African tradition of representation and deliberative democracy is both true and not, depending on how detailed an analysis of Akan family headship structures is on offer. The closer one zooms in, the harder it gets to track straight lines of influence or novelty: where does Casely Hayford proclaim his "Fanteness" for present political effect, and where does he exhibit some real, continuous trait of national politics? Olufemi Taiwo's reading of the Fante Confederation constitution amplifies this interpretive difficulty in its emphasis on how Casely Hayford's father's generation distanced itself from "native" precedents. Taiwo notes that the constitution's "references to progress, education, and industrial pursuits all bespeak eminently modern themes," and that it "did not defend self-government on the basis of reverting to indigenous forms of governance, with which many [Fante leaders] had problems and to which quite a handful had serious objections."[28] Rather than underscore the intrinsic democratic leanings of Fante peoples in the manner of Casely Hayford, Taiwo looks to Articles 4 and 5 of the Confederation constitution as evidence of a radical historical shift from hereditary politics to "the electoral principle."[29] Seen through Taiwo's eyes, Casely Hayford's embrace of indigeneity in the throes of the so-called Gone Fante movement approaching the end of the nineteenth century—with its mannered reclamation of Fante dress, names, and language—tempers the preceding generation's strong endorsement of a "fundamental shift" in governing ethos. Here again, making sense of Fante constitutionalism entails trading off between basic constitutional orientations to description or prescription, recognition or imposition.

Casely Hayford's constitutional advocacy through the NCBWA in the early twentieth century might therefore be seen as a displacement of some Akan precedents and as continuous with others, though he vows a grand allegiance to his heritage. His reclamation of Fante traditions under the banner of regional electoral politics creates a bit of a glass half empty, glass half full situation, whose reception says as much about any reader now as it does about bygone Gold Coast politics of self-rule. While the Gold Coast's social order was no doubt undergoing major change around the zenith of Casely Hayford's political career, in dialogue with and apart from London, his standing in it was multivalent. His worldview was neither radical nor gradualist because it was arguably both, depending on how far any precedent can be seen to stretch. It is no easy feat to determine when a dispensation has enough "new" in it to override its debt to a preceding one, or to distinguish claims made in reaction to loss from threads of determined continuity. The younger Casely-Hayford, for example, makes a poignant case for the dissolution of genealogical bonds in his grandfather's lifetime by way of an anecdote about J. E. Casely Hayford's father, who for years lived and then died alone in London after a fall in 1919.[30] In doing so he also anticipates broader efforts to map family ties' influence on the consolidation of African print cultures, as in Simon Gikandi's reminder, in his recent foreword to *Foundational African Writers*, that in South Africa, too, "we can see how genealogies of cultural production would emerge through family lines."[31] The fact nonetheless remains that family lines made stable by print overwrite chains of practice and belief that are, in life, sometimes hazy, and that Casely Hayford's rise entailed an alchemical mix of legacy and will.

In any event, just as he was publicly burnishing the Fante Confederation's prestige as a local constitutional precedent, the Confederation's leaders found themselves without standing in his more expansive political arena. As wedded as he may have been to Fante cultural inheritance, the transnationalism of Casely Hayford's political ambitions is made possible by—and perhaps contributes to—family genealogy's gradual reworking into a textual one. Gus Casely-Hayford is right to characterize the early twentieth-century moment of Gold Coast politics' regional expansion through the NCBWA as "the confusion of a period of irresistible change," but it is also the period during which a distinctly Fante self-sensibility was, as it were, firmed up.[32] The local does not so much *give way* to the regional, imperial, or global as it coincides with them in a will to textual clarification. Because constitutions can be multiple without detracting from any one constitution's authority, constitutionalism becomes an ideal rallying point for a political bureaucracy that is coordinated across different scales. Even in its boldest assertions of a regional vision—albeit with an imperial bottom line—the NCBWA had to accommodate its internal pluralism. As one practical instance of this, correspondence with London entailed significant and explicit logistical footwork to craft an appearance of "representativeness." The final signatory to a 1920 petition to King George V is listed as one Chief Oluwa of Lagos, Nigeria, who was added "after the Petition had been translated and read over to him in the Yoruba Language by Herbert Macaulay, C.E. . . . and he had signified that he perfectly understood and approved of the same in the presence of [a London solicitor named] E.F. Hunt."[33] A Gold Coast or Lagosian constitution can co-exist with a West African one or, for that matter, with one devised specifically for the NCBWA.

This is not to say that Casely Hayford ever truly got beyond his local allegiances. The nascent constitutional tradition in which he participated was, as I've stated, a decidedly Gold Coast one, and it is notable that his novel's clearest textual precursor was a constitution by title. There is no doubt that as he wrote *Ethiopia Unbound* sometime around 1910, he was keenly aware of John Mensah Sarbah's *Fanti National Constitution* from 1906. As befits its name, *Fanti National Constitution* strives to outline not just particular conventions and beliefs, as did Sarbah's *Fanti Customary Laws* in 1904, but to "trace the broad outlines of Akan-Fante communities, and to explain the principles controlling and regulating the government thereof."[34] A few pages later, in the preface to this detailed exegesis of cases from the Supreme Court of the Gold Coast Colony archive, Sarbah lays out a clear stepping stone to Casely Hayford's nationalized framing of constitutionalism in his NCBWA speech. In answering his own rhetorical question whether Liberia represents West African progress, Sarbah responds with skepticism. "Liberians have wrongly, in my opinion, tried to run a miniature United States Constitution," he writes, "what with counties and shires, American variations of the laws of England, and other institutions and usages of Anglo-Saxon origin. They do not seem to have attempted to develop many important things on the lines of their own nationality."[35] In the postcolonial era, it has become all but axiomatic that constitutions should be tailored to their countries of origin. For Sarbah and Casely Hayford, writing *before* the modern nation-state was secured as a sine qua non of self-rule, fitting political principles to a "nation" was less about actual territory and more about ethnic self-definition.

As such, Casely Hayford's motivating logic of political succession—rather than rebellion, say, or even just the concrete formulation of diffuse long-held norms—has another implication. Drafting a Gold Coast constitution and securing the Fante intelligentsia's political pride of place are for him historically concurrent goals. Referencing a previous Fante "constitutional moment"—the Confederation's founding—thus carries extra weight. It suggests that the guiding principle underlying Casely Hayford's constitutional motivations is *constitutionalism* itself, and that this is in fact tied up with his milieu's ethnogenetic ambitions. To keep pace, once again, with Taiwo's understanding of West African modernization in this period, the political reformers of Casely Hayford's father's moment sought to demonstrate what they took to be an admirable new capacity for progress as they "[reconfigured] their modes of governance in light of the new civilization they had embraced."[36] With Casely Hayford's stronger pull to "Africanness" in reaction to some predecessors' overzealous embrace of British institutions, it makes sense that he would want to identify the progressive Fante tradition with form more than content. To "be constitutional," that is to say, entails for him more than the standardization of steadfast cultural norms and principles *as* text. It is also about carrying forth a cultural idealization *of* text, which sees his writing as the organic culmination of the Fante and, by messy extension, West African political, moral, and spiritual leadership trajectory.

This is a point worth dwelling on for a moment, because none of the more straightforward ways of understanding Casely Hayford's constitutionalism quite accounts for the specificity of how he imagines its Gold Coast lineage. One could, for example, see him as adopting a revered British colonial institution for pragmatic anticolonial purposes, much like his father and the Confederation leaders, working with what tools were available at the time to realize a nationalist agenda. Arvind and Mac Síthigh have called this "constitutionalism of the periphery," which mapped England's civic republicanism onto a "local deliberative tradition" and "native political institutions and political frameworks that had a long pedigree."[37] Taiwo goes further, seeing early West African calls for self-governance as efforts to demonstrate "their capacity for citizenship as British subjects" by "[assuming] responsibility."[38] Stretched for purposes of clarification into the literary arena, this reading of anticolonial constitutionalism resonates with Franco Moretti's famous (and often forcefully rejected) description of the novel form, in his essay "Conjectures on World Literature," as "a compromise between foreign form and local materials," with constitutions as the form and African life as the materials.[39] This would be the generous version of such an account. In a more critical view, Casely Hayford's veneration of constitutional governance might be labeled assimilationist and roped into a full-scale rejection of the "black Englishman" image, even though he saw himself as moving past precisely that.[40]

A second, subtler understanding of his tactics and outlook might hold that he extends the "liberal moment" of the early nineteenth century into the late nineteenth-century consolidation of a transimperial network of jurists and intellectuals. This approach dispenses with a clear-cut distinction between metropole and colonies and is therefore perhaps truer to the formation of the Fante intelligentsia's self-image. Another anonymous *Gold Coast Methodist Times* essay from 1897, which may well have been penned by Casely Hayford, seems to support this view, announcing that the Gold Coast should be an "epitome" of "the fundamental rules and regulations of good and sound Government—the English Government."[41] Here, constitutionalism appears as a nationalist best practice within the British Empire, adherence to which would not need to downplay Africans' active role in the development of legal modernity. As Ian Coller has written, "the history of colonialism, radical resistance struggles, and postcolonial authoritarianism tends to position liberalism as something that is done *to* Africa rather than a form of thought with an indigenous genealogy."[42] Again drawing a parallel with scholarship on world literature, such emphasis on the co-constitution of imperial textual forms has been a powerful trend.[43] But divergent understandings of constitutionalism's "Britishness" aside, including what valence to overlay on Casely Hayford's relation to empire, what demands emphasis here is that he finds something intrinsically textual in Fante history.

Let me extend this slightly further. Far from seeing himself as either adapting a foreign mode of governance *or* helping to generate a global one, J. E. Casely Hayford more likely viewed constitutionalism as a universal language that just happened to suit his distinctive coastal African way of being. Adherence to the prized Roman and later English legal ideal of *ratio scripta*, or written reason, without question aids and abets the rise of his specifically print-intellectual class and could thus be interpreted as self-serving. And yet the *qualities* associated with written constitutions by Casely Hayford and his peers anticipate their actual documentation. King Ghartey was not formally educated—he eagerly learned to read while he worked as a craftsman—and Sarbah in *Fanti National Constitution* compares the long-standing, unwritten Fante tradition of the deliberative council with England's houses of Parliament.[44] "Among jurists there have always been those who take delight in the strict logic of a closely reasoned argument," Arthur R. Hogue observed in 1966 of the common law's appeal, "and who wish to treat law as a science, not as abstract as mathematics perhaps, but similar to mathematics in the timeless certainty of its conclusions."[45] This assessment could well have described Sarbah and

Casely Hayford in their crediting of Gold Coast Africans with a heightened propensity for reason. Since Fanteness had, in their estimation, evolved to revere restraint, learnedness, and structure—in short, the cultivation of a principled self and polity through the deft negotiation of codes—then constitutionalism in a more exact sense was a natural fit.

Such reasoning nuances standard accounts of African constitutionalism in multiple important ways, making Casely Hayford a formidable and overlooked early contributor to African legal theory. First, it marks an illuminating twist on the concept of "constitutional identity"—that is, the identity *of* constitutions—to which some theorists have turned to assess constitutionalism's work across many polities with little in common. Gary Jeffrey Jacobsohn, for instance, argues in his book by that name that any given constitution retains "identifiable characteristics" forged not against but by dint of constitutions' inevitable "disharmonies."[46] In a different but related vein, postcolonial constitutional theorists often emphasize the importance of customizing constitutions to their respective national characters. As Ruth Gordon summarizes this view, "Constitutions can flourish and succeed only if they are firmly planted in the cultural soil from which they gain legitimacy."[47] Gold Coast constitutionalists, in excess of these approaches, contemplated not just their collective defining traits but the very essence of textuality as a means of cultural brokerage. They put forth the view of Fante identity *as* constitutional, by which they meant something like possessing a distinguished propensity for well-ordered written expression.

Casely Hayford's means of doing this—curating Fante history across multiple scales of political agenda setting—escapes most available theoretical frameworks for addressing African constitutionalism writ large. I have noted that Casely Hayford's constitutionalism, like any form of African liberalism, might be read as assimilationist, hybridistic, or as skillfully turning the tools of empire back on itself. Each of these gets at something true about his work without being able to contend with its sheer intellectual density. This reductiveness is paralleled in the Africanist legal arena, which has its own ready-made ways of making sense of African constitutionalism by erecting a firewall between the (post)colonial and precolonial periods. As Berihun Adugna Gebeye explains in his recent *A Theory of African Constitutionalism*, "The major scholarly and policy discussions on African constitutionalism revolve around two main theoretical frameworks: legal centrism and legal pluralism."[48] Where the first focuses on written constitutions and adopts a Western democratic standard of governmental success, the second "posits that there are dual and parallel constitutional systems in African states," one civic and one governed by distinct and largely unwritten indigenous norms.[49] Gebeye proposes a legal syncretic theory of African constitutionalism in place of either of these, which he defines as "the process and the result of adoption, rejection, invention, and transformation of diverse and seemingly opposite legal rules, principles, and practices into a constitutional state with imperial or colonial legacies."[50] J. E. Casely Hayford, it would seem, was way ahead of the game.

This is not to say he figured it all out, as a closer look at *Ethiopia Unbound* within its Gold Coast historical context makes clear. To summarize this first section of this chapter, however, Casely Hayford, Sarbah, and their peers among the Gold Coast intelligentsia grounded their constitutional worldview in a historically compressed local constitutional genealogy, and what they ultimately then suggested was Fantes' innate textual predisposition. Under the auspices of his NCBWA leadership, Casely Hayford then framed his push for an actual Gold Coast constitution as the natural extension of a "constitutional" character already formed. His logic works something like this: the Fante are at heart a constitutional people, as they have tried to prove more than once, and so now require a document to safeguard that fact once and for all. And so while Casely Hayford's British legal training looms large in any account of his multiplaned politics, there is more at stake here than a choice between viewing him through a lens of imperial conquest or one of African agency. At the moment of West Africa's bureaucratic birth, his efforts to "be constitutional" instead distill the challenge of *any* endeavor to solder a record of what has been to a blueprint for what might be.

The Novel and the Constitutionalist

Even if it is now clear why Casely Hayford endorsed constitutionalism as the way forward for the Gold Coast and West Africa, the motivations behind his choice to write a novel as his most ambitious founding document are far from obvious. When *Ethiopia Unbound* was published in London in 1911, Casely Hayford's star had already risen. In addition to his well-known work as co-founder of the Gold Coast Aborigines' Rights Protection Society (ARPS) in the 1890s, he had also co-founded the *Gold Coast Leader* and the Fante National Education Fund in 1902, published *Gold Coast Native Institutions* to great acclaim in 1903, and won the hand of the formidable London-based Sierra Leonean society woman Adelaide Smith in 1904. His legal practice in Axim and Sekondi was thriving, and he argued so prominently against the Forest Bill of 1911—another British effort at controlling

Gold Coast land—in August of that year that his views on it were published as a pamphlet in London in 1912, by request of a group of prominent Gold Coast chiefs. Given Casely Hayford's intentions as recollected by his son, Archie, to "augment the valuable work already undertaken by his esteemed contemporary John Mensah Sarbah" in the legal and political arena, it would be reasonable to surmise that fiction was a garnishing on, rather than an essential ingredient of, his professional and intellectual stature.[51] So why bother?

Several possible answers are partly convincing. Certainly, the cultural cachet of novel writing must have carried some weight in Casely Hayford's allocation of his energies. Colley speculates, in *The Gun, the Ship, and the Pen*, that "many of the constitution-drafters, thinkers and advocates" she treats in that book, briefly including Casely Hayford's Fante Confederation predecessors, "were simply addicted to writing and to the written word."[52] The literary club scene in the Gold Coast was in full swing by the end of the twentieth century's first decade; the Cape Coast Literary and Social Club, of which Casely Hayford would become a patron, was established in 1914. His investment in humanistic education was as deep as the larger Gold Coast interest in "metropolitan culture" was decorative—as detailed in this book's introduction—and *Ethiopia Unbound* is nothing if not a record of the eclectic textual sources by which it was honed. J. E. Casely Hayford was also a celebrity in his day, and though he deeply valued solitude, also participated in London's intellectual scene, both giving and attending lectures on a wide array of topics, including the famous theosophy movement spearheaded by the Russian émigré Helena Blavatsky. As Adelaide M. Cromwell puts it in *An African Victorian Feminist*, "Casely Hayford was a man well accustomed to the ways of the West."[53] A novel would have been one more feather in this cap, and a hallmark of his cultural versatility.

In a more intimate sense, *Ethiopia Unbound* bears the imprint of personal tragedies that would not have found ready expression in Casely Hayford's usual written forms of political treatises, essays, or pamphlets. By this I refer mainly to the death from mastitis (or "breast fever") of his beloved first official wife, Beatrice Pinnock, in 1901, followed by that of their nine-month-old daughter, Muriel. The novel's two successive chapters called "Love and Death" mark a sharp contrast with its academic discussion of religion and philosophy, granting Casely Hayford the space to work through his ideas about posthumous reunion and reincarnation. To the extent that the novel in general, as a form, specializes in demonstrating how character emerges from experience, this representation of grief in *Ethiopia Unbound* matters a great deal. "Yes, he had touched the depths of human happiness and the depths of human sorrow," we read at one point, "and had come to know that the way to God led from the one to the other."[54] Kwamankra, as Casely Hayford's avatar, is able to fulfill his political ambitions only because he is granted the space to come to terms with personal loss.

But even as cultural prestige and personal reckoning are good reasons for Casely Hayford to have written a novel, they cannot fully account for the tremendous intellectual ambition and range of *Ethiopia Unbound*, as it cycles quickly between fictional vignettes, political speeches, Platonic-style dialogues, and extended segments of institutional description and planning (especially of African universities). His larger concerns with self-representation and attaining a constitutional order in the Gold Coast and West Africa suggest a further, more encompassing explanation for his one-off shifting of gears as an author. The novel form, I suggest, in its great flexibility of content and perspective, offers Casely Hayford a unique tool for representing the dual meaning of "constitution" as both character (related to what I have called description) and action (related to what I have called prescription). Turning back to constitutional theory, Hanna Pitkin offers an elegant explanation for how these two interlinking senses of the word shed light on actual constitutional documents. "How do these two uses of constitution—as fundamental character or way of life and as the activity of constituting—illuminate the political and legal sense of 'constitution'?," she asks, before responding, "The latter use serves to remind us that constitutions are *made*, not found."[55] Casely Hayford is a constitution maker, not merely an enforcer. Read as a record of his negotiation between being and building, *Ethiopia Unbound* becomes both a constitutional document and a document about the challenges of implementing constitutionalism within a paradigm of charismatic leadership.

The main constitutional precept that Casely Hayford takes up with his novel is that of restraint. To be more precise, he finds in the novel a way of restraining himself, or at least trying. But before delving deeper into how this actually works in his writing, I want to return briefly to the big picture of constitutionalism. If constitutional theorists agree on any unifying aspect of a constitutional worldview, it is its location of authority in principles and structures of rule, rather than in individual rulers. Phrases like "checks and balances," "separation of powers," and "rule of law" are so commonplace in discussions of constitutionalism as to seem almost banal. Bruce Ackerman rounds out this consensus when he offers, in *Revolutionary Constitutions*, that "constitutionalism . . . involves the imposition of significant legal constraints on top decision-makers."[56] Many scholars have gone so far as to see constitutionalism, therefore, as the governmental mode par excellence of modernity, with that term defined in the broadest Weberian way as the rise of a rational schematization of experiential domains and kinds of knowledge. Taiwo, for instance, sees the Fante Confederation as "quintessentially modern," a phrase he later associates with a "commitment to the rule of law" and the "restraints on the modern state" that it upholds.[57] The separation of a ruler from the ruled and the *rules* is thus cast as part of a profound world historical turn to the logic of categorical clarity and separation. (Weber himself was a constitutional reformer in post–World War I Germany.) This means, echoing Martin Loughlin, that "unable any longer to rest its claims on the charismatic power of a ruler or the unreflective acceptance of traditional practices, a constitutional mode of thinking founds its legitimacy on some notion of consent."[58] As such, what he calls "the incontestable authority of the ruler," or more specifically, "the transcendental notion of kingship," gives way to an ideal of popular sovereignty, or constituent power—or, in short, a constitution's safeguarding by a revolving cast of elected leaders.[59]

Casely Hayford certainly found value in the idea of representative democracy, at least on a limited scale. Whether his own vision of his leadership can persuasively be read through a *constituent*-driven constitutionalist paradigm is another matter. The most influential account of what rule by the people entails within a particular context is probably Carl Schmitt's in *Constitutional Theory* from 1928, in which he reads Germany's Weimar Constitution and its political background in great depth. Its particulars are far outside the scope of Gold Coast history in Casely Hayford's time, and I won't delve into them here. The scholarly literature that Schmitt's work has spawned on constituent rule nonetheless provides a conceptual foothold in this discussion. Again quoting Loughlin, "constituent power is not the expression of the nation operating in accordance with some law of nature; it is a modern concept expressing the evolving precepts of political conduct which breathe life into the constitution."[60] Put otherwise, constitutions understood within the framework of constituent power must be endorsed from the bottom up before they can enforce norms of governance from the top down. In this understanding, the national will precedes its individual leaders in existence and importance. I want to reflect, however, on the appearance of the word "conduct" in Loughlin's definition of constituent power. It suggests that constitutionalism is a matter of *how leaders act*, and by logical extension, that antecedent constituents therefore generate some set of appropriate behaviors on the part of their representatives. As Taiwo writes almost in passing, "constitutions are important" because they are "theoretical and programmatic statements of a society's view of itself, what it wishes to be, *what type of human is expected to inhabit it*."[61] The clean segue from principles to people here is crucial. But specifying a "type of human" presents a further challenge: How are the constitutionally minded constituents who elect constitutionalist leaders meant to emerge, if not through the top-down influence of cultural movers and shakers?

Along with his simultaneously backward- and forward-looking use of text to naturalize his own lifetime as a turning point, Casely Hayford's elite social and political position makes it hard to view his leadership as being downstream of a national shift. There is a chicken-or-the-egg problem haunting any analysis of his moment: the figures who consolidated Gold Coast culture in print, he chief among them, also claimed merely to be channeling (and championing) its norms. What's more, it is difficult to classify the *kind* of leadership that Casely Hayford represented, with representation here a reference both to his writing and to the public figure he cut. Casely Hayford's fictional persona, Kwamankra, is as singular a presence as he is modest in his response to being singled out. His deceased wife, whom he encounters in a religiously nonspecific afterworld in chapter 4, remarks that he is "a god, only thy warfare is not yet accomplished" and so must "carry hence a knowledge which will aid thee in thy work."[62] Casely Hayford thus plants in the reader's mind the idea of his leadership as being divinely sanctioned. Kwamankra demurs, however, replying, "surely, you mock me when you suggest that I am a god. Call me a thinker, a teacher, call me anything that is of the earth, but a god I cannot think that I am one, or can ever be."[63] In this way, a modern constitutionalist could moot and then negate his own suggestion of heavenly legitimation. Two of Max Weber's three canonical forms of authority have been plainly wrought up in Casely Hayford's persona as I have sketched it thus far: the legal-rational (which elevates bureaucracy and procedure) and the traditional (which claims adherence to prevailing practices, however normatively inconsistent). Here, Weber's third form of authority—the charismatic—is also in play.

Turning back to the book's opening pages, even collective Black selfhood is rendered in triumphalist terms of individual spiritual power. The subject of *Ethiopia Unbound*'s first sentence is "men of light and leading," which also reappears in the first numbered section of the third chapter. A few lines later, the "black man" is described as "the scion of a spiritual sphere peculiar unto himself," upon which follows reference to "men like Du Bois, Booker T. Washington, Blyden, Dunbar, Coleridge Taylor and others—men who had distinguished themselves in the fields of activity and intellectuality" as "sons of God, men whom the Gods visited as of yore."[64] And while Weber is a useful point of reference here because his leadership schema has loomed so large in thinking about modernization, we need not even reach that far to find evidence of the spiritual inclination behind Casely Hayford's constitutionalist politics. The novel's very title is an obvious reference to the radical nineteenth-century English poet Percy Bysshe Shelley's 1820 drama *Prometheus Unbound*. A response to Aeschylus's Greek tragedy *Prometheus Bound*, in which the eponymous god of fire is chained up and tortured for defying a tyrannical Zeus, Shelley's version introduces a new emphasis on humanity's redemption through Jupiter's (Zeus's) overthrow. By likening Africa to Prometheus, Casely Hayford also positions his Fante intellectual tradition as heir to a "Western" canonical one extending from ancient Greece to Romantic-era England, suggesting thereby that the empire now risks suppressing the tools of its own redemption. But the figure on which it all hangs is a god, not a lawyer; by suggesting that various Afro-descended leaders are god-like, *Ethiopia Unbound* closes the gap between the two. Scratch a legal functionary, find an immortal flame.

Finally, there are some Gold Coast–specific ways of accounting for the wrench that Casely Hayford's emphasis on spiritual ordination throws in his constitutionalist plans, which can sit side by side with the interpretive lenses that Weber and Shelley provide. Gus Casely-Hayford writes, "Fante oral tradition reveals how the most fundamental organs of government [in Cape Coast] were dominated by charismatic individuals," meaning that "charismatic, clever and well-connected individuals, could rise quickly through the indigenous echelons to positions of great influence."[65] Cape Coast historian Francis Agbodeka makes a similar point, observing that Cape Coast Fante politics had grown *more* rather than less dominated by individual figures leading up to Casely Hayford's political era. "In the nineteenth century," he notes almost in passing, "allegiance [in Cape Coast] became largely personal rather than territorial."[66] The tight bond between sacred and legal authority is further reinforced, following Agbodeka, by Mankessim's centrality to Gold Coast intellectual history. The constitution of the Fante Confederation was in fact first referred to as the Mankessim Constitution for the location of its signing, and the town was also traditionally the Fante religious capital, where kings were appointed.[67] Though King Ghartey signed off as president in his Fante Confederation correspondence, the Fante Confederation constitution designates his office as that of the "king-president"—perhaps based on the Fante word *breyni*—with all the fealty that the first half of that term suggests.[68] His doing so in turn throws Casely Hayford's nickname, the Uncrowned King of West Africa, into bold relief. Where does a kingship end and a presidency begin? In Casely Hayford's lifetime, this was a practical question unresolved by appeals to even the most quintessentially "modern" belief systems.

As kings and constitutionalists are strange bedfellows, so too are novels and constitutions. The novel, as a form, is definitionally amorphous and polyvocal; Russian theorist Mikhail Bakhtin would say that it can "swallow" other genres.[69] In contrast, constitutions are defined by firm guiding principles and constraint. And on top of this difference in hallmark formal identities, Casely Hayford's expression of his politics in a self-consciously literary way raises the question of what to make of his individual authorship. Constitutional scholar Laurence Tribe rightly avers that constitutions are "not the product of any one mind, any one time, any one aspiration," viewing them instead as internally heterogeneous and living documents.[70] But *Ethiopia Unbound* plainly *is* the product of one mind, whatever its ambitions to collective vindication. For that matter, so are *Gold Coast Native Institutions* and Sarbah's *Fanti National Constitution*, to say nothing of the constitution of the Fante Confederation, written by Casely Hayford's older cousin James Hutton Brew. Single authorship would thus seem to be a feature, not a bug, of local constitutional endeavors. The Gold Coast constitutionalist moment of the nineteenth century is thus best seen as moving in lockstep with the consolidation of Gold Coast literary culture, anchored by a roster of prominent patrons. (In Casely Hayford's case this was a literal role as of 1914, with the founding of the Cape Coast Literary and Social Club.[71]) It makes sense, in this context, that Casely Hayford's novelistic and constitutional projects would blur in what sometimes appear to be nonsensical ways.

Ethiopia Unbound therefore exemplifies two orientations, toward explosive heteroglossia on the one hand and studied regulation on the other. It is a chaotic and messianic novel about the even-handed approach to governance required of a would-be constitutionalist leader. On the first score, even its title speaks to the frenetic composition of the text, which moves disarmingly across genres, forms, and plots that then disappear. Within merely the first two chapters of the novel, readers are rushed from grand sociological reflections on the anatomic perfection and historical adaptability of the Black man; to a walking conversation in London between a Gold Coast student and an English one, which winds its way to Fante religious etymology; to, suddenly, a short melodramatic scene of a humble Fante woman furiously embroidering and weeping at the idea that her educated lover might leave her.[72] The meandering between genres continues apace for the rest of the book, all tenuously linked by Kwamankra's intellectual development. It's no wonder that every critic who has addressed *Ethiopia Unbound* as a novel has focused on its scattershot form, seeing it as a reflection of Casely Hayford's cosmopolitan or modernist imagination. And he no doubt was cosmopolitan by any definition of that word, much as it is true that the fragmentary, many-chaptered structure of *Ethiopia Unbound* facilitates a huge range of reference across space and time, earth and afterlife.[73]

On the other hand, the content of the individual squares in this patchwork quilt of a book is often fusty, even conservative, in its clear delineation of texts and lessons, as well as its emphasis on the laws of reason, civic duty, and imperial reform. Casely Hayford credits Kwamankra with an unrivaled respect for the "intellectual, moral, and national training" provided by an education in classics, for instance.[74] Elsewhere, he tells his son during a home history lesson that he "must begin from premises to conclusion, step by step, like the quod erat demonstrandum you were worrying me with the other day."[75] Though the novel might read as experimental or even provisional, Casely Hayford was also a true post-Victorian thinker, a foundationalist and "Man of Reason" to his core. He was a spiritual esotericist, a traditionalist or "liberal conservative," and an advocate for building an advanced constitutional bureaucracy all at once, set on securing what he believed to be universal marks of civilizational advancement. Constitutionalism *was* for him a spiritual calling, because, as he says through Kwamankra, "It becomes . . . the sacred duty of those who can see a little more clearly ahead to point the way."[76] Seen in this light, the restraint or balance that lies at the definitional heart of constitutionalism also characterizes the novel's overarching mechanics. *Ethiopia Unbound* not only reflects each of Casely Hayford's roles or inclinations but engineers equilibrium between them.

To put it a bit differently, just as important as the fact that *Ethiopia Unbound* contains many different elements is that it makes them work together as a founding vision. The novel's descriptions of an ideal education anchor "learnedness" in earlier foundational texts: it finds the path to African self-recognition in an objective relationship with defining civilizational documents. In this way, *Ethiopia Unbound* aspires to *constitute* a constitutionalist outlook among its readers, heeding in advance Kenyan scholar H.W.O. Okoth-Ogendo's oft-cited 1988 warning against "constitutions without constitutionalism."[77] Casely Hayford, consciously or not, knows that advancing constitutional principles of government will require a certain typology of character. The well-known capacity of the novel form to encourage certain sensibilities in its readers is harnessed here to the task of creating a stable West African legal-administrative class. The text's dominant principle, we might then say, across its different dimensions is *balance*, which it expresses by depicting Casely Hayford via Kwamankra as a balancer. *Ethiopia Unbound* indeed gathers many ostensibly contradictory representational modes, systems of belief, and scales of political organization (national, regional, imperial, and universal) in the confines of one text. But it does this by foregrounding—perhaps even in order to foreground—its model of a voracious intellectual who coordinates all these intellectual pieces, with an eye to even-keeled political leadership.

Drawing on Pitkin's comments about how "constitution" invokes both temperament and action, I am suggesting that the guiding ethos of *Ethiopia Unbound* aligns with what the text wants to *do* in its relation to Gold Coast readers. In other words, it is a foundational text that aims to generalize what it views as the ideal kind of political sensibility for a member of West Africa's founding cohort. That sensibility is a constitutional one, in the ways I have already described. Kwamankra exhibits a baseline requirement for constitutionalism in his respect for and focused derivation of first principles from non-African foundational texts, ranging from "the Classics," to Shakespeare's *Hamlet*, to Aesop's "The Wolf and the Lamb" fable and various biblical allusions. At the same time, he casts himself as a consummate modern Fante carrying on a homegrown tradition of text-led sovereignty.

The right kind of leader for the Gold Coast and West Africa is able to hold these convergent trajectories of Gold Coast constitutionalism in balance, a possible god poised ably atop an epistemological seesaw. What it *looks like* to be a "constitutionalist," in turn, at the individual level is chiefly expressed in *Ethiopia Unbound* by its main character's style of reasoning, conveying another key part of Casely Hayford's leadership ideal. To this end, Kwamankra's locutionary style draws on all the sources informing the book to be, in its own right, balance seeking. Cast backward onto the Gold Coast constitutional moment and its novelistic distillation, Bruce Ackerman's notion of "revolution on a human scale" takes on a literal implication. What he calls "the most ambitious collective enterprises that human beings can ever realistically execute" can, for Casely Hayford, be best represented in the form of an actual person who ponders the right combination of reform and overhaul.[78]

This style of reasoning often takes the form of what I will refer to as Casely Hayford's "goldilocks method" of sorting through options as he troubleshoots various challenges. I do not mean this to sound glib. Again and again, he uses Kwamankra to offer brief bits of taxonomic reasoning before settling on an ideal category or position. One good example is from a speech Kwamankra delivers in chapter 18, and whose context now requires some setting up. For its first few pages, Casely Hayford as an omniscient narrator offers general reflections on W.E.B. Du Bois's *The Souls of Black Folk* from 1903 and on the African American plight. He then pivots, with the line "Thoughts like these were stirring in men's minds," to a real-life 1905 meeting in the Gold Coast of a group called the Pan-African Conference, precursor to the more famous Pan-African Congresses that began in 1919.[79] After that, Casely Hayford passes the mic, so to speak, to a different version of himself, in the form of the character he has based on his own history of public speaking and writing. "Among the distinguished speakers at the Conference was Kwamankra," Casely Hayford as narrator writes, at which time Kwamankra launches into a lengthy speech on Edward Blyden and Africa's need to find its distinctive developmental path, offering a series of lessons to this end based on analyses of the Asante Kingdom, the history of Christianity, and Sierra Leone.[80] It is the way Kwamankra *formulates* these pointers to which I draw attention here. In a brief discussion of traditional African marriage norms, he states, "There is the vulgar way of approaching the question of polygamy; there is the scientific way; and lastly there is the spiritual way."[81] Content aside, we can easily read this as "too soft; too hard; just right." A page later, Kwamankra weighs another, similarly structured set of possibilities, situating his ideal type of "the educated native" between "the unsophisticated native" and "the superfine African gentleman," who is, he opines, "no good to anybody."[82]

A few important points get tied together in this reading of Kwamankra's speech along the lines of its formal-rhetorical emphasis on balance. First, by granting his own weightiest historical interventions to a fictional stand-in, Casely Hayford asks to have them read self-consciously *as text*. He creates distance between his vaunted public persona and his views on how best to constitute the Gold Coast public by farming his words out to a made-up source. As an author, he exhibits restraint to depict a model of restrained leadership in his main character; one Casely Hayford is as the other Casely Hayford does. In a memorable scene of such restraint's enactment, Kwamankra instructs his son, based on Casely Hayford's real-life first child, Archie, in how to hold back as part of attaining long-term political change. "Not so fast, my boy," Kwamankra tells him, and then speaks "slowly and deliberately" as he routes his understanding of leadership through "what learned books call the argument."[83] To put it bluntly, Kwamankra teaches his child to read and think like exactly the lawyer that Casely Hayford is. Adopting a veneer of fiction nonetheless remains a meaningful strategy because it echoes the kind of reading, teaching, and bearing for which he advocates through Kwamankra. Constitutionalism always requires self-restraint on the part of the powerful, and in Casely Hayford's world, its viability also requires his self-replication. In sum, Casely Hayford is dedicated to consolidating a new class, in his image, that actively commits to limiting its own power. He finds a way of representing this challenge in the novel's flexibility, because it allows him to split himself into narrator and character. He is an omniscient presence dispensing bedrock principles of reason, equality, and tradition, but that omniscience is then kept in check by its sharing of narrative focus with a fictional protagonist.

Readers of *Ethiopia Unbound* are therefore engaged at multiple levels of what we might call a constitutional habitus, or way of being. We do not just read Casely Hayford as Kwamankra, or read Kwamankra reading; we also read him reasoning through the relationship between textually ingrained principles and desired political outcomes. This adds something specific to a baseline understanding of the range of learning on display in *Ethiopia Unbound* as "eclectic" or "cosmopolitan." Instead of emphasizing multiplicity as such as the text's outstanding trait, a reading with constitutionalism at its center foregrounds the normative dimension of what Casely Hayford intends all this knowledge to *do*. The novel elaborates a constitutionalist way of relating to texts (as interpretable objects containing fundamental principles of social and political organization) to showcase the virtues of a constitutionalist leader (as one who understands and defers to those texts).

Because I have periodically tracked the issues that Casely Hayford's work surfaces in relation to more familiar critical conversations, it is worth briefly flagging how much his representational strategies diverge from those of more recent, and famous, African "founders." Casely Hayford muddled the autobiographical throughline of *Ethiopia Unbound*, while independence-era political leaders more commonly embraced autobiography as what has been called a foundational African literary genre. The historical truth value of, for example, Nelson Mandela or Kwame Nkrumah's autobiographies has been seen as less important than their power to allegorize a new nation, heroic leaders writing Bildungs to become one in their own right. The generic priority on self-narration has in some cases coincided with constitutionalism's wane in the postcolonial period, when, per H. Kwasi Prempeh, "Africa's new managers discarded their so-called independence constitutions."[84] By contrast, Casely Hayford's novel maintains a strict distinction between texts and people, because the state it envisions needs both founding documents and careful readers to enforce them. Allegorizing state and subject, moreover, makes little sense as a kind of constitutional form, since constitutions demand a separability of those elements to underwrite their legitimacy. In *Ethiopia Unbound*, Casely Hayford "brackets" himself and keeps discrete roles and spheres of inquiry in play.

Except when he doesn't. Mostly, the novel offers a transparent device for keeping the narrator and main character separate: "Kwamankra's" views are expressed via philosophical dialogues, political meetings, or in lectures delivered at some institution of higher learning, in part so that readers see him interacting with texts in a scrupulously measured way. But in a short chapter called "Race Emancipation—Particular Considerations: African Nationality," it is unclear whether the narrator or Kwamankra is speaking. Sandwiched between two other chapters in which Kwamankra's place *is* clearly marked, this one begins, "In the name of African nationality the thinker would, through the medium of *Ethiopia Unbound*, greet members of the race everywhere throughout the world."[85] This is the only time that the novel's title is referenced *in* the text, and it is thus left ambiguous whether its authorship should be credited to Casely Hayford or his avatar. Is this another account of Kwamankra's rounds on the tricontinental lecture circuit, or is it a break in that semblance of a plot to reflect on the novel in which he appears? The chapter then goes on to perform an especially substantive example of the goldilocks style of reasoning, applying it at the macro level of carving out a cultural identity. "How extraordinary would be the spectacle of this huge Ethiopian race . . . having imbibed all that is best in Western culture in the land of their oppressors, yet remaining true to racial instincts and inspiration, customs and institutions," either the narrator or Kwamankra espouses. In the parlance of more recent African literary and culture debates, we might say that this vision of African leadership is neither "nativist" (so to speak) nor Western facing but some happy middle ground between the two. What does it mean, then, that Casely Hayford *slips* here, which is to say that he cannot quite keep subject and object, narrator and character in their assigned roles?

In effect, Casely Hayford's efforts to make himself into a replicable "type" of person—that is, a constitutional one—fold back into Casely Hayford the larger-than-life West African political figure. In attempting to replicate or standardize himself through narrative means, he ends up drawing our attention to just how much every bit of the text points back at his own singular reputation. This is, to be clear, a problem. All hail the Uncrowned King of West Africa, we might jest, trying his damndest to make himself slightly less special! To keep up a connection with the bigger picture of legal thought and therefore track Casely Hayford's place in it, I suggest that he wrote himself into what has long been a sticky relationship between esteem for founding documents and allegiance to their enforcers. This tension goes back at least to Aristotle and his emphasis on a "judging agent" class possessed of "right reason" and therefore able to oversee the rule of law, but the twentieth-century legal thinker most often cited to this end is Ronald Dworkin.[86] Dworkin places responsibility for enforcing the rule of law in the hands of technically adept and interpretively dexterous judges typified by an ideal type in his work whom he names Judge Hercules. In his monumental 1986 book *Law's Empire*, Dworkin defines Hercules by his view of "law as integrity," by which he means that he is "a careful judge, a judge of method," who approaches each case by laying out the various interpretive paths to its resolution.[87] Ultimately, Dworkin's point is that an ideal judge within a political system built on the rule of law—that is, by documents—reasons through the far-reaching implications of his decisions. "Law as integrity," Dworkin writes, "requires a judge to test his interpretation of any part of the great network of political structures and decisions of his community by asking whether it could form part of a coherent theory justifying the network as a whole."[88] His prototype has nothing directly to do with Casely Hayford, but it is useful for bringing this chapter full circle back to the NCBWA conference where it began. As Dworkin's emphasis on law begets a profile of judges, Casely Hayford's constitutionalism yields a character study of *himself* as a constitutionalist. His self-exceptionalism is both friend and foe to his politics.

Personality in the Balance

In the realm of ideals, of course, any system of government both nurtures and is nurtured by the kind of citizen required to maintain it. Countless constitutionalist interventions advance this symbiotic or coincident kind of thinking, often, as Frank Michelman explains in his discussion of what he calls legal nonvolitionism, to skirt the question of legal authorship. "It's a nice thought," he writes, "this idea of historical coincidence between the occurrence of a legislative endeavor conforming to a certain (broadly speaking) procedural specification and the coming-into-being of a social practice of attributing legislative efficacy to endeavors falling under that same procedural specification."[89] In sum, while it may be gratifying to imagine that constitutions' origins and norms organically align with people's allegiance to them, this does not obviate the need to reckon with individual constitution writers. Michelman makes this point as part of a dense case for the inevitability of considering a constitution's authorship, which he then takes as a call to continually reevaluate constitutional norms. Constitution writers can "never be conceived as writing on a clean slate"; they are historically formed rather than godlike figures.[90] I introduce Michelman's supple approach to historicizing constitutions alongside their authors to indicate two things. First, contra Tribe, a focus on a constitution's particular authorship is not at odds with the notion that constitutions are "alive" and even internally incoherent.[91] Second, even Michelman's highly nuanced effort to confront the relationship between leaders and publics in legal history would have a hard time with J. E. Casely Hayford. This is because, though his politics won him tremendous respect in his lifetime, it is not clear that they ever really took hold—even, perhaps, in his own predictions about West Africa's future.

Before turning to some of those predictions in the last section of this chapter, I'd like to clarify what I mean by the suggestion that Casely Hayford poses an interpretive challenge to even the most sophisticated thinking about constitutions and constitutionalists. Michelman, as paraphrased here, addresses a persistent question in constitutional thought as to what if any significance should be accorded to actual founders in determining a founding document's meaning and legacy. Pitkin's moving piece on "The Idea of a Constitution" downplays particular authorship as a key part of constitutional meaning, opting instead for a first-person plural narration of "co-founders."[92] While founding documents are, Pitkin grants, "human creations" and "the specific history of a particular people," she then adds that "our capacity for human self-constituting is most fully realized when it is consciously and deliberately exercised, collectively."[93] Meanwhile, debates about America's founding often collapse into political wrangling over whether founders' individual sins discredit a given set of shared ideals or documents; this too informs Michelman's approach. In still another vein, Ackerman's *Revolutionary Constitutions* contemplates "the constitutionalization of charisma," playing on Weber's definition of modernity as a shift to bureaucratic procedure; Ackerman is interested in cases around the world where revolutions culminate in or are appropriated by constitutional orders.[94] Each of these approaches to thinking through the stakes of constitutional meaning imagines constitutional authors as capturing something fundamental to and diffuse in their historical moment; the shared move is to de-exceptionalize them. Pitkin, Michelman, and Ackerman all do this in different ways, and by implication point to the demystification of founding documents. Constitutions and their authors are *of history*, not above it.

But Casely Hayford is neither. The impersonal, well-balanced constitutionalist ethos that he espouses and embodies is upheld by people around him as the grounds of his exceptionalism, with tribute after posthumous tribute to him focusing not just on what he achieved, but on who he was. If Casely Hayford could *almost* sustain a studied separation of his persona from his principles, as "handed over" to Kwamankra in *Ethiopia Unbound*, then his peers did not even try to do the same. Attention to the character of the deceased is obviously part and parcel of any obituary, let alone one for a luminary of Casely Hayford's stature when he died in 1930 in Accra. Regardless, it is illuminating to note what particular aspects of his character were received as distinguishing. In Casely Hayford's case, it is precisely his "constitutionalist" traits as they are developed in his work that were used to single him out. Over and over again, in the paeans that his son, Archie, records, the father's honor and greatness are linked to moderation and self-sacrifice. It can read now as confused and confusing praise: a lawyer and civil servant determined to usher in an era of constitutionalism and civic mindedness is raised to heights befitting an Olympian deity.

Consider, for instance, a letter that an unnamed "very high official" sent to his son, who then presented it in his unpublished manuscript about his father.[95] "As a government official I owe a great deal to him for his disinterested advice of which I frequently availed myself," the letter states, and which Archie considered to be a "great insight . . . into the true character of the man."[96] A year after his death, an occasion that was celebrated in his political hometown of Sekondi for four days, another European official remarked, "Though [Casely Hayford] was extremely tenacious of his points in argument, he was always clear in proving his ease and was studiedly moderate in the language he used in supporting any important matter which he had at heart."[97] In one Lagos newspaper, Casely Hayford was remembered as a "brilliant figure amongst the body of men engaged in the Unification of the Negro forescattered amiss on the shores of Africa."[98] Elsewhere, the tributes were even more breathless. Archie also reprints a Methodist minister's sermon, delivered in Sierra Leone but first published in the *Nigerian Daily Telegraph* in 1930, that calls Casely Hayford a "star of the first magnitude" possessed of "keen vision [and a] well balanced mentality," who was "ready at all times to join forces even with an opponent when truth was on his side." The minister then goes so far as to name him a "prince amongst men," before he segues to a call for West Africans to "reconsecrate [themselves] for duty and service" before Christ.[99]

Even with decades of hindsight, Casely Hayford's political character was imagined beyond his political achievements. Renowned Ghanaian classical scholar L. H. Ofosu-Appiah, in the third and final of his J. B. Danquah Memorial Lectures in Accra in February 1975, associated his predecessor, whom he wrote had "stressed constitutional procedures and a greater respect for the law," with "the era of reasonableness in African nationalism."[100] Ofosu-Appiah had a heavy political axe to grind: his lectures on Casely Hayford were part of a project to restore the legacy of his friend and mentor J. B. Danquah, who was imprisoned by Nkrumah in 1964 and left to die of a heart attack while still incarcerated the following year. Even so, Ofosu-Appiah's use of character-based language in the same breath as he periodizes Ghana's political culture is worth noting because of its resonance with the earlier terms of praise for Casely Hayford. "In the fight for self-government" after the Second World War, Ofosu-Appiah continues, "cool-headed planning had to take second place, while emotional outbursts and the imputation of evil motives to those who could sense danger in such revolutionary tendencies became a cardinal principle of life."[101] Casely Hayford's constitutionalist politics once again become a character profile and indeed a paragon.

In different circumstances, it might be possible to disentangle Casely Hayford's self-perception in *Ethiopia Unbound* from others' perception of him. Casely Hayford could not possibly be held responsible for the terms in which he was praised after his death. And in those different circumstances, Casely Hayford's novel containing sermons would have nothing to do with a sermon about Casely Hayford. But as I have indicated, *Ethiopia Unbound* lays the seed of Gold Coast and West African constitution making as a spiritual calling. Kwamankra declines the suggestion that he is a god, or at least touched by one, but Casely Hayford returns time and again to the messianic dimensions of his political work. In the cryptic fifteenth chapter, he goes so far as to follow a metaphorical description of the Berlin Conference of 1884 (often seen as the official start to the so-called Scramble for Africa) with the following paragraph:

> In the self-same era a god descended upon earth to teach the Ethiopians anew the *way of life*. He came not in thunder, or with great sound, but in the garb of a humble teacher, a John the Baptist among his brethren, preaching racial and national salvation. From land to land, and from shore to shore, his message was the self-same one, which, interpreted in the language of the Christ, was: *What shall it profit a race if it shall gain the whole world and lose its own soul?*[102]

There is no clear-cut way of interpreting this passage because like many parts of the book, it ends before identifying a subject. Nonetheless, it carries a strong suggestion that the figure of Kwamankra, Casely Hayford's vehicle for presenting his ideas while keeping his persona in check, is also all that stands between the author and his deification.

Taken as part of a larger moment of advancing claims to self-determination in the Gold Coast and West Africa, *Ethiopia Unbound* thus leaves anyone trying to come to grips with Casely Hayford's constitutionalism at an impasse. He does not just depict his vision for a Gold Coast constitutional tradition of self-restraint, and institutional checks and balances, by making frequent recourse to individual leaders' charisma. He goes further than that, playing with the idea that modern, "balanced" leadership might even be spiritually ordained. *Ethiopia Unbound* is also his only experiment with the novel form and marks the beginning of the end of his career as a writer. After its publication in 1911, his only work of comparable length and heft is another legal-humanistic treatise from 1913, *The Truth about the West African Land Question*, which I address in the next chapter of this book. But there is a caveat here. In 1915, before he all but abandoned writing to devote himself full time to his work in the NCBWA and on the Gold Coast Legislative Council, Casely Hayford published one slim further "character study" in London: a nineteen-page essay titled *William Waddy Harris: The West African Reformer*. Lifted from the isolated religious history in which this account of Casely Hayford's encounter with a proto-Pentecostal Liberian evangelist has long been considered, its contents speak volumes about his negotiation among forces of personality, spirituality, and measured governance.

Constitutionalism's Spiritual Shadow

William Waddy Harris, read in view of Casely Hayford's constitutionalist interests, is an attempt to square an abiding commitment to public rationality with openness to a civilization-shifting messianic encounter. Its place in Casely Hayford's career also suggests that he could *not* ultimately reconcile the kind of liberal leadership he sought to offer West Africa with the kind of spiritual charisma to which he was drawn. *Ethiopia Unbound* is his first and only effort to sync character typology with political thought; to shore up a constitutionalist worldview, that is, by depicting an ideal constitutionalist. *William Waddy Harris* then marks a split path between Casely Hayford's written vision of leadership and his practical career as a political leader. His reputation in the latter role grows to new renown as his imagination seems to linger elsewhere, reinforcing the image, from the posthumous tributes to him, of a man whose singular esteem eventually outweighs his actual impact on regional politics. *William Waddy Harris* makes clear that the ground began to shift beneath Casely Hayford's feet at the very same time that he broke new institutional ground in his work with the NCBWA. It represents the limits of his ability, as a modern constitutionalist man of letters, to represent a changing West African constitution in a social-descriptive sense. It also reveals the importance of considering Casely Hayford's career holistically, working across parts of his literary and political legacies. Only then can we begin to see where eminence and influence part ways in the history of Gold Coast intellectual life.

Though it is consonant with *Ethiopia Unbound* in its emphasis on individual character, and is in that sense the only real candidate to be considered a "follow-up" to Casely Hayford's novel, *William Waddy Harris* marks a very different formal choice. The characteristic looseness of the essay form—not beholden to even the minimal level of character development found in *Ethiopia Unbound*—made it well suited to capturing what seem like conflicting agendas. As my discussion of *Ethiopia Unbound* has indicated, Casely Hayford affirmed rational modernity while at the same time leaving space for a spiritual understanding of political power. He was not alone in this pairing. Gold Coast intellectuals of his era often rehearsed a distinct kind of liberal secular discourse in the Gold Coast press, to whose flourishing Casely Hayford was so instrumental, and yet in the same pages linked their leadership directly to the church. A 1912 essay in the *Gold Coast Nation*, titled "Our Confession of Faith," moves in the space of three columns from discussing the civic institutions required to sustain "a healthy public opinion" to an injunction to fulfill the nation's mission "in the order of Providence," brought together by "the common God of our Race."[103] *Ethiopia Unbound* nevertheless stands out for its agility in weaving together these tendencies of the Fante legal-political class. Kwamankra's hard-nosed, fact-extolling, eminently reasonable sensibility makes him a methodical and persuasive advocate for the spiritual significance of civic leadership.[104]

But the real Casely Hayford also faced a more delicate challenge in the years between the publication of *Ethiopia Unbound* and *William Waddy Harris*, and approaching the NCBWA's founding in 1917. His leadership cachet, in London especially, stemmed partly from his self-proclaimed insight into "African experience," whose spiritual character began shifting in dramatic ways in the first decades of the twentieth century. Generally speaking, Harris contradicts Casely Hayford's earlier, top-down recommendations for improving Christianity's prospects in the Gold Coast beyond the educated African milieu. In *Gold Coast Native Institutions*, he had written, "There will never be anything like true Christianity on the Gold Coast and in the hinterland till the missionaries have begun from the beginning to build up a national Church on scientific lines—a church wherein the Spirit of Christ will be all in all, and the letter a dead thing."[105] More precisely, Casely Hayford's ability to represent Gold Coast life in both senses of representation—in writing and as its foremost political and cultural arbiter—was stretched to its limit by Waddy Harris's highly influential turn toward direct individual contact with God. Casely Hayford's Methodist mission-educated family was party to a kind of Christianization that was intellectually potent but whose bookishness posed barriers to widespread dissemination, as he himself acknowledges in the quotation above. *William Waddy Harris*, based on the life of the Liberian evangelist William Wadé Harris, portrays his more populist itinerant preaching style as he journeys between his native Liberia, the Ivory Coast, and the Gold Coast, inducting tens of thousands of Africans into the faith through outdoor baptisms performed with only a rudimentary wooden cross, a bowl of water, and what Casely Hayford calls his "tattered Bible."[106] Harris could read English and Grebo, and though involved at different points with both Methodist and Anglican missionaries, he took his religious authority straight from God. "He belongs to no Church," Casely Hayford writes, "Or, if you like, he belongs to the Church universal of which the universal God is both priest and king."[107]

There is confusion surrounding the details of the real Harris's life, but he represents what David Shank refers to as "a new indigenous lay religious movement covering a dozen ethnic groups and involving new patterns of unity in the midst of diversity."[108] His mission was widely seen to mark a kind of halfway point between traditional, pantheistic, and animistic African faith practices and the monotheistic and theocentric tenets of Christianity, and his role in the religious and social history of West Africa is huge. Harris preached against fetishes, or objects of traditional worship, but not against polygamy, for example. The quintessentially "charismatic" qualities of his ministry inaugurated a divergent line of regional development to Casely Hayford and Kwamankra's efforts to find the era's foremost political *and* spiritual calling in clear-eyed constitutionalism. And Harris's geographical reach is also significant: in his appeal across a wide swath of West Africa, he is a more organic regional "founding document" than work that emanates outward from the Gold Coast. In Casely Hayford's essay, he narrates his own encounter with Harris in 1914 as a series of vacillations between persuasion and immersion, as he observes a mode of conversion that he does not undergo but still tries to recount in an experiential way to convince readers of its truth. The "Educated Native" at this moment tries to account for a new African Christian multitude whose path to Christianity he does not, and perhaps cannot, share. Casely Hayford relates to Harris as text and as fact, even as Harris compels him because he operates so far outside an empirical worldview. *William Waddy Harris* thus seeks to convey the richness of a religious ecstasy in whose face he retains the narrative restraint so essential to his constitutionalist politics.

The essay begins by announcing Harris's imperviousness to the place whose religious composition he is single-handedly changing. "To the mystic who lives and thinks in the higher spiritual plane spiritual influences are ever at work," Casely Hayford recounts. "Neither time nor circumstance would seem to have any bearing."[109] In the same breath, he ties those spiritual influences to the "common sense politics" of African self-determination and world progress: "Humanity is in the throes of a new birth. And it does seem as if the movement will begin with West Africa."[110] Quickly, however, the terms of engagement grow muddled, as Casely Hayford searches for a framework that can bridge his propensity for fact-based assertion with the heightened spiritual state he wants to represent. Invoking the educated audience to which all his work is addressed, he parodies their demand for proof. "Where is this God of whom you speak so glibly?," he imagines them asking. "Demonstrate him to us; prove him. Until you do, how can we be sure?"[111] But Casely Hayford believes he knows better, rejoining, "That is hardly a frame of mind for divine intuition." He repeats, "The soul of William Waddy Harris moves in the higher plane," and then adds, "This is so, if you accept the fact or not."[112] Harris's transcendence finds awkward partnership with the very episteme of the fact—recalling this book's previous chapter—whose insertion into Harris's realm Casely Hayford has just mocked.

This odd repurposing of "the fact" is telling. The essay recounts a development in West African religious life that its author has witnessed but not gone all in on, so that the experience of being converted to Christianity by Harris assumes an almost documentary value to him—even apart from his recording it in an actual document. Experience, in a word, becomes something to observe and analyze as much as a name for what it feels like to be inside an event, a noun derived from a verb. The essay is a bravura walk across a perspectival tightrope. But Casely Hayford's ability to find this balance also means that his status in relation to the historical tide of Africa's rise—atop which he had once seen the "Educated Native" boldly poised—is uncertain. The difficulty of interpreting the essay's mix of precarity and prescience comes into bolder relief when it is considered, very briefly, alongside one of the most influential historical narratives of modernity: that of secular "disenchantment," espoused in different ways by figures like Kant in the eighteenth century and Weber in the nineteenth, and influentially developed, in recent years, by the moral philosopher Charles Taylor. In the crowded and lively sphere of debate that the concept has ignited, African spirituality has sometimes been upheld as an "alternative modernity," a counterpoint to any historical narrative that too broadly generalizes the West's relegation of religion to the realm of personal choice and demarcation of worldly from spiritual affairs. In Africa, such arguments suggest, religion remains a pervasive force behind social organization and self-understanding. But while it is easy enough to accept the continent's "problematizing" role in relation to disenchantment in the twentieth century—because of charismatic Christianity's ascent there or the persistence of traditional cosmologies—it is difficult to know where Casely Hayford's generation of liberal-constitutionalist yet charismatically inclined intellectuals might fit into *either* version of things. He was certainly religious, and animated by spiritual interests, but he also internalized key tenets of rational modernity. Does *William Waddy Harris*, with its evocative blending of standpoints, buck disenchantment's trajectory or typify it? Is it, in other words, a full-bodied expression of West Africa's religious rejuvenation, or the product of the very kind of "buffered self" that Taylor argues can draw boundaries between the body and the world?[113]

The essay form takes on greater significance in this light, in its compression of the interplay between what on their face are wholly different historical orientations. To borrow Brian Lennon's terms from "The Essay, in Theory," the "live-wire" or "in time" quality of Casely Hayford's essay on Harris "requires, however provisionally, the re-creation of a position of observation extracted from, taken 'out of,' that time."[114] Though the dynamic—even miraculous—content of Harris's life and work is about as far afield of a textual statement of principles as it could possibly be, the sensibility guiding Casely Hayford's reading of him is more or less in line with Kwamankra's in *Ethiopia Unbound*. The shorter length of the essay helps Casely Hayford draw a tight contrast between a rhetoric of persuasion—narrated "out of time" in the present perfect tense—and an experience of observation narrated in the present tense. He moves from a steady argumentative cadence marked by the phrases "I have spoken of rebellion" and "I have spoken of humility" to describe Harris's Christian tenets into a faster repetition of this formula to describe what it is like to be in his physical presence.[115] "I have heard good men pray. I have heard great men pray. I have heard souls in joy break forth into song," he recites. "But this was a prayer peculiar unto itself. It was short. It was staccato. It abounded in fiery phrases."[116] The paragraph that follows this pulls back from approximating the rhythms of Harris's speech, turning to meet the essay's readers in their skepticism as they are ushered adroitly toward belief. "This man, who and what is he?," asks Casely Hayford rhetorically, before acknowledging, "His works, if they were done a hundred years ago and recorded for our information, few would believe."[117]

Soon after contemplating Harris's significance out loud, so to speak, Casely Hayford pivots to narrating an unnamed woman's conversion experience. His depiction of the scene is punctuated by exclamations of incredulity, reinforcing his observational bona fides at the same time as it stages her transcendent event. "There has been noticed in the crowd a woman who has attempted several times to touch the cross," he writes, "and held back, as if she would rather not. See! She now gets nearer. At last she has touched it, barely touched it. What is this that is happening? Great God! Is it possible?"[118] He describes the woman's agonized convulsions, wild eyes, beastly roaring, and hair standing on end until the prophet's prayer calms her, and he performs her baptism. Harris speaks in a "strange tongue" that some of the crowd then adopt as a seamless response to his demonstrated spiritual power.[119] It is mistaken to call Casely Hayford "an overwhelmed disciple," as Shank does, given the deliberate rhetorical maneuvering by which he brings the experience of Harris's Christian convert to life.[120] Casely Hayford is not overwhelmed but relaying the experience of someone else who is. He is less a disciple than one who argues for the compelling nature of discipleship, ironically by foregrounding the limitations of rational deliberation.

The difference between Casely Hayford's perspective as narrative observer and what we can only imagine are those of the converts whose ecstasy he observes marks the essay's break with how *Ethiopia Unbound* enforces a constitutional worldview. In most of that novel, the "type of human" (to use Taiwo's phrase) required to make a constitutionalist Gold Coast tick is both narrator and character, guiding ethos and specific example of someone who guides. Casely Hayford the author demonstrates his leaderly restraint by granting his views to a separate persona, yet they remain in sync. And while there are bursts of spiritual interest throughout the text, they are by and large absorbed into a larger design of looking *to* text as a stabilizing force. *Ethiopia Unbound*, in other words, shows how texts in general provide founding principles in order to provide its own for the Gold Coast. The "slippage" I have noted between the perspective of Casely Hayford and that of Kwamankra is a revealing exception, as it hints at Casely Hayford's difficulty in getting beyond himself. A vaunted constitutionalist leader, "king-president" or otherwise, does not automatically entail a widespread faith in constitutional leadership. By the time that *William Waddy Harris: The West African Reformer* is published four years later, Casely Hayford as narrator seems to be operating within a wholly different epistemic paradigm to his narrative subjects. Where *Ethiopia Unbound* grants pride of place in advancing democracy to the "men of light and leading in Fante-land," *William Waddy Harris* shows the Christian prophet "leading *them* to fountains of living water."[121]

Much hangs on this use of the object pronoun "them," which erects a firewall between different Gold Coast futures, one constitutionalist and one charismatic. Casely Hayford saw both, and yet between the publication of *William Waddy Harris* and the end of his life in 1930, he all but gave up writing about either. Instead, he worked strenuously to advance the cause of representative constitutional government under the auspices of the NCBWA and the Gold Coast Legislative Council. Without venturing far into the weeds of Ghana's trajectory since then, this parting of ways between two kinds of representation suggests Casely Hayford's increasing nonrepresentativeness. Though the NCBWA looms large in retrospect as the first full-fledged Pan-African organization based on the African continent, it folded soon after Casely Hayford's death. Constitutionalism did not fare much better: as H. Kwasi Prempeh recalls, Kwame Nkrumah as Ghana's first president jettisoned the country's founding document to speed up his own goals.[122] Meanwhile, Pentecostal Christianity since Wadé Harris's day has surged to a dominance in the country—and region—that some have gone so far as to call theocratic.[123] Where is Casely Hayford's constitutionalist vision in all this, and where is his prophetic description of prophecy? Did he anticipate the obsolescence of his constitutional and elite-led politics, even as he further distinguished himself by rightly predicting (and heralding) the coming of a new spiritual age in West Africa? We can only read and wonder alongside his words.

CHAPTER THREE

The Jurisdiction of Morals

THIS CHAPTER, LIKE the last, I enter via one of Casely Hayford's speeches, a sequel of sorts to his 1920 address at the NCBWA's inaugural meeting in Accra. At its second convention in 1923, this time in Freetown, he found himself standing in for fellow barrister Thomas Hutton-Mills as president of the organization. "We are living in a new age and a new order of which we, who participate in them, are hardly aware," Casely Hayford began. "One important element of this new order is the growing consciousness of our race the world over, of which practical statesmanship must take cognisance." A paragraph later, in the speech's printed version, he adds, "One result of this race consciousness is its growing articulateness."[1] The speech then lays out a plan for wide-ranging municipal and judicial reforms at the regional scale, which focus on creating an appellate court for British West Africa as well as a West African Press Union. As earlier in his career, Casely Hayford prizes clarity, discernment, and a pragmatic verging on wonkish approach to West Africans' self-expression and political enfranchisement, hewing to an unflappable standard of precision even in heady times.

Nonetheless, in this speech and elsewhere, Casely Hayford did not take the ascent of a regional consciousness for granted; he understood that it would entail elaborate institutional choreography as well as deliberate suppression of the very nationalist reflexes he had helped nurture. At frequent turns, he remarks on the potential disharmony between advocacy for Africans and allegiance to Africa's constituent parts, noting that even as he has "spoken of the common wants, common claims of our race," he has at the same time "indicated the practical common sense of loyalty to the several flags under which we may live."[2] To bridge this gap between common racial cause and multifaceted geographic composition, Casely Hayford favored a strategy of conscious "cooperation" whereby "this great race of ours, within the British Empire and outside of it, begins to think together."[3] The pluralist turn of his phrase reflects its political objective. In juxtaposing the reality of multiple flags with the ideal of a regional and racial viewpoint, Casely Hayford crystallized his foremost practical challenge: how to steer institutional development across simultaneous, often contradictory-seeming locational and social affinities. How, that is, to forge collective progress from differentiated starting points.

For him and his fellow Gold Coast leaders, coordinating political consciousness across difference was not just a practical necessity—a way to expand Africans' role in the empire's formal political machinery—but a process of moral orchestration. The British Empire, the Gold Coast, West Africa, the Black race, and Cape Coast (co-extensive with Fanteness) all strongly informed Casely Hayford's sense of right and wrong. His navigation of loyalties to "several flags," in the context of his legal-bureaucratic leadership methods, thus yokes urgent disputes about territorial authority to questions of moral metaphysics. To best understand his work, we should ask not which of these scales was most important, but how he arranged and overlaid them in service of a fair and stable polity. In what follows, I turn to "jurisdiction" as the term that best harmonizes these moral and geographical dimensions of Casely Hayford's thought, by drawing out the conceptual and stylistic implications of his concern with different legal norms' distribution.[4] Guided by Bradin Cormack's characterization of jurisdiction as "the infrastructure of the juridical order," I read Casely Hayford's writing about whose standards should apply to which kinds of problems, particularly in *The Truth about The West African Land Question* (1913), with an eye to how his reasoning is itself jurisdictional.[5] Only in studied forms of delimitation, I contend, does Casely Hayford find real liberatory promise.

The Bond of 1844 as Jurisdictional Modernity

I now jump to a small town called Fomena, currently the capital of the Adansi North District in Ghana's present-day Asante region. As of the 2010 census, the district-wide population was just over 107,000. This follows an era of significant growth in the late nineteenth century; Fomena's status as district capital was conferred only in 1875. Once a powerful kingdom in its own right, Adansi is described by Carl Christian Reindorf in his *History of the Gold Coast and Asante* as "the first seat of the Akan nation" and "the enlightened tribe ... from whom the rest acquired wisdom and knowledge."⁶ Whether or not that is true from the viewpoint of other Akan polities, Fomena does occupy a privileged place in the history of Gold Coast claims to sovereignty. It is a hallowed site, in particular, for the formation of a Fante print-intellectual class.

This is due to a momentous, if not much commemorated, textual event that took place there amid rising intraregional tensions seven years into Queen Victoria's reign: the signing of the Bond of 1844. A document of fewer than 150 words, the Bond spelled out three points of agreement between nine coastal chiefs from states now considered Fante and four representatives of the British Crown. The latter group included the popular leader Captain George Maclean, the outgoing governor of Cape Coast and main author of the Bond. Because so much hangs on it, and given that the text is so short, I include all three of its points below:

1. Whereas power and jurisdiction have been exercised for and on behalf of Her Majesty the Queen of Great Britain and Ireland, within divers countries and places adjacent to Her Majesty's forts and settlements on the Gold Coast; we, chiefs of countries and places so referred to, adjacent to the said forts and settlements, do hereby acknowledge that power and jurisdiction, and declare that the first objects of law are the protection of individuals and of property.
2. Human sacrifices, and other barbarous customs, such as panyaring, are abominations, and contrary to law.
3. Murders, robberies, and other crimes and offences, will be tried and enquired of before the Queen's judicial officers and the chiefs of the districts, moulding the customs of the country to the general principles of British law.

In sum, and from a postcolonial perspective, the Fante chiefs erred by granting the British increased dominion over the Gold Coast; Kwaku Larbi Korang has described Gold Coast leaders as party to a Faustian pact.⁷ The Bond has thus often been seen as Fanteland's "selling out" to colonial power in order to secure its own. (The Asante, meanwhile, have gone down in history as staunchly resisting British incursion, including in the series of prominent battles between 1823 and 1831 known as the First Anglo-Asante War.) British control had until this point extended *only* to the coastal forts and immediately surrounding trade settlements, and it would now be permitted to extend beyond them. Crucially, however—and I will return to this point—this extension of jurisdiction was not all-encompassing. It specified only *criminal* matters ("panyaring" was the practice of imprisoning people with unpaid debts), not civil, thus suggesting an implicit distinction between self-evidently moral and more nuts-and-bolts aspects of nation building. But before bridging the jurisdictional metaphysics of the Bond of 1844 with Casely Hayford's work on jurisdiction in the next century, a more detailed explanation of its signatories' vision of modernity is in order.

To start with, it is important to recall that the Asante, not the British, were at the time perceived as the most immediate threat to Fante consolidation.[8] The Gold Coast was undergoing a massive economic and social adjustment in the early to mid-nineteenth century, as rival powers navigated an increased reliance on "legitimate" trade—especially cocoa—following the slave trade's 1807 abolition within the British Empire. As Kwasi Konadu has summarized the situation, "The trade routes that facilitated commerce between the forest interior and the coast remained contested, especially between Asante and Fante, and the conflicts associated with those routes endured.... The nineteenth century opened with Fante efforts to successfully resist Asante expeditions to the coast, in addition to similar incursions, and these encroachments on Fante territory would have been more disastrous if it were not for the help of Europeans established in their coastal forts."[9] Konadu's use of the plural "Europeans" here is telling. To restate a significant point, the European presence in Fante territory was long and variegated: the Portuguese had settled Elmina in 1482, and the Dutch began trading there in 1598. The British were relative latecomers to the region, first under the auspices of the Royal Trading Company (founded in 1752) and then of the African Company of Merchants, before the British Crown withdrew its charter in 1821. Between 1821 and 1828, the coastal forts were administered by the British colonial governor of Sierra Leone; they were in fact something of an afterthought, even an albatross due to their high maintenance costs. For historians of the region these facts are well known. But the quick succession, mutual contestation, and ostensibly ad hoc strategies of European trading powers in the Gold Coast also make up a crucial backstory to Casely Hayford's era and his galvanization of the written word. This history suggests that, for his earliest print-intellectual forebears in the 1840s, Britain's dominance was far from a foregone conclusion. The Fante were not necessarily naive or venal in thinking that they could pick and choose what they took from imperial culture as partners in a robust economy of exchange.

It is impossible, of course, to know for sure what proto-Fante chiefs in 1844 imagined themselves to be doing when they signed the Bond. But the most persuasive accounts of their intentions share an emphasis on Fantes' tactical savvy and self-awareness, a far cry from the familiar colonial-era figure of the African dupe.[10] J. B. Danquah's 1957 lecture-turned-essay "The Historical Significance of the Bond of 1844" remains the most exhaustive and assured reading of the Bond's relevance across the colonial and postcolonial periods, and of the nascent sense of Fante selfhood it helped bring to fruition. The essay refers to the document as that which "recognised the people of the Gold Coast as an independent people," albeit by means of their *witting* self-subjugation.[11] "There should be nothing startling about the use of the term 'bondage' in connection with the Bond of 1844," Danquah's reading continues. "By agreeing to the abrogation or diminution of certain of their ancient rights and liberties, the 'Fante Chiefs' placed themselves under a bounding duty to observe the obligations of the Bond."[12] His interest in the Bond as evidence of a long-standing and distinctive form of Gold Coast African agency, which welds interpretive sophistication to political nous, makes biographical sense. As a member of the so-called Big Six, a nickname for the leaders of the United Gold Coast Convention Party who played the most visible role in winning Ghana's independence from Britain, Danquah in many ways carried the torch of the nineteenth-century Gold Coast intelligentsia. He was born just shy of thirty years after Casely Hayford was, in 1895, and worked briefly with the elder leader to found the Gold Coast Youth Conference in 1929.

More to the point, Danquah had the same sort of intellectual bona fides as Casely Hayford and saw his fine-grained attention to Akan thought traditions as an essential tool for advancing national sovereignty. He had a doctorate in philosophy from University College London—where he wrote, tellingly, about moral character—and was also called to the bar at the Inner Temple in 1926. His most accomplished texts are clear successors to Sarbah and Casely Hayford's efforts at cultural systematization: he published *Akan Laws and Customs and the Akim Abuakwa Constitution* in 1928, and in 1944, *The Akan Doctrine of God: A Fragment of Gold Coast Ethics and Religion*. The similarities don't end there. Danquah, too, returned to Ghana to practice law and there founded an important regional newspaper in 1931, in this case a daily called the *West Africa Times* (later renamed the *Times of West Africa*). But the deeper affinity between Casely Hayford and Danquah is the distinctively *textual* nature of their political commitments. The Bond, in Danquah's telling, inaugurated a movement toward self-conscious modernization that Casely Hayford personified during his lifetime, and that Danquah himself, breaking free of the Bond's "legal effect," then helped see across the finish line of formal independence.[13] Danquah's understanding of the Bond is highly illuminating of "Fanteness" in the Casely Hayford tradition because it attaches the loftiest stakes of the document to its written status; the novelty of the jurisdictional arrangement that the Bond secured is rhetorically wrought up with the novelty of textual agreements in Fante-British dealings. His essay opens by quoting British historian William Walton Claridge to the effect that around the Bond's signing, "documentary evidence of every agreement or arrangement made with the Chiefs and people" was newly necessary because Gold Coast Africans "could no longer be regarded and treated as simple savages as had been the case in the past."[14] Danquah does not assent to the racial denigration of that reading. But he does follow its lead to suggest that the Bond formalized a new kind of fine textual distinction making in navigating the relationship of change to continuity.

Seen in this light, the modern Gold Coast political tradition is about knowing just when and where to *break* with tradition in favor of some new arrangement. It does not mean that any given recalibration of old and new, or "African" and "Western," is necessarily desirable when considered with years of hindsight, but that the willingness to recalibrate in a self-reflective way is definitive. This is the upshot of Danquah's work on the Bond, and it remains persuasive. He sees the Fante chiefs who signed it as having found agreement with their British counterparts around the idea that writing could and should bring clarity to heretofore improvised matters; for them to have seen that their changing conditions demanded such clarification was not credulous but creditable. "The Historical Significance of the Bond of 1844" performs a virtuoso close reading of the Bond to pin down its genre as part of making this case, arguing that it is not a charter, not an act, but a willful and unilateral forfeiting of parts of Fante self-rule with a view to a larger social vision. "By the Bond," Danquah writes, "a free people, who were not subjects of the British sovereign, voluntarily placed themselves under a binding agreement to the British Crown. In thereby diminishing and abrogating certain of their ancient rights and liberties, they secured a better maintenance of their society which was growing more complex by reason of its contact with a society based on a differently organised system of values."[15]

A lot hangs on Danquah's use of "certain" in this passage. He argues not that the Fante signatories to the Bond gave up their freedom wholesale, but that they weighed the trade-offs of exchanging different *kinds* of freedoms for different kinds of social gain. For Danquah, they exercised their self-determination to give some of it up. This is an easy possibility to lose track of amid sharper debates about the Bond and other nineteenth-century Fante-British agreements, which, the historian Rebecca Shumway summarizes, "have variously been used either to argue that the Fante consented to British rule—because the agreements allowed a certain amount of British participation in African affairs—or to argue that the Fante did not yield authority to the British—because the treaties did not grant either sovereignty or landownership to the British government."[16] Shumway, however, offers a different understanding to Danquah's of what the Bond represents, even as she agrees with his view that Fante leaders at the time were "[incorporating] new elements," namely legal ones, as a mark not of cultural corruption but of distinction.[17] Where Danquah sees it as "a world-shaking event," owing both to its contents and written form, Shumway finds continuity with centuries of verbal agreement making between Fantes and Europeans.[18] More specifically, she casts it as one among numerous examples of nineteenth-century treaties that should rightly be understood within the tradition of the palaver, a term that refers to group deliberations among leaders as the cornerstone of "an indigenous African legal code for both local and international dispute settlement and alliance."[19]

Drawing on British attendance at palavers in the eighteenth century, a shared Fante-British priority on rebuffing Asante invasions, and a high rate of Fante intermarriage with Europeans, Shumway makes the case that "the palaver system of the slave trade era continued," in the nineteenth century, "to serve as a necessary mechanism for negotiating the profoundly intertwined affairs of the British and Fante on the Gold Coast."[20] The upshot of this hybrid state of affairs is that it is tough to pinpoint the precise moment, from a Fante perspective, at which it becomes implausible to see the British as allies rather than would-be overlords. Shumway concludes on this basis, "The Bond of 1844 therefore makes much more sense within the indigenous paradigm of the palaver as an agreement among equal parties than it does as a declaration of Fante consent to proto-colonial British rule."[21] To bolster this reading of continuity, she downplays the magnitude of the transition from verbal to written forms of agreement, going so far as to claim, "At the time of its creation . . . the Bond of 1844 was virtually meaningless because it merely acknowledged that criminal cases were sometimes tried in the forts before British officers and African chiefs, a practice that had existed for at least a hundred years."[22] Shumway is right in the sense that the Bond did not mark a neat break with existing Gold Coast judicial practices; Danquah acknowledges as much in his discussion of Claridge, before confirming that the Bond's immediate purpose was to allow Governor Maclean's role in Cape Coast "to be better defined and understood."[23] But there is a *lot* of ground between "world-shaking" and "meaningless" in weighing the document's significance. Even were it notable only for putting what was already true of Fante-English relations in writing, this marks a substantive difference from in-person negotiations and improvised tactics. Getting facts on record here means choosing and deciding how to organize words. Unlike the aggregate "speech act" of an oath, writing is a process of making fine discernments over time.

And discernment, for Casely Hayford, was everything. This is true of both his legal recommendations and his public performance of what it meant to be a new sort of legal-minded African leader, with an intuitive sense of what parts of imperial culture to adopt without harming the salutary aspects of Akan customs. The Bond of 1844, with its suggestion of a willingly modified sovereignty, thus appears through this lens to be an obvious precursor of Casely Hayford's style of reasoning and of his style writ large. It was direct but diplomatic, polished but unadorned. A description of a Cape Coast banquet he helped host in 1913 on behalf of the ARPS, included in an appendix to *The Truth about the West African Land Question* in which multiple other speakers are also recorded invoking the Bond of 1844, sets the scene for this intimacy between legal acumen and Gold Coast personhood. "The dining hall was beautifully lit with incandescent lamps of 1,500 candle power," it begins. "The decorations were simple but tasteful and effective." The elevation of discernment over splendor seems also to have characterized the Cape Coasters' menu, with its "choice and select" wine list.[24] Lamps are not laws, and a wine list is not an organizational charter. My point, in jumping from historians' debates about a mid-nineteenth-century legal document to Casely Hayford's early twentieth-century social environs, is to underscore law's multidimensional presence in Gold Coast life.

A hub of taste making as much as political activity, the ARPS was founded in response to the Lands Bill of 1897, whereby the British tried to gain authority over the distribution of what they wrongly took to be empty or "waste" lands. Though they distinguished between this power to administrate and ownership as such, in effect the move they wanted, to an English system of property titling—and ultimately, a free land market—overlooked an elaborate and self-regulating set of Akan norms around land use.[25] Recalling Fante complaints that British administrators could not be objective, Casely Hayford and his peers read in the Lands Bill a crude misunderstanding of African systems of social and economic regulation.[26] Casely Hayford's contrasting ability to draw clear lines between easily bundled concepts and situations was integral to his tactics on the ARPS front, and later to his refutation of the 1911 Forest Bill, a follow-up British effort to seize control of "uncultivated" Gold Coast lands.[27] He argued against the

Lands Bill in London on behalf of the ARPS and was successful in that his efforts helped bring about the Concessions Ordinance of 1900, which "established the principle that all lands were vested in African communities and chiefs and not in the crown or governor."[28]

But the *way* Casely Hayford argues is most notable here, in view of his multivalent understanding of distinction, or discernment, as a social aura and intellectual methodology. In writing about British efforts to override Gold Coast land norms, he is more a pedant than firebrand, finding profound insights in subtle terminological differences. "And here we must carefully distinguish between Paramountcy; and Ownership," he announces in *The Truth about the West African Land Question* (hereafter abbreviated in this chapter as *Land Question*).[29] Casely Hayford then illustrates this distinction with extended discussion of a hypothetical plot of land that is farmed by one person, possessed by another, and owned by yet a third. Understanding the difference entails distinguishing between the Fante term *abusa* (one-third payment of profits or commodities to an owner in exchange for land use), and an "occasional contribution" made on relevant occasions to a paramount chief. From there, he suggests a further distinction of "tribute" from "allegiance fee," which he contends would save "much confusion of ideas."[30]

It's distinctions all the way down. Casely Hayford, accordingly, also forges West African unity by recounting the details of other jurisdictional crises: if the British have made unreliable maps of "West Africa," then specific accounts of their misprision now create the territory. He describes flawed and generic kinds of British territorial delimitation in Sierra Leone by using a metaphor, which contrasts with the fastidious place linking his own prose performs. "The direct object was to bring civilisation into Africa," he writes of Sierra Leone's founding in 1787, before adding drily, "It was not a time for *discrimination*."[31] He then figures the misguided British enterprise of maintaining a separate Sierra Leone colony (coastal and settled by freed slaves) and protectorate (inland and inhabited mostly by indigenous groups) as a project of building "hermetically sealed" glass houses, in which plants were laid out and labeled "as in a museum."[32] The simile works powerfully to level a charge against Britain of dividing to rule, and it shows off Casely Hayford's rhetorical prowess. But figuration here is reserved for effect rather than for urgent matters of persuasion, so that likening a specific thing to a generic other appears at odds with identifying permutations of a common cause. When *Land Question* moves on from Sierra Leone to Nigeria in querying how "the land question has aroused all West Africa," Casely Hayford prefaces a dense analysis of

Lagos's Cession to Britain in 1861 with "Now for the facts."[33] In the section as a whole, then, he counterposes figurative and factual-historical descriptive tactics, setting up a suggestive alliance between, on the one hand, sameness and separation, and on the other, distinction and solidarity. West Africa could not be sloganeered into existence; it had to be carefully drawn from flag to flag.

Even where other factors were on his side, such as with the ARPS defeat of the Public Lands Bill of 1897, it is hard not to see Casely Hayford's trademark distinction making as having had real force in the world.[34] In a speech at the 1913 ARPS banquet, the acting principal of the Mfantsipim School (S. J. Gibson) remarked on the persuasive effect of this hyperanalytic disposition. He commended the society for "[seeking] to preserve the old, not because of its antiquity but because of its intrinsic value," as it avoided "degenerating into a permanent opposition."[35] Casely Hayford emphasized differences when building a unified front, insisting that no association go unquestioned. As one kind of jurisdiction in the Bond of 1844 did not entail another, Casely Hayford gave automatic assent neither to British nor Akan principles of social organization. Avoiding unearned generalizations on even the most hot-button topics was part of the "seriousness" that he and his fellow ARPS leaders sought to cultivate in their broader presentation, especially after the advent of a more interventionist style of indirect rule in 1912. "The Aborigines Society is a serious political organization and should be taken seriously," reads an unsigned editorial in the March 28, 1912, issue of the *Gold Coast Nation*. The style of Gold Coast leaders' banquets buttressed the style of their rhetoric.[36]

Whether or not the Bond had an objective "world-shaking" effect, per J. B. Danquah, because it documented and conventionalized Africans' propensity to pick and choose, the Fante movers and shakers of later generations wrote and acted as if it did. It is not possible to separate fully the Bond of 1844 from the Gold Coast modernity that rose in its image; how Casely Hayford and his ilk read their history was of a piece with the day-to-day, practical details of their legislative leadership style. To be a modern Fante leader meant subscribing to a legislative brand of politics not just because it was prudent, but because it was *hard-nosed*; staking (or ceding) a claim on paper suggested to them a new kind of integrity. A particular instance of ARPS pushback on British governance, published in the *Gold Coast Nation* on March 28, 1912, underscores this dynamic. The society's ire, in this case, was provoked by colonial officials' having undermined its legal authority to collect dues from its members, by publishing a letter to "Kings and Chiefs" that advised them of their right to "refuse [to contribute to the

ARPS] with impunity." Galled at the underhanded affront to their lawful and methodical way of doing things as well as to their membership pedigree, the ARPS published a rejoinder. "A Society some of whose founders are the lineal descendants of the very Kings who nearly Seventy years ago, signed the Historic Bond of 1844 thereby giving England a firm footing in this Country," it reads in part, "ought not to be trifled with and the writer before committing his burning thoughts on paper should have given them credit for a little good sense." They did not simply acknowledge that the Bond of 1844 entailed a choice to give up part of their self-governance to England; they were proud of what this meant for Fante judgment.

It is unsurprising, therefore, that Casely Hayford's reading of the Bond anticipates Danquah's more than it does Shumway's, in that he sees in it the clear start of a new Gold Coast era. He frames it, moreover, much as Danquah later and more famously does: as an effort to organize *different kinds* of authority, some of which are continuous with predocumentary Fante norms, and some of which require Fante leaders' judicious acquiescence to British ones. In *Gold Coast Native Institutions*, he writes, "The Bond had no reference to territorial acquisition; it did not extend the Queen's possessions beyond their former limits. In brief, such jurisdiction as it conferred was restricted to criminal matters."[37] The discussion that follows in *Land Question* is more involved. After citing ample but miscellaneous evidence, in the form of dispatches and reports, of British officials' acknowledgment that they did not have rights to Gold Coast African lands, Casely Hayford reflects on the Bond's importance in codifying this precedent. He is responding, specifically, to a report on Gold Coast land policies by British Special Commissioner H. Conway Belfield, who had little experience there and recommended the potentially catastrophic "transference of jurisdiction in Land Grants from the Supreme Court to the Executive."[38] From Casely Hayford's perspective, the fact that Fante chiefs in 1844 assented in print to *giving up* criminal jurisdiction proves by omission that they did not relinquish civil authority. He writes, for example, "For it will be remembered that the Bond of 1844, which gave Her Majesty for the first time criminal jurisdiction in the country, was silent as to jurisdiction in civil matters."[39]

Making such distinctions necessarily risks getting them wrong, and it is easy to find fault now with the Fante signatories of the Bond of 1844 or with Casely Hayford's endorsement of it, as well as with his legal-reformist tactics more broadly. This is truer still given Danquah's prominent place in the history of the Bond's interpretation, as well as his connection to Casely Hayford: Danquah is arguably Ghana's most famous loser, dramatically imprisoned unto death under Kwame Nkrumah for his alleged involvement in an assassination attempt, and long an emblem of a banished constitutionalist, legal-elitist style of rule. With almost two centuries of hindsight, it seems clear that allowing British officials to oversee the administration of justice in an effort to "mould" Gold Coast customs only to *certain* "general principles of British law" would open the door to more encompassing colonization. And yet as Olufemi Taiwo insists, "African theorists of the nineteenth century acknowledged their debts to their conquerors. They may have been mistaken in their identification of the antecedents of the principle of political governance to which they subscribed. But we should not read back into the past our current nationalist predilections."[40] To deny Gold Coast modernizers the possibility of having miscalculated—of giving up in order to gain—would be a kind of intellectual insult.

A Rightful Order

Casely Hayford's repeated references to the Bond of 1844 in his writing about land administration in the early twentieth century make "jurisdiction" an obvious place to look in mapping his Gold Coast intellectual tradition. Jurisdictional debates, in a straightforward sense, make up a substantial chunk of the contents of early Anglo-Fante writing. But jurisdiction is also a guiding *principle* of Casely Hayford's work, and so warrants further fleshing out before a closer look at *Land Question* in this chapter's final section. What does jurisdiction offer, conceptually, that related ideas like legal pluralism or sovereignty do not? As Renisa Mawani puts it aptly in *Across Oceans of Law: The Komagata Maru and Jurisdiction in the Time of Empire*, "Unlike sovereignty, which assumes a coherent and homogeneous unity of legal and political authority, jurisdiction points to the multiplicity and heterogeneity of law."[41] Mariana Valverde similarly invokes the term to identify the many authoritative paths that coalesce as a single state. While political theorists have remained transfixed by sovereignty, she bemoans, and encouraged thereby to unhelpful generalizations "about law, about science, or about 'modernity,'" the fact is that "governing projects and the power-knowledges that make them work are differentiated from one another and kept from overtly clashing by the workings of the machinery of 'jurisdiction,' which instantly sorts governing processes, knowledges, and powers into their proper slots."[42] In Casely Hayford's hands, this overt condition of legal multiplicity, and linked emphasis on sorting as a leadership skill, had metaphysical implications.

Distinction making and boundary drawing were *moral* operations for him, in the sense that they facilitated explicit discussion of how moral absolutes fit into a big picture of Gold Coast development. Certain concerns were marked as matters of right and wrong regardless of political calculation, even as they were enfolded into a larger plan for African-led political change. When he turns to the Bond of 1844 in *Gold Coast Native Institutions*, for example, Casely Hayford punctuates his breezy, matter-of-fact tone with an emphatic moral vocabulary. "Now, a careful reading of this Bond makes it clearly evident that its main object was to enable Her Majesty to exercise jurisdiction in suppressing heinous offences committed within districts adjacent to the forts. In the exercise of such jurisdiction, the Queen's judicial officers were to act conjointly with the Chiefs of the districts."[43] The effect is to make it appear as if certain transgressions—the "heinous" ones—are beyond locationally determined dispute or explanation, and so warrant whatever sort of legal arrangement will get the job of punishing them done. As Luke Bennett and Antonia Layard note in their work on legal geography, which they root in the truism that "Law comes alive applied to space," some things nonetheless confound place-based understanding. "A lack of space-talk may be a clue that location should not excuse culpability," they admit, "that murder is murder wherever it happens."[44] In Casely Hayford's formulation above, "to exercise jurisdiction" could, as concerns both grammar and content, be replaced with "to exercise discretion," meaning that *these* crimes, but not others, summon right-thinking leaders to acknowledge and prioritize shared and immovable values. The question of where to prioritize universal over place-based values also arose around questions of legal process, with acute importance for regional cooperation. As a notable example, trial by jury for criminal cases was practiced in the Gold Coast long before it was in neighboring Asante.[45]

Knowing just where to draw lines, furthermore—how to sort ideas and subjects into separate compartments—was key to an *order-seeking* anticolonial politics that sought the stability required for long-term reform. It is not, of course, anomalous for morality to be a Victorian- or Edwardian-era public preoccupation; it is the subject of too many books and articles to count. But it *is* notable to see as clear and casual a linking of moral rhetoric, minute practicality, and transnational ethnic ambition as that supplied by the Cape Coast print sphere in Casely Hayford's lifetime. A single General News column in the *Gold Coast Leader* on June 13, 1912, glides from emphasizing Gold Coasters' global credentialing, to reporting on failures of municipal management, to affirming the justice of legal sentences. "At the request of Mr. Casely Hayford," the first item notes, a number of Gold Coast leaders were introduced at a conference in Liverpool as "Princes of

West Africa." Meanwhile, back home, "letters and telegrams [were being] kept for days at the store of the local Post Agent," and a "notorious convict" was sentenced to a "well deserved" punishment of five years of hard labor. Distinguishing between proper and improper, or right and wrong, on a situational basis was definitive of a Fante rhetorical style and social bearing, and essential to the long-term and mundane functionality of Gold Coast self and state.

In Bradin Cormack's magisterial *A Power to Do Justice: Jurisdiction, English Literature, and the Rise of the Common Law, 1509–1625*, he provides a strong theoretical scaffolding for how "jurisdiction amounts to the delimitation of a sphere ... that is the precondition for the juridical as such, for the very capacity of the law to come into effect."[46] He means that drawing boundaries between one place, temporality, or genre and another is essential to granting them any legal "content" at all; in other words, the act of deciding who or what has authority over which sphere becomes inseparable from an account of how power works inside it. Cormack offers a number of further descriptions of jurisdiction that fit the Casely Hayford context, despite the gap in location and period. Naming jurisdiction as "a principle of distribution" and "the infrastructure of the juridical order," he recognizes the intimate connection between legal-administrative minutiae and habits of mind.[47] As the versatile figure he was, Casely Hayford sought to distribute roles and purpose with utmost precision, slotting things into their rightful place because he had a view of the whole. If his distinction-making bent can seem fussy, perhaps rigid, this is only part of the dispositional picture. In fact Casely Hayford was a kind of bird's-eye-view manager, "whose policy," noted the younger Gold Coast barrister and editor Magnus J. Sampson in 1948, "was based not on mere theories or ideals but on practical politics."[48] He was steeped in legal practice on a day-to-day level but worked all the while to refine "the law's" role in a multifaceted and expanding regional federation. He moved dexterously between law's real and its ideal. When Cormack observes that some literary texts' "orientation toward law will, critically, so express itself as a meditation on the mechanics of legal authority," we might just as well say that Casely Hayford's legal texts meditate on the meaning of literary form, as well as a literary pedigree.[49]

The volume of his interests and influences can obscure the fact that Casely Hayford was a highly *ordered* thinker. He wanted West African institutions that worked, led by men whose racial consciousness was geared toward "coming together for practical purposes" and building beyond "loose" organizations.[50] A brief return to *Ethiopia Unbound* illustrates this propensity to see order, not chaos, as the natural state of Gold Coast society, as well as law's ready availability for metaphoric use. In a scene of genteel socializing and drinking populated by "a body of learned men ... including the members of the Diplomatic Service, one or two doctors, with a fair sprinkling of coloured barristers," a debate about jurisdiction takes center stage. It concerns cemetery protocols in particular, namely whether people of different races should be buried side by side. When a British official scoffs at the idea of integrated internment, Kwamankra, as the Casely Hayford figure, explains that this position defies the political "reciprocity" on which the British presence in the Gold Coast depends. Assuring the official that he is not personally offended, Kwamankra points out the foolishness of segregation for all parties. His own view is that "if you took mankind in the aggregate, irrespective of race, and shook them up together, as you would the slips of paper in a jury panel box, you would find after the exercise that the cultured would shake themselves free and come together, and so would the uncouth, the vulgar, and the ignorant"[51] Legal procedure, and specifically the form of the jury, provides a set of practical conventions to support social self-sorting.

Adjacent to the literary arena, Casely Hayford's pragmatic orientation was in full force in the 1920s regarding the development of a regional judiciary, as he advocated for the creation of a single court of appeal for the Gold Coast, Sierra Leone, and the Gambia. Cormack's understanding of jurisdiction falters here as a tool for understanding the Gold Coast intellectual milieu because of its emphasis on boundaries' porousness and instability. His book takes its tonal cues from a poststructuralist slate of thinkers, including Agamben, Derrida, Rancière, and Foucault, whose high conceptual register chafes against Casely Hayford's desire for rational order and airtight argument. An important underlying point of *A Power to Do Justice* is that jurisdiction, or the formal allocation of authority, "entails the fundamental juridical dynamic by which the distribution of a given authority both stabilizes and makes contestable that authority's norms," as it "makes visible a governing and productive instability in the law . . . because jurisdiction marks any norm whatsoever as the recursive expression of an ongoing, practical processing of disorder."[52] To see jurisdiction as a "fantasy" or a "haunting" as Cormack does isn't necessarily wrong; no authority outside that of a true sovereign operates without a shadow.[53] All the same, it is an explanatory mismatch with jurisdiction's unrivaled normative power as Gold Coast leaders from 1844 through the creation of the NCBWA in 1920 perceived it.

Lauren Benton offers a more historically intuitive account of jurisdiction as a culture-shaping force in *Law and Colonial Cultures: Legal Regimes in*

World History, 1400–1900, which sees West Africa as a crucial node in the movement away from legal pluralism and toward state hegemony (and ultimately an interstate international order) in the nineteenth century. Her discussion of "cultural intermediaries" in the practice of *"jurisdictional politics"*—by which she means "conflicts over the preservation, creation, nature, and extent of different legal forums and authorities"—in many ways fits the Fante intelligentsia to a tee.[54] Benton elucidates two of the baseline conditions I have emphasized about the Gold Coast legal class's sense of their lettered tradition as it emerges from the Bond of 1844. First, that "the structure of legal authority and the creation of cultural hierarchies were inextricably intertwined" with jurisdictional debates, therefore affording "fine distinctions among groups ... an importance that appears exaggerated to observers outside a particular time and place."[55] And second, that the world before the rise of the nation-state was full of "legal regimes in which actors immersed in different legal systems nevertheless constructed a shared understanding of legal power as a basis for exchanges of goods and information, even in the absence of an overlapping authority or a formal regulatory structure."[56] She backs away from a purely macrostructural understanding of intra-imperial politics to adopt a more sensitive approach focused on how legal boundary drawing and collective self-understanding interacted at key historical junctures.

Globalization, in Benton's recounting, was not a foregone conclusion; colonizing and colonized groups of legal professionals could inhabit shared roles with substantive engagement, even amid rising administrative inequalities (especially after Britain's formal colonization of the Gold Coast in 1874). It follows from Benton's analysis that agency would have been *perceived*, at least, to be "real" at the level of the individual as well as the community. This is no doubt consonant with Casely Hayford's understanding of the Bond of 1844, which he described as having set forth a new and morally compelling opportunity for British and African legal personnel to work "conjointly."[57] Legal systems in Benton's analysis were not "stacked" but rather existed, for a time, side by side, permitting what she calls "rampant boundary crossing" not just of "legal ideas and practices" but also of "legal actors," who "[appealed] regularly to multiple legal authorities and [perceived] themselves as members of more than one legal community."[58] This is certainly true of Casely Hayford, whose boundary crossing was legendary even during his lifetime. Cape Coast newspapers tracked his regular comings and goings, and he was, to all appearances, equally at home drinking whiskey at London's Inner Temple as quietly practicing law in the small town of Axim.[59]

What demands some historical recovery, en route to sharpening the normative edge of jurisdiction in this frame, is the sheer brio and decisiveness of his and his peers' dealings with British administrators. Reading the Bond of 1844 and the cultural style it inspired through this lens can then get beyond a familiar injunction to restore "African agency" and examine the particular claims that such agency in fact advanced. In this case, it was that British norms around criminality and criminal procedure were morally desirable in the Gold Coast while British norms around land use were not. An unsigned October 30, 1897, editorial in the *Gold Coast Methodist Times* puts forth its outlook as such: "To call a spade a spade has always subjected men to temporary inconvenience, but later events have without exception justified those who unflinchingly refrained from indulging in linguistic dodges to cover their meaning." The piece is indeed unflinching, alternating between fulsome praise of British legal traditions and scathing criticism of then-current land legislation. "The national greatness of the English people has been determined by their national laws and institutions," it continues. "We too are anxious to march *en masse* after the great English Nation; We want to do so willingly, voluntarily intelligently and gradually. We refuse to be dragged whipped or cajoled to it. We refuse to rise, in any except the only way prescribed by the Constitution of England." Each of these elements must be understood through the other; admiration without anger might seem like pandering, and anger without room for admiration, like dogma. When the editorial proclaims, in conclusion, that "we cannot soften the truth or smooth our tongue to please friends or foes," its confidence feels earned.

The fact that Gold Coast leaders were so forthright in their criticisms of British policy marks the degree to which West African circumstances in this period diverge from broad expectations around colonial power dynamics. Put bluntly, there is no compelling reason to read Fante admiration for parts of the British imperial system as coerced or insincere, because condemnation too was given so freely. Subversion is not the operative framework here; discernment is. And where discernment is possible, any given choice packs real punch in the normative crafting of character. In short, it has to be taken seriously. Casely Hayford did not simply, rotely adapt his British legal training to Gold Coast nationalist ends because it is what he happened to have at his disposal, though of course his options, like anyone's, were limited by time and place. He also *evaluated* Gold Coast legal history and tactics on a (literal) case-by-case basis, with acute awareness of his own historical position. This normative weight, in turn, tightens the connection between jurisdiction's intrinsic assumption of multiplicity (because one jurisdiction is defined vis-à-vis others) and the possibility it implies of interjurisdictional mobility. In this way, Casely Hayford's jurisdictional way of working through problems becomes the enabling condition of his Fante cosmopolitan self-styling; his legal training and disposition have far-reaching cultural effects.

In legal scholar Richard T. Ford's terms, we might say that Casely Hayford was skilled at navigating the narrow space between "organic" and "synthetic" forms of jurisdiction, with the former "a natural outgrowth of circumstances, conditions, and principles that, morally, preexist the state," and the latter "imposed on groups of people from 'outside' or 'above.'"[60] Fante nationhood, in the nineteenth and early twentieth centuries, was in the process of highly visible self-invention in both a cultural and a political sense (as detailed in this book's introductory discussion of the Gone Fante movement). At the same time, Casely Hayford's studied performance of his "Educated African" role—in relation to traditional chiefs on one end and the broader Gold Coast population on the other—meant that he was comfortable with a top-down kind of legislative politics. Awareness of the inexact fit or, more optimistically, complementarity between Ford's two jurisdictional variants was central to his efforts at a regional Pan-Africanism. Casely Hayford was part of engineering an organic "Fanteness" on the Gold Coast at the same time as he advocated for a synthetic "West African" polity. A suitable leader had to know which was which and be able to move nimbly between them.

So where does the element of placeless moral truths fit in, the "heinous offences" whose wrongness transcends politics and yet contributes forcefully to their definition? This chapter's steady reference point of the Bond of 1844 makes it easier to make good on its promise of moral-metaphysical engagement. Subsequent Gold Coast leaders' pride in the Bond, including Casely Hayford's rhetorical replication of the consequential distinction making he took it to represent, exemplifies as well as complicates Ford's organic/synthetic equation. The Bond's negative claim, that it did *not* entail civil jurisdiction for the British, no doubt spoke to a Fante desire to "[safeguard] tradition and legacy" in conformity with Ford's understanding of an organic jurisdiction.[61] Its positive claim to extended British criminal jurisdiction likewise fits his understanding of a synthetic one, in that it corresponded "with the *regularization of the body politic*" that "encourages citizens to understand themselves as rational and objective utility maximizers and to conform to a set of activities that facilitate the free alienability of land, individual freedom of action, and geographic and social mobility."[62] But Casely Hayford prioritized "individual freedom of action" and "geographic and social mobility" only up to a point: "the free alienability of land" was off the table because land falls under the "organic" jurisdiction of Akan norms and traditions. The mobility Casely Hayford envisioned, then, was not only or even mainly territorial; rather, it entailed knowing movement between different *kinds* of jurisdiction within the same space. In his discussion of how "jurisdictional presence is not physical but *metaphysical*,"[63] Ford writes, "territory is . . . a container that holds a bundle of individuals and resources, just as fee simple ownership of real property consists of a bundle of rights. Moreover, the relationship between a territory and the individuals and resources it 'holds' is not a natural or necessary correspondence. It is not a relationship of empirical fact but one of positive design."[64]

I have already likened Casely Hayford to a manager in an effort to capture his ability to keep tabs on the many moving parts of social and political change. But "designer" is perhaps a better fit: it draws attention to the importance of sensibility as opposed to mechanization. Gus Casely-Hayford writes in his foreword to the 2024 critical edition of *Ethiopia Unbound* that Casely Hayford "did not just implore Africans to fight for their freedom but crafted an apparatus to imagine how they might deliver it."[65] The emphasis on craft as statesmanship's bulwark is apposite here, in its suggestion that building stable social forms is more art than science. To use Ford's phrasing, Casely Hayford was indeed a key agent in "regularizing" the West African body politic, but it also still had a long way to go before assuming a self-sustaining structure. The Bond of 1844 was imprinted on successive generations of Gold Coast leaders as an exercise in getting a new and multiply sourced legal design *just right*. This "rightness," in turn, can be construed in two strong senses: as a project of fitting parts together to make a functional whole (e.g., arranging individual colonies and protectorates into a region, or ensuring the complementarity of common and customary legal systems), and as an accompanying challenge of fixing certain moral laws in writing. Doing both at once required, in the first place, a strong empirical understanding of West African conditions. As follows from this book's first chapter, Casely Hayford felt able to be objective about Africans' place in the British Empire because of where he was from and what he had seen, not because of who he was in some essential sense. But combining the managerial and the moral also required a great deal of finesse, a distinguishing knack for knowing when to marshal which terms.

Casely Hayford's role thus once again exceeds that of an intermediary, or one who shuttles between places or cultures. A successful designer in this frame is not so much a hybrid figure as a chameleonic one, sometimes a scientist and sometimes an interpretive virtuoso. Martin Chanock, in his work on legal culture in southern Africa, has memorably written that nationalist historians of the continent have focused more on "what was said about change than what was said about order."[66] This observation still holds water, but the choice it replicates as critique is ultimately a false one. A better way to conceive of Casely Hayford's overarching objective is as the careful determination of what kind of order was essential to the change he desired. In other words, sustainable change entailed elements of fixity, and the role of the scholar-leader was to figure out what those were. Fixity, crucially, was for Casely Hayford a dynamic and active ideal—a value can *be fixed* given the leaderly insight and wherewithal. The Fante signatories of the Bond of 1844, in whose image Casely Hayford worked, aimed to fix new forms of criminal jurisdiction. In contrast, by now infamously, the British imagined Akan traditional rule as fixed in a different way: not as responsive to history as it was made, but as its mere affixation. The best-known version of this argument is Mahmoud Mamdani's, developed across many years but captured most succinctly in *Define and Rule*. In it, he postulates indirect rule as a system whereby "*native administration* claimed to be faithful to tradition and custom, which it defined in the singular, more or less unchanged since time immemorial."[67]

In broad strokes Mamdani is correct, and the British in the Gold Coast, as elsewhere, ramped up their investment in "native custom" from the 1880s onward. As others before me have noted, however, Mamdani's understanding of indirect rule relies on a binary that is more persuasive in the context of settler colonialism in eastern and southern Africa than it is in a West African colony like the Gold Coast, where there were such long histories of racial intermingling and sophisticated legal politics. Mamdani—anchoring his discussion in the work of influential Victorian-era jurist and legal historian Henry James Sumner Maine, who based his understanding of so-called primitive customs mostly on his experience in India—outlines a general theory of nativism.[68] Maine, he writes, "distinguished the West from the non-West and a universal civilization from local custom." This entailed first the theorization, then the institutional enforcement of a series of co-constructive oppositions: "If the settler was modern, the native was not; if history defined the settler, geography defined the native; if legislation and sanction defined modern political society, habitual observance defined that of the native. If continuous progress was the mark of settler civilization, culture was best thought of as part of nature, fixed and unchanging." Ultimately, Mamdani concludes, these all fed a "bifurcation between civil and customary law."[69] The tragedy of this cultural turn in British imperial thought is its on-the-ground reification, as colonized peoples came to believe in their own reduction to the status of traditional curiosity.

Conventionally, the counter-move to this frozen ethnographic one has been to insist on culture's dynamism or fluidity, particularly among those who may seem excluded by terms like "cosmopolitanism" because of its European origins and presumption of mobility.[70] Casely Hayford and his Gold Coast intelligentsia are, to that end, often seen as both cosmopolitan and Creole, with the first emphasizing their refusal of territorial boundaries and the second homing in on the formative, centuries-long history of intercultural contact in West Africa's coastal cities and towns. The Fante, in this understanding, may by the nineteenth century be considered a Creole people. Were these the only two paradigmatic options for understanding the figure and moment at the center of this book—culture as enforced stasis versus some version of culture as dynamic or in flux—then the latter is clearly more apt. But to read Casely Hayford through a standard of "culture" at all misses the wood for the trees of his pointed, densely historiographic brand of written engagement. If, as Mamdani offers, imperialist nativism "[claimed] to protect authenticity against the threat of progress," then defying it by asserting *non*-authenticity is a fair but rather feeble response. Françoise Lionnet discusses "Creole identity" as "an accident of birth: a mode of belonging that connects one to a history of coerced contact that produced unpredictable cultural formations and linguistic variations."[71] This is true enough, well and good. But the available critical language in this case falls vastly short of its subjects, for whom the patient distillation of elements was of paramount political importance. Whatever Casely Hayford was, he was renowned for what he did. And what he did best was eloquently argue.

The 1920s Gold Coast was a ripe time and place to bring this talent to bear on discussing and designing new legal infrastructure. British officials, in tense public dialogue with the Gold Coast journalistic and legal elite, had spent the preceding decades quite literally rewriting their understanding of the relationship between traditional Akan and "modern" imperial rule. British official William Brandford Griffith, who was governor of the Gold Coast from 1880 to 1881 and between 1885 and 1895, in 1917 acknowledged that "Prior to the Ashanti War of 1873 our rights and powers on the Gold Coast were of a most indefinite character."[72] That all changed in 1874, the year of the Gold Coast's formal colonization, when the British gave its Legislative Council the power to make ordinances in the queen's name. The resulting legal paperwork came fast and furiously, giving the

Gold Coast an unusually strong association with text: Griffith wrote that he knew of no "colony with so short a life as the Gold Coast which has had so many editions of its Ordinances compiled."[73] In 1883 the council passed the Native Jurisdiction Ordinance, which firmed up the function of native tribunals overseen by local chiefs but now ultimately accountable to a British-administered justice system with the Supreme Court at the top.[74] Writing of an earlier, 1878 version of the ordinance, R. Addo-Fening notes that "one cannot help but conclude that by granting the Governor power to 'dismiss' Chiefs and thereby abrogating their right of jurisdiction the Ordinance clearly sought to establish that the jurisdiction of the Chiefs was to cease to be inherent and henceforth become derivative instead."[75] Gold Coast legal history in this sense tracks with Mamdani's well-known argument, as Gold Coast chiefs grew increasingly central to British colonial administration.[76]

By the time that Gordon Guggisberg was appointed governor of the Gold Coast in 1919, a policy of indirect rule there was in full effect. In Roger Gocking's words, this meant that by the 1920s. "the seemingly rigid boundary between customary and common law was far less so in practice than it was in theory."[77] Such increasing interpenetration, coupled with the consequential distinction between (British) criminal and (African) civil law that the Bond of 1844 had bequeathed to successive generations, further urged an expressly moral vocabulary around questions of jurisdiction. After the amended Native Jurisdiction Ordinance was passed in 1910 and all customary law–based courts became native tribunals, meaning that they were now uniformly under British colonial dominion, debates around degrees of harm within the Gold Coast justice system were paramount. "Europeans in general concluded that there was no real distinction between tort and crime in customary law," Gocking continues, which then took on a "self-fulfilling quality."[78] Any so-called serious offense—including murder, robbery, and slave dealing—was referred to British-administered courts, while the native tribunals "dealt mostly with disputes arising out of the ownership and possession of land, customary marriage, fetishism, witchcraft and debt cases." In sum, common law courts could imprison, while customary law courts could fine.[79] Needless to say, this raised all manner of epistemological concerns around what counted as "serious," for example with regard to whether supernatural methods of causing death qualified as murder. Ironically and perhaps tragically, the criminal/civil distinction that the Fante signatories of the Bond of 1844 had insisted on as a means of asserting their equal status echoed in the early twentieth century as a tiering of justice.

Governor Guggisberg was also a vigorous supporter of African cultural development beyond the legal sphere, even following Casely Hayford's lead in advocating for African language instruction; both were instrumental, as discussed in this book's introduction, in the founding of Achimota College. So too did they cooperate to bring about the return of the Asante King (Asantehene) Prempeh I from his exile in the Seychelles in 1924, before restoring him to a lesser position (Kumasehene) in 1926.[80] At the same time, however, Guggisberg prohibited Africans from joining the political service, maintaining that "the African child must learn to walk before attempting to run."[81] As such, his intentions now appear more paternalistic than cooperative. But this is only part of the story of the era of indirect rule, and to tell it with Casely Hayford at the center means drawing out the full and unmuzzled force of its contestation. Far from being a smooth process of top-down enforcement, with African interlocutors "pinned down, localized, thrown out of civilization as an outcast, confined to custom, and then defined as its product," the patronizing British valorization of African "custom" and "tradition" was a topic of high-profile mockery and suspicion over many years.[82]

An editorial in the June 6, 1912, issue of the *Gold Coast Nation*, "The Personnel of the Deputation to Downing Street, London," is a prime example of such early pushback against culturalist thinking in politics. It scoffs, "An exaggerated idea is being industriously instilled into the minds of some people to the effect that unless Kings or Chiefs are sent to Downing Street, London, [officials there] would be inclined to give short shrift to our Deputation." The English, it opines, must surely not be that gullible. "Our inherent rights to the soil of our ancestors," the piece continues, "our time-honoured claims to the land of our birth must not be confused with the demands of idle curiosity and the passing craze for spectacular scenes. If we are incapable of proving our case to the hilt by actual presentation of irrebuttable facts, figures and arguments, it would be madness to suppose that the barbaric splendour of a dozen of Bowlers' loin-cloth Chiefs executing war dances in the streets of London ... could so impress the people of England by their mere presence as to force concessions which cannot be supported by customary law and constitutional rights."

Whoever voiced this particular opinion in the *Nation*, it speaks to a broader propensity among the Gold Coast editorial class to distinguish between custom and culture, and culture and history in the early twentieth century. The understanding of "culture" that Casely Hayford worked with was some combination of located, time-tested best practices and deep-seated civilizational ideals. His understanding of history was as an engagement with the present that fused the most grounding, closely studied parts of the past with an openness to new traits and ideas. Much of his work can be cherry picked to score points for either "Fante nationalist" or "imperial modernizer," and, at different points, he was arguably both. But the heft of his writing comes through only with due attention to how tradition and innovation temper each other. Another unsigned editorial from the March 4, 1911, edition of the *Gold Coast Leader*, which Casely Hayford co-founded and later edited, spotlights this delicate interface. Titled "The Atavistic Tendencies of the Age: A National Asset" and situating itself amid "the age of Transition," the piece announces, "The Gold Coast native . . . will invariably 'Go Fante' in his intellectual evolution and therein lies his national salvation," a process that "marks the mental terminus of the Gold Coast native and describes his ultimate Reversion to the primitive simplicity of his ancestors sobered and matured with all that is excellent in Western civilization and Religion." This quotation, on its own, might suggest a fairly straightforward notion of "African plus"—indigenous customs embellished with some European comforts.

In fact, it is more profound in its grappling with what moral laws to sanction or jettison, hearkening back expressly to the language of "moulding" character from the Bond of 1844. "But let us not be misunderstood," the piece continues. "We do not countenance or advocate anything destructive or subversive of Twentieth Century civilization or refinement which forms the warp and woof of the life of so many. We do not in any conceivable way bolster up the exploded fallacies, anomalies and incongruities of prehistoric times, neither do we repudiate the hallowed influences and associations that have so largely contributed to mould and are moulding, albeit slowly and imperceptibly the character of our people." It ends, by now unsurprisingly, with a directive to "cultivate the art of assimilating new things with the utmost discrimination and discretion." When read in its totality, the "primitive simplicity" that the editorial invokes to describe the Fante past seems to register a minimalist aesthetic more than nondevelopment, though the latter implication is certainly present. Moral progress has an elegant cut.

Casely Hayford in his major works was likewise attuned to the shortcomings of "culture"—in either a frozen or a fluid iteration—as a position from which to advance his political vision for a unified West Africa. In addition to his awareness of the footwork involved in finding accord between the region and its constituent nations, he distinguished between tradition and history as the bedrock of nationhood. In *Land Question*, he addresses the Native Jurisdiction Ordinance head on through numerous of its revisions and amendments, taking particular care to preserve the difference between a static, easily co-opted account of Akan customs and his own championing of time-worn and yet flexible local norms. The stakes of this juxtaposition are clearest when Casely Hayford explains why the default British assumption of chiefly jurisdiction over land was flawed, affirming instead that "it is abundantly clear that the paramount Chief of a Native State is in no sense the *ultimus haeres* [ultimate heir] to any land to which there is no succession, since in the Customary Law care is taken to continue the *persona* of the family."[83] Chiefs as such, he is emphasizing here, simply did not represent what British officials under a system of indirect rule wanted them to; the fact that chiefs are traditional rulers as against "modern" legal ones did not mean that they are the buck at which all things African stops.

The concept of "persona" here also carries substantial weight for understanding the bond between literary and legal concepts in Casely Hayford's thought. "Persona" is defined as character in the widely used *Black's Law Dictionary* and understood not as synonymous with but rather related to the concept of personhood. Whereas "one man may unite many characters ... as, for example, the characters of father and son, of master and servant," the persona of the family in Casely Hayford's usage can inversely be kept alive by any number of (types of) people, be they blood relations, long-serving domestic workers, or a "tribesman" selected "by adoption and commendation" in the absence of the other two.[84] He spells out the different categories of Akan affiliation in play when determining property ownership, which are easily and wrongly conflated in a deferral to "traditional culture" imagined as a thing or image, rather than an unfolding narrative. "Again," Casely Hayford attests patiently, "it is of considerable importance to note that the words 'tribe' and 'family' are not synonymous terms in the conception of the Customary Law." As a result, the whole British understanding of Akan social life, and the laws that govern it, is in error. He continues, "it would seem that in the remote past there was some visible tangible connection between the members of a tribe, but such connection is lost in tradition; and it is enough to say that in property considerations one goes hopelessly wrong in the conception of the Customary Law when he applies the terms 'family' and 'tribe' synonymously."[85]

When Casely Hayford elects persona rather than tribe as the right lens to make sense of Gold Coast property succession, he prioritizes character over culture. And through character, he emphasizes a capacity for evaluation as a vector of Gold Coast history, namely in his repetition that family "persona" can be advanced, when needed, through the considered selection of an unrelated heir. The upshot of all this—considered alongside the emerging legal hierarchy of the postcolonization Gold Coast and the vigorous public contestation of cheap ideas about culture—is that Africans' ability to pick and choose the terms of their modernity had to be preserved at all costs. On this point, characterological ideals and legal advocacy converged. Where there is no room for fine categorical distinction making, there is no way to choose a better arrangement over a worse one. And where choice is inconceivable, so too is the sort of moral discernment by which the Gold Coast intelligentsia defined itself. The push for a moral vocabulary around jurisdiction was part of Casely Hayford's career-defining quest to harmonize statements of intrinsic value with the pragmatic aspects of building a modern African legislative state. Nuts and bolts, rights and wrongs, were all mixed up together in his project of drawing clear lines.

Citation's Moral Lines

One of the trademarks of Casely Hayford's style is his tendency to copious citation. This is on full display in *Ethiopia Unbound*, with its bounty of literary and cultural references, ranging from ancient Greece to the American poet Edwin Markham. But it is also an impressive feature of his nonfiction writing, including *The Truth about the West African Land Question*. While the variation, frequency, and considerable length of the quotations in both texts can sometimes seem a bit overwhelming, perhaps jumbled, a closer look at Casely Hayford's citational practice reveals the "clear lines" of his chaos. The care with which he weaves other texts and positions into his own in *Land Question* therefore means that it rewards "literary" attention, which traces the sentence-level crafting of its argument against the British misappropriation of Gold Coast lands. Even amid quotations nested within quotations, Casely Hayford maintains strict boundaries between speakers and through them, between right and wrong. A reading of how, not just who or what, he cites puts the moral underpinnings of jurisdictional disagreement in bold relief.

In its focus on particular land bills and ordinances, *Land Question* makes the most targeted legal and political intervention of all Casely Hayford's major works, even in comparison with *Gold Coast Native Institutions*' long-view account of Akan political traditions. It opens with four epigraphs attributed to the British (though French-born) writer and politician Edmund Dean—or E. D.—Morel, who had risen to prominence as an imperial voice of conscience due to his pacifism around the First World

War and outspoken condemnation of abuses in King Leopold's Congo. An ally, by default, of Casely Hayford's ARPS in the latter cause, Morel was best known in the Gold Coast as the founder of a Liverpool-based magazine called the *West African Mail* in 1903, with financial backing from merchant and shipping mogul John Holt.[86] *Land Question* trades on Morel's moral credentials in the first epigraph especially, which reads in part, "There can be no justification whatever for the break-up of land tenure, or for the alienation of native property, under any pretext. It is morally indefensible, and what is morally indefensible is seldom politically wise."[87] Casely Hayford sets up Morel as an advocate of the Gold Coast African cause on Morel's *own* terms, stacking multiple expressions of his respect for African authority atop one another. The third epigraph even matches Casely Hayford's political model of "cooperation," which I invoked in the first pages of this chapter. "If the native can feel that he is secure in his tenure of land," Morel states in a 1906 interview with the French colonial minister, "he will become a willing and eager co-operator."[88]

Morel's moral credibility as the liberal imperialist par excellence does not last long, at least as far as *Land Question* is concerned. By only the seventh page of the book, Casely Hayford has accused him of being ready to "kill [West Africa's] soul to save her life," owing to his "ambiguous" position on how to build a regional political entity.[89] In Morel's proclamation of duty to respect both West African autonomy and the "Colonial Office"—the latter term distinct in Casely Hayford's use from "the Crown" and its associated ideals—Casely Hayford likens him to a man "trying to please two mistresses."[90] And his loyalties are not just divided but poorly formed; Morel's politics of indirect rule strike Casely Hayford as incoherent. I use this term intentionally: what we might think of as the "puzzle pieces" of Casely Hayford's worldview, sourced from multiple traditions and indebted, in their innovative arrangement, to the Bond of 1844, do not fit together for Morel. In contrast to Casely Hayford's emphasis on maintaining West Africa's discrete national units as part of its collective political mobilization, Morel copies-and-pastes strategies from one place onto another. "Of course, Mr. Morel is anxious that British dominion should be universal in West Africa," Casely Hayford writes of Morel's fascination with northern Nigeria as a model for indirect rule in the Gold Coast. "And he has one patent for it. He can conceive of none other."[91] He then replicates the *Land Question* epigraphs' effect by other means, quoting yet another British colonial minister (one Mr. Harcourt) quoting Morel on the point that land policies must vary from one colony to another. Morel appears to regularly betray his own most thoughtful positions.

What we might call nested quotation is a multifaceted strategy for Casely Hayford. Making good on the Fante intelligentsia's claims to situated objectivity, he walks readers through the scaffolding of his positions, source by source. It is not enough only to summarize key political turns and offer eloquent commentary on them; *Land Question* demonstrates that its author has "done the reading" in a literal sense. A prominent case in point foregrounds the stakes of such effortful, reconstructive prose. In the book's fourth chapter, also titled "The Truth about the West African Land Question," Casely Hayford accuses Morel of effacing crucial details of Gold Coast land tenure debates in his writing for the *West African Mail*. More to the point, Morel had neglected to acknowledge that there *was* no live debate about who could administer Gold Coast lands after 1898, at which time, Casely Hayford writes, "the Government had withdrawn from the position" that there were any "Crown lands on the Gold Coast."[92] Rather than just leave it there, Casely Hayford then declares that "the necessity ... has arisen for a calm and clear statement of the full facts of the situation."[93] Providing such a statement entails chasing down a source—an article by an MP named Josiah Wedgwood in *The Anti-Slavery Reporter and Aborigines' Friend*—that Morel cites only in passing. It turns out that Wedgwood presents in no uncertain terms the challenge posed by African land ownership to the British imperial hunger for cheap labor. He goes so far as to note that "the Congo system is the best yet invented" from this angle, directly undermining the liberal position on which Morel made his name.

These citational webs hold immense historical interest in their own right, not least because Casely Hayford's work captures the quote-by-quote construction of the imperial public sphere. By chronicling British-African intellectual exchange in such detail, including impressions of in-person meetings and events, it also spotlights the contingency of what may look like public consensus given a greater level of generalization. Here, however, I am more concerned with how Casely Hayford operates as a writer. Typically sensitive to the needs of his readers, he is willing to risk the tedium of citing documents within documents, for many pages at a stretch, because it permits him to pinpoint where and by what paths people go wrong. Be that as it may, his meticulous reading habits and attention to more and less forceful versions of arguments that others have articulated across years give all players their due. Casely Hayford, to that end, consistently trains his criticisms on E. D. Morel *as a writer*, refusing ad hominem insults to focus on how he conducts himself in print. Of Morel's thinned-out representation of land matters in the Gold Coast, and specifically the Legislative Council's having been persuaded years before that the British did not have land jurisdiction there, Casely Hayford writes: "It was inconvenient for him, perhaps, to inform the public that the Government had given way on the matter of compulsory acquisition. But he still found it possible to write from week to week as if nothing had happened; nor did he, even after his own views upon the 'educated native' had been somewhat modified by force of circumstances, condescend to take his readers into his confidence as to the causes which had led to such modification."[94] Morel's patronizing African politics carry over to his dealings with his readers.

When Casely Hayford showcases the contrasting soundness of his own research practices, he beats E. D. Morel at his own game; the latter's liberal paternalism toward Africans cannot withstand the pressure of this punctilious Gold Coast interlocutor. A cautious and inductive reasoner, Casely Hayford reconstructs long-term patterns in Morel's published writing before consigning him to a general trend of humanistically veiled British rapaciousness. Only after catching Morel in the associative act of praising the Belgian Congo's administration does he posit an underlying motive in the form of a rhetorical question. "Is it possible that, in varying forms, the root idea at the back of even 'E.D.M.' and his friends is the production of wealth by depriving the natives of free land?," Casely Hayford asks.[95] As he speaks at length through Casely Hayford, Morel comes across not so much malicious as lacking in acumen, exploitative by default of his smug and summary handling of complex information amid shifting political sands. In glossing over the dehumanizing details of the liberal-sounding discourse he advances around African rights, he empties his moral ideals of meaningful content. Morel, by taking citational shortcuts and thereby failing to distinguish his own position from that of Josiah Wedgwood's, can instead plausibly be cast as an example of what Casely Hayford calls "the philanthropist who, posing as the heaven-born guardian of native interests, would restrict the people from directly and freely dealing with their lands by placing all business negotiations under Government control and management."[96] Casely Hayford, meanwhile, takes his reader with him into the citational weeds, frequently sign-posting his intentions and addressing whomever occupied that role. Phrases like "It will occur to the reader that . . .", "It is necessary to explain that . . .", and "We must patiently follow the special correspondent . . ." pepper this section of *Land Question*.[97]

Even still, its tenor slowly rises to a boil. Once he has revealed Morel's ideological "tell," so to speak, in his having so readily associated himself with Wedgwood's bald analysis of Britain's economic needs, Casely Hayford begins to introduce more explicitly moral language. He notes, for starters, that "it is necessary to emphasize the root evil in the fallacy" that the

British Crown has any right to oversee Gold Coast lands.[98] A bit later, in emphasizing the Gold Coast's uniqueness vis-à-vis other British territories, he enjoins, "You cannot, for the sake of a so-called uniformity, break solemn pledges, and wrench from the hands of those who have trusted you that which is indisputably theirs."[99] One *can*, of course, do just that. But Casely Hayford's willingness to posit inviolable moral laws serves here as a rhetorical payoff for his scrupulous citation habits. It also works in reverse order from how Casely Hayford represents E. D. Morel's position in the chapter's design, starting with the bold moralism of its epigraphs and then steadily undermining it with further quotation. Morel, as a result, comes to stand in for a liberal imperialism whose political parts don't add up to its professed moral whole, whereas Casely Hayford works incrementally toward moral plausibility. At no time, however, does he become monologic. The second half of the chapter quotes a British *West African Mail* correspondent named G. D. Hazzledine, who writes about the timber industry in southern Nigeria by "fairly and fully" summarizing a set of proposed protectionist policies there.[100] Ultimately, Hazzledine disagrees with the proposals and with the idea that the British should act as intermediaries in West Africa; Casely Hayford agrees with Hazzledine. The salient point here is that Hazzledine gets even more space in *Land Question* than Morel does, meaning that ample citation is more than a means that gives way to an argumentative end. Casely Hayford does not just find his moral voice in relation to Morel's failings, that is, but interweaves his own considered views with those from other sources, while maintaining clarity around who says what.

It should be clear by now that citation and quotation matter a *lot* to Casely Hayford's work, in ways that exceed box checking or pedantry. *Land Question* earns its moral credibility with citational care; Casely Hayford both treats his print interlocutors with generosity and subjects them to his own standard of review. Seen in this light, his analysis of land politics in the Gold Coast is intimately linked to his compositional practices. In this book's first chapter on objectivity, I show how Casely Hayford's historical (including geographical) position allowed him to see facts where British officials did not or could not. Here, his extensive and attentive citations carry this claim into the realm of form, so that the driving concern becomes not how to see but *tell* the truth. Jonathan Kramnick's recent apologia for professional literary criticism might appear to be an odd intertext for a West African treatise on land from 1913, but it offers insightful commentary on the relationship between referencing and rectitude. He writes that "much of literary criticism turns on the art of quoting well: pointing to lines or words of interest to your argument; placing new words up against or around them; describing how quoted words sit among words unquoted or in the tradition of scholarly discussion. In this way, quotation is the art of moving across two orders of writing, one's own and someone else's."[101]

Elsewhere, Kramnick elaborates a practice that he calls "critical free indirect discourse," which he defines as "silently matching a text's tone and idiom."[102] But quotation as described above is *not* so much about creating a seamless appearance of one "voice," so much as it is a practice of overt negotiation between two. As Kramnick continues, "The skilled practice of in-sentence quotation consists in embedding the words of another so that the apt form is something of a weave."[103] Such weaving leaves open a space for moral judgment. When Casely Hayford performs a line by line reading of the 1911 Wedgwood editorial on the economics of land tenure—the one that E. D. Morel mentions without revealing its angle of exploitation—he "matches" its tone in the act of naming it, praising Wedgwood's candor in contrast with Morel's elision. "Indeed," he observes after frankly summarizing Wedgwood's argument for the British dependence on African cheap labor, "[Wedgwood] states the case with a *naïveté* which is perfectly refreshing."[104] Casely Hayford then credits Wedgwood for "frankness" even as he rejects the ideas he brings to light, because here, at least, he can meet his print opponent in awareness and good faith.[105] He digs up Wedgwood *through* Morel to show how a thorough and honest style of intertextual reference is a precondition for hashing out the details of the Gold Coast's fairest jurisdictional arrangement. It is not quite accurate to call the layers of reference in *Land Question* a moral language in its own right, but it is certainly the structural apparatus by which moral language rises or falls.

Amplifying the literary dimensions of *Land Question* in this way also builds on and fills out one of Casely Hayford's most substantial (if brief) recent scholarly treatments, in Musab Younis's *On the Scale of the World: The Formation of Black Anticolonial Thought*. Younis argues astutely that West Africans made early and overlooked contributions to the advent of what is now known as economic structuralism, a brand of thought directed to understanding "the machinery of global order" by combining "historical analysis with contemporary global politics."[106] What interests Younis most in this approach is its mobility across scales: by foregrounding Africa's impoverishment within a set hierarchy of powers, it can be used to recuperate globality as it was constructed by, rather than as it has effaced, local forms of anti-imperial struggle. He rescues Casely Hayford from passing consignment to the dustbins of romantic nationalism and pre-independence elitism on this basis. Focusing on his work at the *Gold Coast Leader* through the 1920s, Younis notes that "an analysis of writing about race and the economy [there] casts a different light on [Casely Hayford's] thought and that of his milieu. It points to a body of writing far more attuned to race as *structure* than the 'nativist' label implies."[107] He sees the citational work of Casely Hayford and peer writers, much of which reprinted and commented on journalism from British publications, as meaningful in this context. Younis writes, "Citations from metropolitan newspapers assisted this move—away from the specific and singular, and towards the broad and theoretical."[108]

This is correct, and it is rare to see Casely Hayford's detailed engagement with intra-imperial legal politics acknowledged for its conceptually generalizing impulse. Younis does well to point out that racial ideology in Casely Hayford's work, in the *Leader* but also beyond it, was a tool of broad economic critique and not a vain exercise in cultural nationalism. This angle of analysis also opens up strains of Gold Coast economic thought that complicate an anticapitalist recuperation of early Fante state builders. In his stand against regulating the Gold Coast's timber industry, which he thought would disrupt Africans' ability to profit from it, Casely Hayford would have made an interesting addition to Marc-William Palen's cast of characters in *Pax Economica: Left Wing Visions of a Free Trade World*.[109] For all this, however, *On the Scale of the World* does not broach the next level of Casely Hayford's efforts at generalization, namely that assigned to the moral code (of "root evil," "solemn pledges," and "fair" summary) in whose name *Land Question*'s economic analysis advances. Citation in Younis's reading, as well as in the earlier work on West African print culture to which he makes reference, is unrelated to authors' metaphysical interests.[110] But what he calls "the worldliness of the *Leader*'s anticolonialism" ultimately offers a very partial view of the Fante intelligentsia.[111]

Without veering too far into ethnographic explanation, it is crucial here to note that Akan societies, of which Fante is one, have long been understood to be heavily honor based. In Kwame Appiah's words, "a person of honor cares first of all not about being respected but about being *worthy* of respect," meaning that "honor itself is the thing that matters, not honor's rewards."[112] A political and economic bottom line for understanding why Casely Hayford's writing is significant—in other words, because it was among the first bodies of work to lay bare the systemic injustice of British imperialism in Africa—by definition thinks in terms of outcome or reward, even if, as for Younis, it does so in order to underscore new sources of anticapitalist critique. More specifically, this version of economic structuralism emphasizes the unjust and racist denial of a reward in proportion to one's labor. *Land Question* is, without doubt, an innovative work of political economy along these lines. But Younis is too quick to want to move past the "quasi-aristocratic pan-Africanism" that others have seen in Casely Hayford to get to the "real" materialist goods, in the process downplaying the deep-rooted social morality of his milieu.[113] The sophistication of Casely Hayford's oeuvre lies in its dexterity as it moves across different kinds and scales of value, tempering economics with honorability.

A firm understanding of what it meant to be Fante is elemental to this movement, and J. B. Danquah's exegesis of Akan norms is here once again a rich explanatory source. His classic *The Akan Doctrine of God* devotes a chapter to "The Nana (or Exemplar)," in reference to the human paragons of virtue traditionally anointed by the Akan. Danquah takes honorable personal conduct—behaving as "a man of dignity, one without disgrace, in nature like a son of [the] Akan"—to be the lifeblood of their religion.[114] Whereas a Christian Messiah was "expected to come as the divine agent to fulfill a promise or covenant of delivery or triumph," the Akan Nana, or exemplary person, is "produced, invented, fashioned or hewed out by his community."[115] Even more significant is Danquah's description of the Nana as having been "selected the fittest person to rule and lead his community," since it suggests that maximum respect is reserved not for suffering and servitude, but for a leader's "[embodying] in his person the positive qualities of a citizen of the moral and civil estates, as a present fact of the 'practical' life."[116] A Nana leads by continuous example, rather than dying on the cross. As such, the role casts individual honor as the building block of the public good, or the starting point for what Danquah calls "the practical expansion of patriotic devotion to a personal ideal of dignity that sustains the common life."[117] Elaborating years later on the masculine facets of Akan morality, Stephan Miescher likewise points to honor's centrality to the role of the *opanyin*, a term in Twi and Fante meaning elder or figure of authority. The men he interviewed during fieldwork in Kwawu (or Kwahu) Ghana all stressed that "*opanyin* need to continue to prove their worthiness," and that "conduct, behavior, and speech are considered decisive."[118]

Though Miescher notes, "Ideals of elderhood and big-man status have formed a continuity in Akan societies since the nineteenth century," J. E. Casely Hayford's cosmopolitan Cape Coast is a long way from the Asante region in the early aughts.[119] Nor is Danquah in *The Akan Doctrine of God* discussing the early Fante intelligentsia in particular. My intention here is not to conflate these examples, but simply to illustrate that political economy only gets us so far to understanding the virtuosic feat of social, historical, and metaphysical synthesis that Casely Hayford's writing about jurisdiction represents. He frequently uses English terms whose heft is made legible only through reference to their Fante counterparts and the system of values they entail. This is in evidence when he speculates, in *Land Question*, on the future of the new Gold Coast Governor Sir Hugh Clifford, who accedes to the office in 1913. Casely Hayford contrasts Clifford's "courtesy and tact" with the nervous anxiety of a lower-ranked British official who had previously denigrated Africans, noting that the governor's "regard for [their] self-respect and self-esteem" was the "simple act of a gentleman."[120] And he goes even further in the importance he attributes to gentlemanly conduct, continuing, "We badly want real gentlemen in His Majesty's West African Civil Service. It would be half the solution of the administrative problem."[121] Without understanding the socially definitive role of the *opanyin*, also sometimes translated as gentleman, Casely Hayford's faith in the power of respectful British behavior to right the wrongs of indirect rule would seem grossly exaggerated.[122]

Casely Hayford's elaborate but exacting citational practice is, in the context of these Akan moral values, a form of honorable conduct. Taking stock of it thus demands a set of terms that can toggle between its "merely" informational, or even analytic, value and its overtly moral dimensions. One recent source for such terms is Matthew Sussman's work on what he calls "stylistic virtue" in Victorian-era literary criticism, which posits that "the persistence of the belletristic lexicon throughout the nineteenth century offers evidence of the widespread influence, both explicit and implicit, of Aristotelian virtue ethics on matters of aesthetic perception and judgment."[123] Looking away from more obvious sources of ethical thought in the British nineteenth century, namely utilitarianism (based in consequences) and Kantianism (based in adherence to immoveable norms), Sussman argues, "Aristotelian or virtue ethics relies upon a much broader conception of moral life that refers to excellence in character," and thus appealed to writers who "understood aesthetic excellence as inhering in the constitutive 'virtues' of a work or text, whether these were moral, stylistic, or both."[124] He is writing about canonical British figures like Ruskin, Arnold, and Pater, but the sensibility he describes fits Casely Hayford in many ways. Casely Hayford's connection to antiquity is spelled out in *Ethiopia Unbound*, when it likens Fante civilization to that of the ancient Greeks based on a shared aristocratic and yet earthy sensibility, as well as their systems of gods. Danquah may well have had Casely Hayford in mind in concluding his own chapter on Akan exemplarity with a section on "The Greek and the Akan Parallels," which holds that "the Greek ideal would be a better parallel for the Akan [than Christianity] because it did not involve a man losing the whole world for the sake of gaining his own soul. The Greek ideal, like the Akan, was one made for human nature."[125]

Whatever the trajectory by which virtue ethics have come to seem descriptive of Akan moral codes, the redolence of the *Ethiopia Unbound* chapter on the subject, "A Similitude: The Greek and the Fante," provides an ideal if slightly belated case in point for Sussman's culminating claim. "Style assumes a central importance during the nineteenth century not because it offered an alternative to ethics," he concludes, "but because it offered an alternative ethics to the hedonic utilitarianism that seemed to empty life of those humanist values—beauty, flexibility, individuality, and feeling—that artistically inclined and educated Britons naturally associated with Hellenism."[126] Casely Hayford's connection to virtue ethics could be drawn out by many routes, including the continuation that Danquah attempts of his cultural-cosmological comparison. What makes stylistic virtue the most appealing in the present frame is its attention to how certain descriptors are marked as virtuous by certain writers. When Ruskin refers to an object as "chaste," for instance, in his 1846 book *Modern Painters*, Sussman writes, "artistic style resembles action in Aristotelian ethics, being the mode through which underlying moral dispositions and principles are given tangible external form; chasteness, as a stylistic virtue, is essentially reducible to 'moderation' as a moral one."[127] The underlying idea is that the pursuit of excellent character can be *expressed as*, not just *described by*, an aesthetic, true to a "broader ethical principle of dispositional authenticity—a condition of right feeling and attitude—that applies to life as well as art."[128] In effect, a critic can weigh in on questions of ultimate right and wrong by attending closely to a text's formal attributes. This is a provocative framing in view of the fact that Casely Hayford comments not only on other texts, but on texts about the core "text" of the Gold Coast's jurisdictional configuration. Jurisdictional lines are proactively authored and so must be assiduously read.

What then are Casely Hayford's comparable terms to Ruskin's "chaste" in *Land Question*? Which words, for him, describe an aesthetic trait and thereby invoke a consonant characterological virtue? Not surprisingly, they all point back to distinction making. He frequently describes authors in *Land Question* as "learned," and theories or principles as "sound." Texts, more often than not, he introduces without fanfare. What praise for writing itself *is* present homes in on its power to demonstrate that one thing rather than another is correct. Casely Hayford refers to an illustration in the *West African Mail* as "significant," and to the paper's correspondent

Mr. Hazzledine's sentences as "well-chosen."[129] When he relates an intense legal exchange around the Forest Bill that took place in 1912 in Cape Coast, he refers to one response as having had "sufficient importance to be reproduced."[130] The most forceful description is reserved for a "masterly and telling" speech by the high-ranking legal official who introduced a delegation of Gold Coast lawyers in London that same year.[131] Conversely, he accuses articles in the *West African Mail* of making "idle" suggestions.[132] In each of these examples of a text's brief aesthetic assessment, the emphasis is on knowing how to ascertain what matters; Casely Hayford has no room for pomp or frivolity. This tendency echoes, among other things, the impatience with "the barbaric splendour" of African cultural display expressed in the June 6, 1912, *Gold Coast Nation* editorial, itself symptomatic of a general aversion to confusing spectacle with politics. The virtue being conjured can best be called "discernment," or perhaps "seriousness"—a capacity to tell wheat from chaff and then sort them in public view.

By surveying how a moral virtue of discernment is encapsulated in *Land Question* term by term, this chapter comes full circle back to the Bond of 1844 as a watershed moment for Gold Coast modernity. The Bond committed a jurisdictional map of Anglo-Fante partnership to writing, and thereby enshrined a willingness to pick and choose the best parts of different legal systems as an influential brand of Fante state building and, by extension, selfhood. A modern Fante leader, it held, should be able to draw lines between different *kinds* of legal authority as well as its different sources, carefully weighing both practical and moral situational demands. Casely Hayford's generation of a Gold Coast legal intelligentsia looked to 1844 as a moment of what he called "frank co-operation" between British and African leaders, even where that meant giving up some aspects of Fante autonomy.[133] Given the centrality of jurisdictional debates to the broader print consolidation of the Gold Coast intelligentsia, it is not surprising that such studied distinction making also became Casely Hayford's stylistic calling card. Distinguishing one concept from another, in writing, was the mark of a distinguished character, the expression of a deeper ability to tell right from wrong and so arrive at the best possible social arrangement. It is an ideal of personhood that resonates to this day. In the tradition of the Fante naming ceremony, the head of family, or *abusuapanyin*, instructs a newborn child in seeing things for what they are: "*Nsu a, nsu. Nsa a, nsa*" (Water is water, and spirits spirits). Look well and name correctly, the tradition suggests; let no outside noise or circumstance blur the line. J. E. Casely Hayford took the injunction much to heart.

EPILOGUE

Where in the World Is J. E. Casely Hayford?

IN JANUARY 2024, I took a last research trip to London in preparation for completing this book. I was there, in the main, to visit the archives at the Inner Temple, in the hopes that some of its 1890s records would help sharpen my picture of Casely Hayford's legal and social education (as indeed they did). While I was there, I happened to wander past the Brunei Gallery on the SOAS University of London campus, just a few blocks from my hotel. It was hosting an exhibition called *Building Africa*, curated by Julia Gallagher and Kuukuwa Manful, on the relationship between architectural landmarks and political culture in Ethiopia, South Africa, and Ghana.[1] Ghana's portion of the installation focused heavily on secondary schools, complete with matching his-and-her uniforms and a large display of colorful school crests. This is not as offbeat an emphasis as it might seem to readers from elsewhere: in Ghana, where one goes to high school occupies something like the niche that university affiliation does in the United States or even in the UK. As an anonymous Ghanaian put it in one of the sticky-note responses to earlier versions of the exhibition, which were then woven into its London iteration, "The secondary schools really moulded our lives. That is where most students learnt what the outside world meant in a person's life. You learnt the social etiquette from there." This sentiment no doubt applies in bolded form to the oldest of Ghana's state-run secondary schools, most prominently including Achimota and Mfantsipim, or "Motown" and "The School" to their familiars.

J. E. Casely Hayford was not mentioned anywhere by name in "Building Africa," but his legacy was present all the same. One placard, titled "Nation-Building: Secondary Schools," noted that "Africans," and not just

European missionaries, had "established and built many secondary schools in the country," implicitly invoking Casely Hayford's work as an educational steward and theorist alongside compatriots like John Mensah Sarbah and J.E.K. Aggrey. His vision for an African and cosmopolitan national university, which found practical intention in his co-founding of the Fante National Education Fund in 1902 and more stirring expression in *Ethiopia Unbound*, was realized, at least in part, during his lifetime. Spearheaded by Sarbah and brought to fruition with the help of his fellow ARPS leaders, the Mfantsipim School was founded in 1905 to build on the foundation laid by Cape Coast's Wesleyan Boys High School, where Casely Hayford had been headmaster in the early 1890s. Casely Hayford was involved from start to finish in various ways, and Mfantsipim's curriculum evolved to include the local languages Fante, Twi, and Ga alongside core subjects like history and the sciences.[2] When he helped get Achimota College off the ground in 1927, Gold Coast languages beyond English featured even more prominently.[3] It has, in the decades since, become a revered and proudly African stomping ground for all manner of political and cultural leaders, including six Ghanaian heads of state and Zimbabwe's beloved former first lady, Sally Mugabe.

What I took from this London encounter with such a forceful yet anonymized testament to Casely Hayford's influence on Gold Coast liberal educational culture is that in today's Ghana, he is both everywhere and nowhere. Many people are vaguely aware of his achievements, and in Accra and the Central Region, nearly everyone recognizes the stature of the surname Casely-Hayford (now hyphenated). In Cape Coast, he remains literally visible in the form of an austere-looking statue outside a rowdy men's university dormitory named in his honor.

Here, though, I acknowledge that this kind of point-by-point legacy tracing may seem less than urgent, given the extensive intellectual work still remaining to situate Casely Hayford even *within* his time. There are books yet to be written that compare him with other African intellectuals of the (pre-)colonial period, perhaps most notably the Tswana South African writer Sol Plaatje. Born in 1876 and laid to rest in 1932 (in comparison with Casely Hayford's 1866 to 1930), Plaatje's major nonfiction work, *Native Life in South Africa*, responded in 1916 to the Natives' Land Act of 1913, which reserved the vast majority of state lands for white ownership. Like his Gold Coast legal-humanistic counterpart, Plaatje took white legislators to task for their careless reading of life-altering documents and traveled across his region to map the suffering that resulted. And this only scratches the surface of looming Casely Hayford–related research prospects. Zooming out further, it is just as easy to imagine a study of *Ethiopia*

Unbound alongside other, contemporaneous novels of imperial intellectual manners, for example, E. M. Forster's *Howards End*, with its low-key but definitive commentary on how British masculine *anti*-intellectualism was shaped by relations with West Africa. And this is to say nothing of the many obvious points of connection between Gold Coast and South Asian intellectual history, some of which appear in this book's notes. One of my course syllabi, in fact, features Casely Hayford alongside Forster and Gandhi, and it is my hope that as earlier African texts and figures become better known beyond specialist circles, they will mix and mingle with all sorts.

Nonetheless, and for better or worse, these are not the lines of inquiry to which I am drawn in this epilogue, nor am I interested in using its pages to make one last go at a focused argument. I would like, instead, briefly to extend my reflections on the present-day space between the ubiquity and implausibility of Casely Hayford's legacy in Ghana, because it is something around which I still have trouble wrapping my mind. People there still *live in* institutions he founded and recite ideals of Africa's modernization via its own traditions that he was among the first to articulate publicly; *Gold Coast Native Institutions* is often taught at the University of Ghana's School of Law and cited as an authoritative work by both lay and professional historians. In this sense, Casely Hayford is an outstanding example of "the nineteenth century's dogged persistence into the present through its structures," in Zachary Samalin's words, "whether institutional, ideological, discursive, or more obviously material."[4] And yet for all his iconicity in channeling cultural esteem, as the subject of countless, freely circulated heritage blog and social media posts extolling the proud and anti-imperial Akan past, virtually nothing about his constitutional vision for the Gold Coast's political progress has persisted in Ghana's official halls of power. As Kwasi Prempeh observed in 2007, "The postcolonial tradition of an imperial president [has] survived the initial round of democratic and constitutional reforms in Africa," carrying forth only the worst aspects of Nkrumah and his cohort's rush to bypass legislative process and multiparty democracy in the name of radical reform. And to follow Richard Rathbone in *Nkrumah and the Chiefs*, Ghana's First Republic also marked a violent break with Casely Hayford's nuanced respect for traditional leadership structures, as well as his political cooperation with traditional rulers, especially in the early days of his work with the ARPS.[5] If Casely Hayford used law to expertly weave past institutions with emergent ones, Nkrumah sought to manufacture a whole new kind of thread.

Whether Casely Hayford's more gradualist approach to African liberation was a starting point for or hindrance to later, more "successful" independence movements is an open question, a kind of Rorschach test for a reader's own politics. Attempting to answer it, even in my own head, often reminds me of a heated debate in an undergraduate Russian history seminar, when the professor asked us students whether Stalin's excesses were continuous with or at odds with Leninism; we quickly staked out vehement positions that spoke to our own, mostly American sense of the world. What is, either way, indisputable is that beginning with Nkrumah's administration and across the ensuing so-called Coup years, between 1966 and 1979, modern Ghana was engineered without functional legislative guardrails. Though it underwent what is widely viewed as a successful transition to electoral democracy in the 1990s, the country's government still heavily favors the executive: its president has overwhelming authority over both legislation and ministerial (as well as municipal) appointments.[6] And with a precedent set in the 1960s of rebuilding constitutions, per Prempeh, to "suit the instrumental needs of particular regimes," it is perhaps to be expected that electoral politics' hold would be tenuous.[7]

The idea that someone as publicly disciplined and "academic" as Casely Hayford could be a major political player is almost laughable. As contemporary Ghanaian politicians herald upright forefathers, like him, who brandished African causes on the world stage, their armies of ministers are busy finding ever more creative ways to use state funds as home decor.[8] Indeed, the clearest current successors to Casely Hayford's style of anticolonial civic work—in its steadfast regard for "good governance" based on sound and transparent processes, the rigorous tracking of facts, and a willingness to wield big ideas before a public by which one's leadership rises or falls—are the *non*governmental organizations that endeavor to hold the state accountable. The Center for Democratic Development, where Prempeh is employed, is my own outstanding example, and the place in Accra where I can best imagine Casely Hayford conversing at length across administrative minutiae and first principles. Perhaps he would now design surveys there, or give speeches, or write level-headed reports about the curtailing of representation by, this time, Ghana's own Jubilee House instead of British administrators. Who can say, and why bother to try? The answer to the second question is simple: it is that legacy matters, because it is so easily co-opted or expunged.

I am skipping a huge amount of political history here, and needfully so. Postindependence Ghanaian politics—and really, global politics, period—are so far removed from this book's erudite and versatile fin de siècle subject as to demand a whole different kind of scholarly training for their explanation. Political scientists and historians are on the task, and as a literary comparatist, I have little of substance to add.[9] The salient fact for this book's story is that Casely Hayford's oeuvre, in contrast, is not at all outside the literary scholar or intellectual historian's wheelhouse, because his style of leadership was so wrought up with his style of writing. As a novelist, legal philosopher, and rhetorician, he made every political move into a public exercise in textual craft. And *as* such a multifaceted intellectual figure—for whom sound reading was truth, and truth, action—he demands a kind of disciplinary promiscuity to be well understood. With its flexible boundaries and training, literary studies is ideally suited for this undertaking. Part of the task of working through Casely Hayford's ongoing resonance is asking precisely about how parts of his protean profile get parceled out to different *kinds* of lineages across the century (or so) after his death. If Casely Hayford's mark is barely legible in West African politics with a capital *P*, and only partly so in the nongovernmental sphere, where has the rest of it gone? It is here that tracing his legacy is most poignant, as doing so must reassemble a shattered, holistic conception of the African elite. It follows down separate paths, that is, an ideal of African leadership that once used law to "bundle" ethnographic, civic, governmental, philosophical, spiritual, and aesthetic callings. I am interested in and moved by the more atomized social portrait that emerges in its wake, even if I do not feel able to pin down clear causes and effects in what is ultimately a highly overdetermined history.

One way to illustrate this separation of elements in Casely Hayford's professional aftermath is with a quick glance at the careers of his own descendants, as governance and "culture" come into increasingly detached relation across successive generations. His son, Archie Casely Hayford, was a barrister who followed a successful stint in Gold Coast municipal politics with three ministerial positions in Kwame Nkrumah's administration (of Agriculture and Natural Resources, Communications, and the Interior). But while he represented what was perhaps the last gasp of J. E. Casely Hayford's elite-minded civic ethos within formal politics, a kind of noblesse oblige that saw service rather than innovation as its north star, even Archie did not publish any groundbreaking literary works. *His* two oldest sons then offer an on-the-nose illustration of the forked path that starts to separate the "man of letters" from the man of state. Beattie Casely-Hayford trained as an engineer before becoming the inaugural director of the Ghana Arts Council, and then of the television division of the Ghana Broadcasting Corporation (he also co-founded the Ghana National Dance Ensemble). His brother, Louis, was the Volta River Authority's third CEO.[10] My point here is not that energy industry officials cannot be "cultured"—Louis certainly was—or that arts administrators lack political ideas. I mean simply to illustrate how quickly a life like Casely Hayford's becomes unrealistic, even for those who plainly inherit his combination of interests and ideals. The expansion and firming-up of Ghana's postindependence institutions, as elsewhere, necessitates more focused professional tracks.

Among present-day Casely-Hayfords, the range of prominent careers likewise spans the arts, the law, communications, business, and fashion design, parceled out to different depoliticized spheres (depoliticized, that is, in a formal sense). The London-based Casely-Hayford brand, founded in 2009 by the father and son team of Joe and Charlie Casely-Hayford, retains many elements that would be recognizable to students of their famous ancestor's work. Joe Casely-Hayford, who died in 2019, was a legendary figure in his own right, pioneering what his son has called an "anarchic but incredibly traditional style," which fused the strict tradition of British sartorialism with culturally eclectic streetwear influences. Even J. E. Casely Hayford's interest in Meiji-era Japan, in *Ethiopia Unbound*, lives on in the elegant Marylebone shop: much of the Casely-Hayford collection has long been crafted there, honing a shared orientation to detail across a formidable language barrier.[11] And the family homage is also explicit, with Adelaide Cromwell's 1986 book on Adelaide Smith Casely Hayford, *An African Victorian Feminist*, proudly displayed in the Casely-Hayford boutique. Sydney Casely-Hayford, who died in 2023, was a financial expert and columnist who for years worked through complex economic ideas for Ghana's general public, as well as playing a prominent role in the nonpartisan political and economic watchdog group OccupyGhana. It is also hard not to think of Ekra-Agyiman tirelessly making the rounds of local meetings in Cape Coast and Axim when his grandson Gus Casely-Hayford, the inaugural director of London's V&A East museum, rides his bicycle to engage with students at hundreds of underserved local schools.[12] Last but by no means least, Margaret Casely-Hayford has turned a prestigious British legal career in the direction of higher education and the arts, serving as the first woman chancellor of Coventry University and the chair of the board of Shakespeare's Globe theater. J. E. Casely Hayford's sensibility, then, remains palpable in different ways in various corners of Ghana and its London diaspora.

The list of the family's aesthetic and civic achievements could no doubt go on, and there is much that is meaningful in foregrounding Britain's formative Black elite lineage. J. E. Casely Hayford is mentioned in nearly every article on the family at large and sits prominently in the background of the intact Fante diasporic milieu. But the ways in which he cannot be recovered, and can never exist again, are just as meaningful to ponder. He was a jack of all leadership trades, moving deftly across legislation, legal scholarship, journalism, and diplomacy—as well as multiple scales of literary and aesthetic innovation. All the while, he maintained not just substantive but influential interests in popular religion and material and organizational infrastructure. He was, so to speak, a Gold Coast Renaissance man, living out this role through what now seems like an almost impossible balance of public and private deliberation and confidence. This does not mean he never miscalculated, or that he should now be treated with kid gloves. It does mean that this kind of career, and maybe this kind of person, are simply no longer plausible in the cultural and economic hubs of the Anglophone world, and that along with many gains, this represents a real loss.

Across the decades since Casely Hayford's death in 1930, through the fiercer nationalisms of the 1950s and '60s and the economic contractions of African "structural adjustment" programs in the 1980s and '90s, each of the spheres folded into his historical self-styling has been discretely professionalized. Writers write (or teach writing), legislators legislate (or block others' efforts to do so), and arts administrators run arts organizations (assuming they have not been replaced by someone with an MBA). There are, inevitably, exceptions—lawyers still write fiction; some writers are acknowledged by some states—but no one in today's London or Accra could be expected to occupy the highest step on so many professional ladders at once. Try, for a moment, to envision how this might look: a member of British Parliament who is also a dedicated small-town lawyer, pathbreaking novelist, and cultural attaché, and whose dense legal monographs win praise at state galas and local book club meetings alike. A high-ranking Ghanaian public official who dedicates countless hours to philological and philosophical understanding alone in Axim and ultimately gives up a celebrated writing career to be absorbed into the grinding daily work of regional capacity building. A Pan-Africanist cultural luminary whose behind-the-scenes, long-haul institutional vision lives up to their exalted public rhetoric. It's not that no one now would *want* to fulfill such a multipronged version of success, or bring together such a diverse set of traits and pursuits in their public personhood—it's just hard to imagine being able or allowed to do so. So we try to imagine and fail. Then try again.

NOTES

Introduction: The "How" Behind the "Who" of Gold Coast Letters

1. The title of first African novel in English has one other viable contender in Liberian writer Joseph Jeffrey Walters's *Guanya Pau: A Story of an African Princess*, which was published in 1891 and is available in a 2004 Broadview edition edited by Gareth Griffiths and John Victor Singler. *Guanya Pau*, however, was written at Oberlin College, likely with an American audience in mind, and does not seem to have circulated beyond its point of origin until the 1990s, aside from a serialized version in Monrovia in 1905–6. Casely Hayford lived and wrote in West Africa, where his books were also advertised and circulated. *Ethiopia Unbound* thus still lays a persuasive claim to this mark of distinction.

2. At minimum, in West Africa, these would include the Creole Sierra Leonean military surgeon and research scientist James Africanus Beale Horton's *West African Countries and Peoples* (1868); the Ga historian, physician, and minister Carl Christian Reindorf's *The History of the Gold Coast and Asante* (1889 in Ga, and 1895 in English translation); the Gold Coast's first barrister John Mensah Sarbah's *Fanti Customary Laws* (1904); and, a bit further afield, the Yoruba Anglican minister and historian Samuel Johnson's *The History of the Yorubas* (completed in 1897, though not published until 1921).

3. Casely Hayford was a fixture of the "News in Brief" section of the *Gold Coast Nation*, for instance, the official print organ of the ARPS. The April 4, 1912, installment describes his weekend trip to the small town of Abakrampah to attend a service at the Wesleyan Mission Chapel there, meant to encourage the local pastor in his "strenuous efforts" to teach local children to "chant the Psalms in the vernacular." And in the space of only a single two-column section in the April 25, 1912, edition of the paper, he is mentioned twice. The first item announces that, "Barrister Casely Hayford's Second Pamphlet published at the request of the Amanhin's is out and may be had at 6d a copy from the Secretary of the Aborigines Society," and the second that "Mr. Casely Hayford is expected here within a fortnight to meet the members of the Executive Committee." Similar entries elsewhere chronicle his travels with his second wife. As Adwoa Opoku-Agyemang and I note in our introduction to *Ethiopia Unbound*, he was treated practically like a head of state. "The Cape Coast Literary and Social Club, founded in 1914, did not hesitate to broadcast Casely Hayford's position as their patron," we explain there. "One printed program from the period, which advertises 'Dances, Conversation, Musical Games, Speeches & Toasts, Theatrical Performances,' puts [his] profile-raising function in bold relief. The card accords as much space to listing the upcoming events as to naming the club's twelve patrons, and places Casely Hayford directly after His Excellency the Governor and the Provincial Commissioner" (xxii–xxiii).

4. Nkrumah's indebtedness took more than one form. In addition to citing "the great Casely-Hayford" in his autobiography (*Ghana*, 205), he was joined by Casely Hayford's son, Archie Casely Hayford, when he delivered his famous Midnight Speech declaring Ghana's independence in 1957. Archie was later appointed Nkrumah's minister of agriculture and natural resources. In a less obvious sense, Nkrumah was also influenced by the early twentieth-century literary culture and emphasis on "vernacular" education that Casely Hayford was instrumental in consolidating, including via Nkrumah's admiration for Casely Hayford's slightly younger peer J.E.K. Aggrey, a fellow force behind the founding of Achimota College and its first vice principal, from 1925 to 1927.

5. High-profile recent books on global Black political thought by Adom Getachew (*Worldmaking After Empire*) and Musab Younis (*On the Scale of the World*), for instance, make great strides in recounting the transformative ambition of Black postcolonial and Global South thinkers. But for all such books' welcome ambition in unearthing a broader archive of political thought forged around ideals of economic justice and liberation, it is also easy to see them as invitations to leave area-specific, often more politically variegated work to regional specialists with smaller readerships.

6. Earle, "African Intellectual History and Historiography."

7. Diouf and Prais, "Casting the Badge of Inferiority," 205.

8. Diouf and Prais, "Casting the Badge of Inferiority," 207.

9. Casely Hayford to Du Bois, June 8, 1904, https://credo.library.umass.edu/view/pageturn/mums312-b002-i385/#page/1/mode/1up.

10. See, for example, Casely Hayford to Du Bois, September 21, 1921, https://credo.library.umass.edu/view/full/mums312-b017-i241. Upon J. E. Casely Hayford's death, furthermore, Du Bois writes to his son Archie Casely Hayford that he "never had the pleasure of meeting" his late father; October 25, 1930, https://credo.library.umass.edu/view/full/mums312-b185-i345.

11. Mark Hayford was accompanied in Alabama by his fellow Reverend F. A. Pinanko, who published his "Report on the International Conference on the Negro Held at Tuskegee, Ala, April 17, 18, 19, 1912" in the February 6, 1913, issue of the *Gold Coast Nation*, along with a transcript of his own address. He notes that the "Gold Coast as a nation has never entered into the mind of the Afro-American and, therefore, it was my special opportunity to touch on that subject in my address." The most comprehensive overview of Mark Hayford's life remains G. M. Haliburton's essay "Mark Christian Hayford: A Non-Success Story," which chronicles his numerous but disappointing religious fundraising campaigns in the United States and England.

12. J. E. Casely Hayford, *Ethiopia Unbound*, xxviii. This speech in the novel is a modified version of Casely Hayford's introduction, written in Axim, to Blyden's 1905 collection of speeches, *West Africa before Europe*.

13. Blyden, "West African Problems," 101.

14. Archie Casely Hayford, "Man and His Work," 16. Even Ghana's capital city, Accra, in this period was more a place where one had to do business than an imaginative hub. It is telling, in this light, that though Casely Hayford died in Accra, he wished to be buried alongside his first wife, Beatrice Pinnock, in Axim.

15. Gold Coast newspapers in the 1910s and 1920s contain many reports of Casely Hayford's work with civic organizations, but a couple of representative examples will

suffice to show just how involved he was at the municipal level. The *Gold Coast Leader* reports on February 4, 1911, in its "General News" section, that "Mr. Casely Hayford has been paying a round of visits to the schools in [Cape Coast]," teaching about "love of country" and even distributing prizes for the "best essays on [his] remarks made on Mr. [John Mensah] Sarbah's life and work." The *Gold Coast Nation*, on April 11, 1912, notes that he was "Master of Ceremonies" at "a most interesting and instructive ceremony" in Kotokuraba (part of Cape Coast), where the results of an ARPS officer election were announced.

16. Ateko went on to establish Accra's first Theosophy Lodge in 1935. (The first theosophy study group in West Africa was founded in Lagos in 1908.) Unsurprisingly, given his era and social stature, Casely Hayford was also a member of multiple Masonic lodges. These were St. George's Lodge 3851 in Sekondi, the Victoria chapter in Accra, and an additional lodge in Lagos. See Casely-Hayford and Rathbone, "Politics, Families and Freemasonry," 143–60.

17. Scott, *Conscripts of Modernity*, 12.

18. Scott, *Conscripts of Modernity*, 16.

19. My orientation here is more in line with Jane Burbank and Frederick Cooper's in *Post-Imperial Possibilities*, which parses the formation of "large-scale, transcontinental projects that could unite peoples of different origins in productive, attractive, and strong political units" (3), guided by the idea that "The conventional notion of sovereignty as an all-or-nothing proposition corresponds poorly to the complexities of power relations in world history" (11).

20. Newell, *Literary Culture in Colonial Ghana*, 136.

21. J. E. Casely Hayford, *United West Africa*, 42.

22. Many readers will recognize that this maxim is derived from Jesus's words in Mark 2:27 of the Bible, translated in the King James Version as "The sabbath was made for man, and not man for the sabbath." The point stands, since the passage, which describes Jesus's rebuttal of the Pharisees' concern that his disciples are breaking holy rules, shows how he wields his authority for worldly adaptation.

23. Cover, "Folktales of Justice," 191.

24. See Kwasi Wiredu's essay "Towards Decolonizing African Philosophy and Religion." I discuss the implications of its argument at length in *The African Novel of Ideas*, noting there that "Wiredu arrives at a vision of God as one who fashions a world from previously extant but unformed materials ... to indicate in turn a priority on an *ordering function* rather than a miraculous intervention" (43–44).

25. Cover, "Folktales of Justice," 196.

26. For a detailed reconstruction of Brew's life and its significance to the rise of a mixed-race Fante elite through trade relations (including the slave trade) and intermarriage, see Priestley, "Richard Brew."

27. By far the most granular and persuasive account of "class" (or some version of it) in emergent structures of Fante social organization in the nineteenth century is the 1992 PhD dissertation "A Genealogical History of Cape Coast Stool Families," by Casely Hayford's grandson, Augustus (or Gus) Casely-Hayford. In it, he describes the mislabeling of a complex set of divisions among Cape Coast lineages—most prominently between matrilineal and patrilineal forms of succession—as a straightforward opposition between the literate and traditional elites on the one hand, and

the educated elites and the Fante masses on the other (17–18). Casely-Hayford draws meaningfully on David Kimble's *Political History of Ghana* but adds significant depth to connections between the Cape Coast intelligentsia and traditional Akan chieftaincy structures.

28. J. E. Casely Hayford, "The Foundations of Self-Government: Historic Speeches by The Late Honourable Joseph Ephraim Casely Hayford, Leader of the West African Congress," unpublished manuscript, compiled by Admirer, SOAS special collections, 68.

29. Greenblatt, *Renaissance Self-Fashioning*, 6.

30. Greenblatt, *Renaissance Self-Fashioning*, 3–4.

31. Benton and Ford, *Rage for Order*, 2.

32. Korang, *Writing Ghana, Imagining Africa*, 206.

33. Casely-Hayford, "Prosopographical Approaches to Fante History," 50.

34. Casely-Hayford, "Genealogical History of Cape Coast Stool Families," 20–22.

35. Casely-Hayford, "Prosopographical Approaches to Fante History," 49.

36. Casely Hayford is characteristically blunt on this point regarding both African and European intellectual shortcomings. In *Native Institutions*, he explains that the okyeame "was called a linguist first by a half-educated native interpreter, tasked to explain his position to the white man, and as 'linguist' he has been known ever since in the language of law and politics on the Gold Coast" (68). He briefly suggests "spokesman" as an alternative but determines that it is not worth trying to buck such strong precedent.

37. Yankah, *Speaking for the Chief*, 1.

38. J. E. Casely Hayford, *Native Institutions*, 68–69.

39. J. E. Casely Hayford, *Native Institutions*, 70.

40. J. E. Casely Hayford, *Ethiopia Unbound*, 85–86.

41. J. E. Casely Hayford, *Native Institutions*, 70.

42. Kwesi Yankah translates the Asante *anona* clan's associated saying as, "When you see a lone bird, do not throw a stone; it may belong to a multitude" (*Speaking for the Chief*, 49). Kwame Arhin's essay "Rank and Class among the Asante and Fante in the Nineteenth Century" offers an extended discussion of how education became the basis for Fante "social excellence" in the nineteenth century. According to Arhin, "An Asante, however well educated or rich, aims at some kind of chiefship as the supreme index of social achievement. The Fante aims at the acquisition of repute as a highly educated man" (2).

43. As one instance of this, the *Gold Coast Nation* on June 6, 1912, under "Our Editor's Notes and Comments," announced Casely Hayford as part of a "Deputation to England in connection with the Forestry Ordinance" with "Joseph Ephraim Casely Hayford Esq., Barrister-at-Law, a Prince of Cape Coast District and a member of the Executive Committee of the Gold Coast Aborigines Rights Protection Society."

44. J. E. Casely Hayford, *Native Institutions*, 199.

45. Nkrumah, *Ghana*, viii. Nkrumah applies this diagnosis of elitism specifically to the National Congress of British West Africa. Some outstanding and field-directing studies of non-elite textual and literary cultures in West Africa are the volume *Africa's Hidden Histories*, edited by Karin Barber; Ato Quayson's *Oxford Street, Accra*, specifically its discussion of tro-tro slogans; and Stephanie Newell's recent *Newsprint*

Literature and Local Literary Creativity in West Africa, 1900s–1960s. A similar shift away from elite print intellectuals has occurred in the field of Ghanaian intellectual history, marked most notably by Kwasi Konadu's *Our Own Way in This Part of the World*, which charts the multi-imperial, intraregional dynamics informing the work and thought of Kofi Dɔnkɔ, a blacksmith, farmer, healer, and thinker in present-day Ghana's Bono region. I would go so far as to say that to focus on a figure as privileged as Casely Hayford now approaches taboo status in the field of African literary studies.

    46. J. E. Casely Hayford, "Foundations of Self-Government," 47.

    47. J. E. Casely Hayford, *West African Leadership*, 48. On the differences (and in some cases, rifts) between Garvey's Universal Negro Improvement Association (UNIA) and Casely Hayford's NCBWA, see, for example, Yekutiel Gershoni's essay "Common Goals, Different Ways." For more on the dissolution of Adelaide Casely Hayford's relationship with the UNIA in Sierra Leone, see Rita Okonkwo's essay "Adelaide Casely Hayford: Cultural Nationalist and Feminist."

    48. J. E. Casely Hayford, *Correspondence Relating to the National Congress of British West Africa* (hereafter *NCBWA Correspondence*), 50.

    49. Casely Hayford did ease up on his skepticism of Garvey's methods in response to Garvey's dubious 1923 criminal conviction for mail fraud in the United States, and he opposed the banning of Garvey's *Negro World* newspaper in British colonies on liberal grounds; African readers, he felt, should be free to make up their own minds about Garvey. On December 1, 1923, Casely Hayford (presumably) used the *Gold Coast Leader* to advocate for Du Bois and other Black leaders to "sink all personal questions and squabbles, and attend to the great constructive work before them," recognizing the importance of Garvey's global stature and charisma for advancing a broader agenda of African self-governance. At the same time, he looked to Liberia—and not his own country—as the UNIA's rightful destination, noting in the *Leader* on April 12, 1924, that "[Liberia] is marked out for great things in the careful and gradual absorption of useful African element, which would form the nucleus of a great nation." In another *Leader* editorial from May 17 of the same year, he goes so far as to position Liberia within a grand providential plan to unify Africans by means of enslavement, so that they might, like the biblical Israelites, "be led out of Egypt a peculiar people with a great spoil." That said, it would be a serious stretch to call even this later, more receptive Casely Hayford a "Garveyite," as some cultural historians have done. Even as he urged Liberia in the May 17, 1924, *Leader* piece—and in another on August 9, 1924—to fulfill its racial destiny by welcoming small and orderly delegations of UNIA members, he stipulated there, "The new African shall not be aggressive. He shall not be an offense to any one. His motto will be: Live and let live." In a similar spirit, yet a further *Leader* editorial from July 19, 1924, takes Du Bois to task not for the substance of his distaste for Garvey, but for the "exhibition of ill-temper" by which the usually "distinguished, refined, and cultured editor of the *Crisis*" had conveyed it.

    50. Archie Casely Hayford, "Man and His Work," 13.

    51. Ferguson, *Papers of George Ekem Ferguson*, xi.

    52. Fitzmaurice, *King Leopold's Ghostwriter*, 22.

    53. Fitzmaurice, *King Leopold's Ghostwriter*, 22.

54. Casely Hayford's understanding of "culture" deliberately conflates its ethnographic and social-hierarchical dimensions. The quotation, in full, from his 1919 short book *United West Africa*, is: "Be as wise as serpents and gentle as doves. There is no need for race antagonisms. And if such there must be, prove that by your superior culture such considerations are beneath you" (15).

55. See, for instance, Kimble, *Political History of Ghana*; July, *Origins of Modern African Thought*; Okonkwo, *Heroes of West African Nationalism*; and Falola, *Nationalism and African Intellectuals*. These are all important books, needless to say, from which one might have expected a more extended treatment of Casely Hayford to emerge. The closest thing to a book-length study of Casely Hayford's career is the Ghanaian classicist L. H. Ofosu-Appiah's *Joseph Ephraim Casely Hayford: The Man of Vision and Faith*, which is actually a series of lectures that he delivered to the Ghana Academy of Arts and Sciences in 1975 and totals only thirty-one pages.

56. J. E. Casely Hayford, "Foundations of Self-Government," 66.

57. J. E. Casely Hayford, *West African Leadership*, 41.

58. J. E. Casely Hayford, *West African Leadership*, 73.

59. J. E. Casely Hayford, *West African Leadership*, 79.

60. J. E. Casely Hayford, *West African Leadership*, 79.

61. J. E. Casely Hayford, *West African Leadership*, 68.

62. J. E. Casely Hayford, *West African Leadership*, 95.

63. J. E. Casely Hayford, *West African Leadership*, 114.

64. Waldron, *Dignity of Legislation*, 2.

65. Gewirtz, "Narrative and Rhetoric in the Law," 2.

66. As two accomplished recent cases in point, see the edited volume Constable, Volpp, and Wagner, *Looking for Law in All the Wrong Places*, and Rohit De's 2018 monograph *A People's Constitution: The Everyday Life of Law in the Indian Republic*. The editors of the former work note, in their introduction, that their approaches "place the humanities front and center in the study of law," by "turning to materials that range from the most conventional legal works and routine documents to novels and photographs, from police courts to theater scripts, from ethnographic practices to road signs, [to] expand the range of sources that are relevant to law" (3–4).

67. J. E. Casely Hayford, *West African Leadership*, 116. Even as Casely Hayford's legal practice sacrificed considerable profitability, it brought in enough income to help him forgo profit in other intellectual arenas. In Archie Casely Hayford's unpublished book about his father, he notes that J. E. purchased his own printing press to improve the quality of the *Gold Coast Leader* newspaper, and that "he was constantly augmenting [the press] with his own private funds obtained from his legal practice. The business side of it was forgotten and neglected in the zeal to do a public service and hence it did not pay" (14).

68. Waldron, *Dignity of Legislation*, 7.

69. J. E. Casely Hayford, *West African Leadership*, 116.

70. Pocock, "Virtues, Rights, and Manners," 355.

71. Pocock, "Virtues, Rights, and Manners," 364.

72. Pocock, "Virtues, Rights, and Manners," 357, 359.

73. Pocock, "Virtues, Rights, and Manners," 361.

74. Pocock, "Virtues, Rights, and Manners," 367.

75. Pocock, "Virtues, Rights, and Manners," 365.

76. Lest there be any doubt concerning Casely Hayford's position on the social importance of lawyers, he states in this same speech: "I think that the Bar should be supported rather than discouraged. Even if they do make enormous fees it is not undesirable, for after all what do they do with the money? Do they not educate and train their children to become good citizens, and to provide you with Legislators capable of following your debates? Do they not build good houses and improve your cities? Do they not invest in articles of merchandise and make money circulate? In what way therefore are they undesirable? I hold no special brief for them. I have nearly come to the end of my own career, but I think it is not right that the Bar in this country should be discouraged" (*West African Leadership*, 118).

77. J. E. Casely Hayford, *Ethiopia Unbound*, 148–50.

78. J. E. Casely Hayford, *Native Institutions*, xiv, xv.

79. Du Bois, "Talented Tenth," 75; J. E. Casely Hayford, *Ethiopia Unbound*, 17.

80. Du Bois, "Talented Tenth," 60–61, 45.

81. J. E. Casely Hayford, *Ethiopia Unbound*, 8.

82. Take, for instance, a Legislative Council speech from March 21, 1923, in which he raises numerous matters of transportation maintenance and development, including what was then the significant "question of tarmetting roads," that is, making them suitable for motor traffic, especially between cocoa farms and ports (J. E. Casely Hayford, *West African Leadership*, 147). Tarmetting and car use were huge topics of concern in the 1920s and '30s Gold Coast. See also *Gold Coast: Report for 1929–30*, Annual Colonial Reports No. 1504 (London: H. M. Stationery Office,1930), https://libsysdigi.library.illinois.edu/ilharvest/Africana/Books2011 -05/5530214/5530214_1929_1930/5530214_1929_1930_opt.pdf.

83. J. E. Casely Hayford, *Ethiopia Unbound*, 46. The protagonist, named Kwamankra, focuses especially on streets, observing the fluid transitions between "a busy, noisy thoroughfare" and "a number of peaceful avenues, wearing a beautiful green, like unto moss, which met in one grand broadway." He adds, "The different walks seemed designed with an eye to quiet contemplation. Now and again the avenues ended abruptly in an ingeniously laid-out garden from which again avenues continued to the broadway" (42).

84. Michaelmas is the British academic term that extends from fall (September or October) to the Christmas holiday.

85. According to documents held in the official Inner Temple archives, as are all references here to the specifics of Casely Hayford's Inner Temple education, these subjects were: constitutional law; legal history; Roman law and jurisprudence; public and private international law; english law and equity, including criminal law; civil and criminal procedure; evidence; real and personal property; contracts and torts; and equity, trusts, and easements.

86. As one case in point, the scant notes for an Inner Temple luncheon on July 27, 1896, state that "Suggestions and complaints were made as to the quantity and quality of the whiskey and various other matters." Ren Pepitone looks in depth at the culture of British colonial legal training in *Brotherhood of Barristers*, in which they remark that "the Inns were professional associations whose primary function was to preserve

the prestige of the bar by regulating the admission and behavior of law students and barristers. That is to say, the societies were more invested in members' social standing and conduct than their knowledge of the law" (xi). That said, the book also chronicles the Inns' turn to a more academic understanding of legal training beginning in the mid nineteenth century, which was accompanied, to maintain their authority over the Bar, by their taking "active steps to make it seem as if the Inns fulfilled public obligation and served the public good" (5).

87. Directly anticipating Casely Hayford's social leadership on his return to the Gold Coast (in the immediate sense of hosting and curating events), which I discuss at greater length in chapter 3, Inner Temple members also planned their own balls and oversaw the distribution of cigars. A full list of standing committees in 1894 included those designated for: Finance and Domestic Management; Library; Choir; Chamber; Nine; Luncheon; Dispensation; Building and Land East of Temple; Hall Building; Reading Room; Fire; Garden; Education; Electric Lighting; and a Standing Joint Committee on the Duties, Interests, and Discipline of the Bar.

88. Korang, *Writing Ghana, Imagining Africa*, 206.

89. Higney, *Institutional Character*, 3.

90. Higney, *Institutional Character*, 8.

91. J. E. Casely Hayford, *United West Africa*, 8.

92. J. E. Casely Hayford, *United West Africa*, 50.

93. All of text quoted above is from *United West Africa*, 48.

94. J. E. Casely Hayford, *United West Africa*, 49.

95. Fitzmaurice, *King Leopold's Ghostwriter*, 25. For Skinner's deft summary of conceptual history (or the history of concepts) as distinct from earlier forms of intellectual history, which also touches on its latter-day marginalization within history departments (as opposed to philosophy or politics), see "Quentin Skinner: 'Concepts only have histories,'" interview by Jacques Lévy and Emmanuelle Tricoire, *Espaces-Temps.net*, 2007, https://www.espacestemps.net/en/articles/quentin-skinner/.

Chapter One. A Matter-of-Fact Kind of Man

1. Korang, *Writing Ghana, Imagining Africa*, 16.

2. Scott, *Conscripts of Modernity*, 7.

3. J. E. Casely Hayford, *Native Institutions*, 172.

4. *Native Institutions*, 173.

5. Laumann, "Compradore-in-Arms," 126; Limberg, "Economy of the Fante Confederation," 83.

6. Limberg also notes interestingly, "The Constitution marks the end of the active economy of the Fanti Confederation"—which included road duties, and directed funds mainly to "messengers, fees, and salaries" ("Economy of the Fante Confederation," 89)—"and the beginning of a new period when the economy of the future was being discussed, planned, and re-planned. The Confederation survived for about one year more, but during this year its economy was only an abstraction, beautifully packed in detailed schemes" (101).

7. Agbodeka, "Fanti Confederacy," 83, 86.

8. Johnson, *Towards Nationhood in West Africa*, ix.

9. Korang, *Writing Ghana, Imagining Africa*, 179.

10. For one recent example that builds on Kwame Anthony Appiah's well-known book *Cosmopolitanism: Ethics in a World of Strangers*, see Esperanza Brizuela-Garcia's essay "Cosmopolitanism: Why Nineteenth Century Gold Coast Thinkers Matter in the Twenty-First Century." Brizuela-Garcia argues, contra David Kimble's 1963 classic *A Political History of Ghana*, that while "the conventional wisdom about intellectuals like Casely-Hayford [*sic*], Reindorf and Mensah Sarbah tends to oversimplify the nature of their contributions," by seeing them as part of a nationalist continuum, "the work of synthesis they endeavored did not involve a facile understanding of European and/or African ways, but rather an interpretation of them" (208–9).

11. Zachernuk, *Colonial Subjects*, 32–33.

12. Johnson, *Towards Nationhood in West Africa*, xi; Korang, *Writing Ghana, Imagining Africa*, 206.

13. Tenkorang, "John Mensah Sarbah," 67–68.

14. Tenkorang, "John Mensah Sarbah," 65–78. For a detailed discussion of the ARPS' interest and participation in early twentieth-century race congresses, see S.K.B. Asante's essay "The Neglected Aspects of the Activities of the Gold Coast Aborigines Rights Protection Society."

15. *Native Institutions*, 319.

16. Cooper, "Possibility and Constraint," 169.

17. Cooper, "Possibility and Constraint," 174.

18. Attoh Ahuma, *Gold Coast Nation and National Consciousness*, 2.

19. J. E. Casely Hayford, *Ethiopia Unbound*, 71.

20. Gikandi, *Maps of Englishness*, xix.

21. Collis-Buthelezi, "Under the Aegis of Empire," 121, 127. Gaurav Desai also provides a good illustration of just how taken for granted as a political macro-structure the British Empire still was in this period in *Subject to Colonialism*. In his analysis of the origins of London's International Institute for African Languages and Cultures in 1926, he quotes the prominent British colonial administrator Frederick John Lugard as, "in almost the same breath," describing the institute as "entirely non-political" and tasking it with assisting "colonial agents" (100).

22. Getachew, "Problem of Liberal Empire Reconsidered," 168.

23. Goyal, "Africa and the Black Atlantic," v.

24. Taylor, *Empire of Neglect*, 143.

25. *Native Institutions*, 5–6.

26. *Native Institutions*, 128.

27. *Native Institutions*, 129. For a broader overview of African and Caribbean intellectuals' position *within* London in the first few decades of the twentieth century, see Matera, "Colonial Subjects."

28. Wenzel, "Zones of Occult Instability," 336–37.

29. Wenzel, "Zones of Occult Instability," 338–39.

30. Taiwo, *How Colonialism Preempted Modernity in Africa*, 126.

31. *Native Institutions*, 182.

32. *Native Institutions*, 22. While the Confederation typified this highest state form, Casely Hayford here describes earlier attainments of it, including what he calls the Fanti Union (an informal precursor of the Confederation).

33. *Native Institutions*, 24. Casely Hayford's discussion of kingship under the broad heading of "native institutions," by virtue of its generalizing intentions, does not paint a full picture of how variable the determination of Akan stool succession can be. While Fante polities often have a mix of matrilineal and patrilineal inheritances, Asante is famously matrilineal. Even within Asante, however, beyond the decidedly unique office of the *asantehene*, there are considerable differences across kinds of stools. Kwame Arhin has observed that "the bases of ranking," and thus procedures around succession, both among and within the three kinds of Asante authority of *adekrofo*, *ahemfo*, and *amanhene*, "were the antiquity of stools, distinction in war of former stool holders, and relationships of stools to the head stool of the state" (Arhin, "Rank and Class among the Asante and Fante," 5–6). Casely Hayford's account of Akan kingship—not incorrect but generic and concerned with emphasizing the in-built guardrails around Akan power—begins as follows: "The office of king is elective. No king, that is to say, is born a king. There are a number of circumstances which may prevent the nearest to the stool from ever sitting thereon" (*Native Institutions*, 3).

34. *Native Institutions*, 186.
35. *Native Institutions*, 187.
36. *Native Institutions*, 187.
37. *Native Institutions*, ix.
38. *Native Institutions*, xiii, 8.
39. *Native Institutions*, 8.
40. *Native Institutions*, 26.
41. *Native Institutions*, xiii.
42. *Native Institutions*, 127.
43. Nagel, *View from Nowhere*, 74.
44. Sarbah, *Fanti Customary Laws*, ix.
45. Sarbah, *Fanti Customary Laws*, ix (italics added), x.
46. *Native Institutions*, xiv.
47. Poovey, *History of the Modern Fact*, 6.
48. Poovey, *History of the Modern Fact*, 9.
49. *Native Institutions*, 99, 239.
50. Sarbah, *Fanti Customary Laws*, 5.
51. Casely Hayford cites *Fanti Customary Laws* extensively in *Native Institutions*, also writing there, "With kind permission, reference has also been made to 'Fanti Customary Laws,' the able work of my learned friend, the Honourable John Mensah Sarbah" (xiv).
52. *Native Institutions*, 80.
53. Anderson, *Powers of Distance*, 9.
54. Anderson, *Powers of Distance*, 12.
55. Anderson, *Powers of Distance*, 12.
56. Its introduction, however, was written in 1903.
57. Attoh Ahuma, *Memoirs of West African Celebrities*, x.
58. Attoh Ahuma, *Memoirs of West African Celebrities*, xiv.
59. The *Memoirs of West African Celebrities* epigraph in full is: "The life of a people grows, it is knit together and yet expanded, in joy and sorrow, in thought and action; it absorbs the thought of other nations into its own forms, and gives back the thought as new wealth to the world; it is a power and an organ in the great body of the nations.

But there may come a check, an arrest; memories may be stifled, and love may be faint for the lack of them; or memories may shrink into withered relics—the soul of a people, whereby they know themselves to be one, may seem to be dying for want of common action. But who shall say, 'The fountain of their life is dried up, they shall forever cease to be a nation?' Who shall say it? Not he who feels the life of his people stirring within his own. Shall he say, 'That way events are wending, I will not resist?' His very soul is resistance, and is as a seed of fire that may enkindle the souls of multitudes, and make a new pathway for events" (unpaginated). The scene in *Daniel Deronda* takes place in chapter 42.

60. Eliot, *Daniel Deronda*, 444–45.
61. Attoh Ahuma, *Memoirs of West African Celebrities*, 254, 256.
62. *Native Institutions*, 178.
63. Levine, *Dying to Know*, 3.
64. Levine, *Dying to Know*, 92.
65. Rorty, *Objectivity, Relativism, and Truth*, 7.
66. Daston and Galison, *Objectivity*, 196.
67. Daston and Galison, *Objectivity*, 38.
68. Daston and Galison, *Objectivity*, 34.
69. Daston and Galison, *Objectivity*, 35.
70. For a countervailing discussion of the rise of the British essay as a secularizing form, see, for example, Gee, "'Such Opinions Cannot Cohere': Swift's Inwardness"; and Gualtieri, "Essay as Form."
71. *Native Institutions*, 247.
72. *Native Institutions*, 247.
73. *Native Institutions*, 249.
74. Diouf and Prais, "Casting the Badge of Inferiority," 205.
75. Diouf and Prais, "Casting the Badge of Inferiority," 208–9.
76. Du Bois, *Souls of Black Folk*, 3.
77. Du Bois, *Souls of Black Folk*, 156.
78. Du Bois, *Souls of Black Folk*, 90.
79. Du Bois, *Black Reconstruction*, 722.
80. Du Bois, *Black Reconstruction*, 722.
81. *Native Institutions*, 240.
82. Levine, *Dying to Know*, 7.
83. Levine, *Dying to Know*, 5.
84. See Mignolo, *Darker Side of Western Modernity*.
85. Levine, *Dying to Know*, 18.
86. *Native Institutions*, 80, 81.
87. *Native Institutions*, 101.
88. *Native Institutions*, 118.
89. *Native Institutions*, 125.
90. *Native Institutions*, 125.
91. Levine, *Dying to Know*, 14.
92. Goodlad, "Moral Character," 132.
93. Goodlad, "Moral Character," 141.
94. *Native Institutions*, 263.
95. *Native Institutions*, 239–40.

96. Goodlad, "Moral Character," 141–42.

97. Goodlad, "Moral Character," 146.

98. Collini, "Idea of 'Character' in Victorian Political Thought," 34.

99. Collini, "Idea of 'Character' in Victorian Political Thought," 44.

100. K. M. Parker, "Law 'In' and 'As' History," 590.

101. K. M. Parker, "Law 'In' and 'As' History," 596.

102. K. M. Parker, "Law 'In' and 'As' History," 597.

103. Attoh Ahuma, *Gold Coast Nation and National Consciousness*, 2.

104. Attoh Ahuma, *Gold Coast Nation and National Consciousness*, 2.

105. K. M. Parker, "Law 'In' and 'As' History," 603.

106. K. M. Parker, "Law 'In' and 'As' History," 602.

107. Sarbah, *Fanti Customary Laws*, x.

108. Newell, *Literary Culture in Colonial Ghana*, 7.

109. Newell, *Literary Culture in Colonial Ghana*, 8, 19, 44.

110. Newell, *Literary Culture in Colonial Ghana*, 204. Newell's longer explanation of different forms of Gold Coast English sheds further light on the distinction between literate Africans broadly and Casely Hayford's position at its uppermost rung. "Highly educated members of the African elite did not express themselves in the florid English of the lower orders," she continues. "The most elaborate English stemmed from the least educated social class, the 'scholars', who were socially and economically differentiated from the elite and occupied a different place within the colourful spectrum of 'West African English' styles" (204).

111. Frank, "Casely-Hayford's Inherited Resistance."

112. Cromwell, *African Victorian Feminist*, 68.

113. Cromwell, *African Victorian Feminist*, 80. The vesting of aesthetic snobbery in Fante rather than English was characteristic of Casely Hayford's milieu. A representative piece called "The Fanti Language" in the October 22, 1888, issue of the *Gold Coast Echo* pronounces that "the reduction of the Akan language, based . . . on the awkwapim dialect, could never be popular; inasmuch as the Akwapims, as a nation, form but a very small part of the Akan family; their dialect unpopular; and, unlike the Fanti dialect which is full of life, entirely restricted within their own narrow limit." "Awkwapim" is an earlier version of what is now typically spelled "Akuapem," the name of a people and language concentrated mainly in the southeastern part of present-day Ghana. It is also the version of Twi into which the Bible was first translated in the 1870s by the Basel Mission.

114. *Native Institutions*, 249–50.

115. "Africanus" is almost certainly a reference to Africanus Horton, who adopted it during his years of study in Britain. John Bull is a character who symbolizes Great Britain, akin to the United States' Uncle Sam, who first appeared as a well-to-do farmer in the eighteenth century.

116. Du Bois's actual description, in the first chapter of *The Souls of Black Folk*, is: "It is a peculiar sensation, this double-consciousness, this sense of always looking at one's self through the eyes of others, of measuring one's soul by the tape of a world that looks on in amused contempt and pity. One ever feels his twoness,—an American, a Negro; two souls, two thoughts, two unreconciled strivings; two warring ideals in one dark body, whose dogged strength alone keeps it from being torn asunder" (3).

117. Korang, *Writing Ghana, Imagining Africa*, 220.
118. Korang, *Writing Ghana, Imagining Africa*, 52.
119. Korang, *Writing Ghana, Imagining Africa*, 47.
120. Daston and Galison, *Objectivity*, 6.
121. Daston and Galison, *Objectivity*, 10.
122. Daston and Galison, *Objectivity*, 52.
123. Daston and Galison, *Objectivity*, 52.
124. *Native Institutions*, 75.
125. *Native Institutions*, 75.
126. *Native Institutions*, 175.
127. *Native Institutions*, 179–80.
128. De, "Jurisprudence of Decolonization," 122.
129. Daston and Galison, *Objectivity*, 34.
130. John Mensah Sarbah is acutely aware of this fact, remarking "I have endeavoured in some instances to state the Customary Law in a few simply worded positions, embodying what a careful analytical study proves to be the principles running through it. I am quite alive to the danger of reducing Customary Law to a condition of fixity in a semi-developed state of society, the effect of which may hinder the gradually operating innate generation of law by a process of natural development, independent of accident and individual will, which best accords with the varying needs and spirit of a people so circumstanced as the inhabitants of the Gold Coast" (*Fanti Customary Laws*, xi).
131. *Native Institutions*, xi.
132. *Native Institutions*, xii.
133. *Native Institutions*, 93, 98.
134. *Native Institutions*, 44.
135. *Native Institutions*, 46.
136. I reprint these hypothetical cases here in full, so that they can be referenced, if needed, as my own argument develops: "In Ashanti, where a stranger kills big game on another's land, the licensee takes to the licensor a portion of the meat, the latter, in turn, taking to the Head-Chief a leg of the animal killed. Again, where a nugget is found in mining, the licensee brings to the licensor a portion of the gold with the nugget, the licensor sending the nugget to the King. In the two cases, the licensor would be the person having the right *to* possess, the Head-Chief or King merely having a claim to the allegiance of the licensor" (*Native Institutions*, 49).
137. *Native Institutions*, 61–62.
138. *Native Institutions*, 101–2.
139. *Native Institutions*, 102.
140. *Native Institutions*, 103.
141. *Native Institutions*, 104.
142. *Native Institutions*, 104.

Chapter Two. A Gold Coast Constitution

1. *NCBWA Correspondence*, 50–51. As John Parker also discusses in *In My Time of Dying*, the letter to which Casely Hayford refers, dictated by Ghartey to his English-speaking public just days before his death, was published in the *Gold Coast Methodist*

Times. "Be constitutional" is in fact its penultimate line; it is followed by "GOD bless you, our country and the Queen" (243).

2. *NCBWA Correspondence*, 51.
3. Colley, *The Gun, the Ship, and the Pen*, 12.
4. Taiwo, *How Colonialism Preempted Modernity in Africa*, 186.
5. *NCBWA Correspondence*, 47.
6. *NCBWA Correspondence*, 43.
7. *NCBWA Correspondence*, 50.
8. Sedley, "Cloudy Horizon"; Loughlin, "Constitutionalism."
9. Stark, "Nenabozho's Smart Berries," 347–48.
10. This is in contrast to the most common twentieth-century critical story of how novels are foundational to nationhood, which suggests that the nation, like all social commonalities, is constructed by being "smuggled in," so to speak, by fiction. The ur-text for this way of thinking about the novel as a tool for enforcing national affinity is Benedict Anderson's 1983 book *Imagined Communities*. As Jonathan Culler explains in a useful essay called "Anderson and the Novel," Anderson's interest in ways of depicting lives lived separately but bound together makes the novel one of his favorite objects of analysis. The most famous technique he elaborates for doing this is the "meanwhile," or the ability of an omniscient narrator to show readers what different characters are doing at the same time.
11. McIlwain, *Constitutionalism*, 7.
12. Tully, *Strange Multiplicity*, 60.
13. Aristotle's constitutional categories are laid out most famously in his *Politics*, but his approach to political constitution by way of historical narrative is typified by *The Constitution of the Athenians* (sometimes translated as *The Constitution of Athens*, or *The Athenian Constitution*, and possibly also authored by one of his students). The most famous analysis of US constitutional character is probably Bruce Ackerman's, whose exposition of what he calls "constitutional moments" presents constitutional change as something that occurs over time through the judicial synthesis of intended guiding principles, at key moments of social coalescence around their contestation. See his 1993 book *Foundations*, the first volume of his trilogy *We the People*, as well as Michael W. McConnell's extremely helpful response essay, "The Forgotten Constitutional Moment."
14. In addition to McIlwain, see Giovanni Sartori's much-cited essay "Constitutionalism."
15. Taiwo, *How Colonialism Preempted Modernity in Africa*, 208.
16. *NCBWA Correspondence*, 50
17. J. E. Casely Hayford, *Ethiopia Unbound*, 151.
18. *Ethiopia Unbound*, 8.
19. Casely-Hayford, "Genealogical History of Cape Coast Stool Families," 290.
20. Editorial Notes section, 2.
21. Colley, *The Gun, the Ship, and the Pen*, 10.
22. On the historical porousness of customary legal systems throughout British Africa, see T. Olawale Elias's seminal *The Nature of African Customary Law* from 1956, specifically its chapter "Impact of English Law upon African Law." As he reviews key elements of various customary systems, Elias moves freely between the terms of

English legal conventions' "absorption" by Africa and the idea that "the African was already familiar" with many of them "under his own customary law" (283).

23. McIlwain, *Constitutionalism*, 16.

24. Writing on this topic is too abundant to survey here, but see, foundationally, Arthur R. Hogue's 1966 book *Origins of the Common Law*. It is also interesting, per J. B. Danquah's 1957 speech-turned-essay "The Historical Significance of the Bond of 1844," that numerous scholars of Gold Coast history have likened that jurisdictional agreement (in his view, wrongly) to the Magna Carta.

25. Aravind and Sítigh, "Constitutionalism in the Periphery," 217.

26. Casely-Hayford, "Genealogical History of Cape Coast Stool Families," 290.

27. *NCBWA Correspondence*, 27.

28. Taiwo, *How Colonialism Preempted Modernity in Africa*, 209, 211.

29. Taiwo, *How Colonialism Preempted Modernity in Africa*, 210. Article 4 stipulates the election of Confederation officers (president, vice president, secretary, undersecretary, treasurer, and assistant treasurer), and Article 5 that "the president be elected from the body of kings, and be proclaimed king-president of the Fanti Confederation."

30. Casely-Hayford, "Genealogical History of Cape Coast Stool Families," 290.

31. Willemse, *Foundational African Writers*, xiv.

32. Willemse, *Foundational African Writers*, 293.

33. *NCBWA Correspondence*, 26.

34. Sarbah, *Fanti National Constitution*, viii.

35. Sarbah, *Fanti National Constitution*, xx.

36. Taiwo, *How Colonialism Preempted Modernity in Africa*, 206.

37. Aravind and Mac Síthigh, "Constitutionalism in the Periphery," 215.

38. Taiwo, *How Colonialism Preempted Modernity in Africa*, 209.

39. Moretti, "Conjectures on World Literature."

40. Even his second wife, Adelaide Smith, lends weight to this reading. She describes him as possessing "the finesse of English gentlemen" compared with most "African" suitors (Cromwell, *African Victorian Feminist*, 64).

41. September 15, 1897, issue of the *Gold Coast Methodist Times*, 2.

42. Coller, "African Liberalism in the Age of Empire?," 530.

43. As one strong example of this approach, see DiGiacomo "Assertion of Coevalness."

44. Sarbah, *Fanti National Constitution*, 236.

45. Hogue, *Origins of the Common Law*, 9.

46. Jacobsohn, *Constitutional Identity*, 4.

47. Gordon, "Growing Constitutions," 530.

48. Gebeye, *Theory of African Constitutionalism*, 1.

49. Gebeye, *Theory of African Constitutionalism*, 10.

50. Gebeye, *Theory of African Constitutionalism*, 10.

51. Archie Casely Hayford, "Man and His Work," 10.

52. Colley, *The Gun, the Ship, and the Pen*, 12.

53. Cromwell, *African Victorian Feminist*, 68.

54. *Ethiopia Unbound*, 35.

55. Pitkin, "Idea of a Constitution," 168.

56. Ackerman, *Revolutionary Constitutions*, 2.
57. Taiwo, *How Colonialism Preempted Modernity in Africa*, 122, 157, 170.
58. Loughlin, "Constitutional Imagination," 3.
59. Loughlin, "Constitutional Imagination," 4.
60. Loughlin, "Concept of Constituent Power," 221.
61. Taiwo, *How Colonialism Preempted Modernity in Africa*, 204, italics added.
62. *Ethiopia Unbound*, 45.
63. *Ethiopia Unbound*, 45.
64. *Ethiopia Unbound*, 7–8.
65. Casely-Hayford, "Genealogical History of Cape Coast Stool Families," 16.
66. Agbodeka, "Fanti Confederacy," 87.
67. Agbodeka, "Fanti Confederacy," 89–90.
68. Agbodeka explains Ghartey's position thus: "To the office of the king-president the Fantis elected King Ghartey, who thus became President of the Confederate Court (Dec. 1868) and enjoyed supreme power in the nation. Ghartey resided in Mankessim, the traditional capital of Fantiland, where we find cases being referred to his court. This does not merely show us how the judiciary worked but is also proof positive of the untainted loyalty Ghartey enjoyed as a Fanti magistrate. Ghartey's office did not bear the title of the head of state of the entire Fantiland, but in the estimation of the Fantis he was nothing other than that" ("Fanti Confederacy," 117).
69. Bakhtin makes this argument in his essay "Epic and Novel," originally published in Russian in 1941, and in English in Caryl Emerson and Michael Holquist's 1975 collection *The Dialogic Imagination: Four Essays by M. M. Bakhtin*.
70. Tribe, "Idea of the Constitution," 173.
71. As Adwoa Opoku-Agyemang and I write in our introduction to *Ethiopia Unbound*, "One printed program from the period, which advertises 'Dances, Conversation, Musical Games, Speeches & Toasts, Theatrical Performances,' puts [literary clubs'] profile-raising function in bold relief. The card accords as much space to listing the upcoming events as to naming the club's twelve patrons, and places Casely Hayford directly after His Excellency the Governor and the Provincial Commissioner. In a different document dated 11th April 1921, the Cape Coast Literary and Social Club requests the use of the Government Gardens from the Commissioner of the Central Province: they would like to organize a reception to celebrate the safe return from England of 'the Honourable Casely Hayford, M.B.E., Barrister-at-Law and [Patron] of our Club'" (xxii–xxiii).
72. *Ethiopia Unbound*, 7–16.
73. I have already written at length about the shortcomings of and alternatives to reading *Ethiopia Unbound* mainly as "unconventional" or non-novelistic. See chapter 1, "*Ethiopia Unbound* as Afro-Comparatist Novel," in *African Novel of Ideas*.
74. *Ethiopia Unbound*, 147.
75. *Ethiopia Unbound*, 83.
76. *Ethiopia Unbound*, 136.
77. Okoth-Ogendo's 1988 paper "Constitutions without Constitutionalism: Reflections on an African Political Paradox" was first delivered at a conference in the United States in 1988 and has been republished many times since. But the title phrase is in much wider use and predates Okoth-Ogendo's intervention. Political theorist Shannon Stimson sums its common use up as follows in her *Oxford Handbook of Political*

Theory chapter "Constitutionalism and the Rule of Law": "On this view, without a commitment to limited government, which is then identified as government under rule of law . . . a state might be said to have a constitution in the mechanical sense of offices and administration, but lack *constitutionalism*" (323).

78. Ackerman, *Revolutionary Constitutions*, 28.
79. *Ethiopia Unbound*, 135.
80. *Ethiopia Unbound*, 136.
81. *Ethiopia Unbound*, 142.
82. *Ethiopia Unbound*, 143.
83. *Ethiopia Unbound*, 89.
84. Prempeh, "Africa's 'Constitutionalism Revival,'" 473.
85. *Ethiopia Unbound*, 125.
86. Aristotle's quintessential exposition of the restrained, moderating figure of the judge is from Book 5 of the *Nicomachean Ethics*. Aristotle writes there, "This is why, when people dispute, they take refuge in the judge; and to go to the judge is to go to justice; for the nature of the judge is to be a sort of animate justice; and they seek the judge as an intermediate, and in some states they call judges mediators, on the assumption that if they get what is intermediate they will get what is just. The just, then, is an intermediate, since the judge is so."
87. Dworkin, *Law's Empire*, 239, 240.
88. Dworkin, *Law's Empire*, 245.
89. Michelman, "Constitutional Authorship by the People," 1617.
90. Michelman, "Constitutional Authorship by the People," 1628.
91. Tribe, "Idea of the Constitution," 172.
92. Pitkin, "Idea of a Constitution," 168.
93. Pitkin, "Idea of a Constitution," 168.
94. Ackerman, *Revolutionary Constitutions*, 8.
95. I use Archibald Casely Hayford's first name in this chapter not as a sign of an overly casual bearing toward his work, but in order to avoid what would otherwise be unavoidable confusion with the elder Casely Hayford.
96. Archie Casely Hayford, "Man and His Work," 22.
97. Archie Casely Hayford, "Man and His Work," 26.
98. Archie Casely Hayford, "Man and His Work," 37.
99. Archie Casely Hayford, "Man and His Work," 38–39.
100. Ofosu-Appiah, *Joseph Ephraim Casely Hayford*, 21, 24.
101. Ofosu-Appiah, *Joseph Ephraim Casely Hayford*, 24.
102. *Ethiopia Unbound*, 119.
103. "Our Confession of Faith," *Gold Coast Nation*, April 18. 1912.
104. Interestingly, Ofosu-Appiah even classifies *Ethiopia Unbound* as being among Casely Hayford's "main scholarly works" in *Joseph Ephraim Casely Hayford* (9).
105. J. E. Casely Hayford, *Native Institutions*, 105–6.
106. J. E. Casely Hayford, *William Waddy Harris*, 10.
107. *William Waddy Harris*, 6–7.
108. Shank, "Prophet Harris," 174.
109. *William Waddy Harris*, 5.
110. *William Waddy Harris*, 5.

111. *William Waddy Harris*, 6.

112. *William Waddy Harris*, 6.

113. The scholarship on Taylor's version of disenchantment alone is truly voluminous, to say nothing of Weber's or Kant's. Extensive debate on the topic—including where Africa and the postcolonial world are concerned—can easily be found with keyword searches on the Social Science Research Council's blog the *Immanent Frame*, which is devoted entirely to questions of secularism and religion. The notion of the buffered self is developed most prominently in Taylor's 2007 book *A Secular Age*, and it is also summarized nicely in a short 2008 essay for the *Immanent Frame*, "Buffered and Porous Selves."

114. Lennon, "Essay, in Theory," 71, 73, 83.

115. *William Waddy Harris*, 8–9.

116. *William Waddy Harris*, 10.

117. *William Waddy Harris*, 10.

118. *William Waddy Harris*, 11.

119. *William Waddy Harris*, 12.

120. Shank, "Prophet Harris," 130.

121. *Ethiopia Unbound*, 17; *William Waddy Harris*, 12, italics added.

122. "Kwame Nkrumah, who had led the Gold Coast (Ghana) to become sub-Saharan Africa's first sovereign state, famously disparaged Africa's independence constitutions as neocolonial devices designed to ensure 'the preservation of imperial interests in the newly emergent state.' Specifically, Nkrumah identified 'constitutional rigidity' (the 'obnoxious entrenched clauses'), 'political separatism' (Nkrumaism for the limited constitutional role reserved for regional assemblies), and 'a civil service apparatus insulated from the new political power' as key features of Africa's independence constitutions that had been designed (as 'schisms') to impede 'speedy development.' Rejection of the independence constitution was, therefore, to be regarded as 'the starting point in the process of consolidation [of the people's power].' In line with this political diagnosis, the gist of which was shared by Nkrumah's peers in other newly sovereign African states, postcolonial Africa's first constitutions were soon replaced by constitutions designed to suit the instrumental needs of particular regimes. Between 1960 and 1962 thirteen newly independent African states, beginning with Ghana, amended or replaced their independence constitutions." From Prempeh, "Africa's 'Constitutionalism Revival,'" 474. Ghana's constitution was revisited four times since its first version at independence in 1957, most recently in 1992, partly amid a succession of coups between 1966 and the end of military rule in 1992.

123. Prempeh has in fact been one of the Ghanaian scholars to level this accusation. See his op-ed "Have We Traded Our Republic for a Theocracy?" on the Ghanaian news and commentary site myjoyonline, February 23, 2021, https://myjoyonline.com/h-kwasi-prempeh-have-we-traded-our-republic-for-a-theocracy/. On Pentecostalism in Ghana broadly, see, for example, Meyer, "Going and Making Public."

Chapter Three. The Jurisdiction of Morals

1. J. E. Casely Hayford, *West African Leadership*, 67.

2. *West African Leadership*, 75. Though its authorship is anonymous, the Editorial Notes of the March 4, 1911, issue of the *Gold Coast Leader*, of which Casely Hayford

was editor, had expressed a similar concern. "'West African Readers' is a misnomer," one note reads. "We have no common nomenclature for the Gold Coast, Sierra Leone, Lagos and the Gambia."

3. *West African Leadership*, 75.

4. Ebony Coletu, in her chapter "Pan-African Logistics" in *Assembly Codes*, adopts a similar approach to theorizing the relationship between returned members of the Black diaspora and their Gold Coast hosts around 1915. She writes, "Understanding the Pan-African imagination in this [logistical] light reveals a contingent set of experimental propositions exploring the fit between distinct spheres of law" (67).

5. Cormack, *Power to Do Justice*, 7.

6. Reindorf, *History of the Gold Coast and Asante*, 44.

7. In *Writing Ghana, Imagining Africa*, Korang describes Casely Hayford as part of "an African middle class discovering, relative to its own native sphere of belonging, its alienated messenger status" (178).

8. The point at which we can properly begin to speak of a unified "Fante" polity is controversial and a subject of ongoing debate among historians of the region, with 1844 a strong contender.

9. Konadu, "Euro-African Commerce and Social Chaos," 266.

10. A prominent example of this is the Ndebele King Lobengula, who signed away the exclusive mining rights to his land to Cecil Rhodes' British South Africa Company in the Rudd Concession of 1888. Lobengula claimed after the fact that he had been deceived as to the terms of the agreement, which is now widely seen as having paved the way for Rhodesia's founding.

11. Danquah, "Historical Significance," 5.

12. Danquah, "Historical Significance," 6.

13. Danquah, "Historical Significance," 3. Danquah's role in Ghanaian history has been a topic of renewed controversy in recent years, and I do not wish to wade into debates over his symbolic use in party politics there. It is interesting, nonetheless, in the context of this chapter that they have centered on the degree of Danquah's involvement in the founding of the University of Ghana, and by extension on the question of whether he is the rightful inheritor of the Casely Hayford generation's educationist legacy. At an event marking the 75th anniversary of the university's founding in 2023, Ghana's President Nana Akufo-Addo paid tribute to Danquah as its "founder" and floated the idea—not for the first time—that the University of Ghana might be renamed in his honor. This did not go over well with many members of the Ghanaian public, not least because Danquah was Akufo-Addo's maternal uncle. For one among many write-ups of the speech in Ghanaian media at the time, see "What Akufo-Addo Actually Said about Renaming UG after JB Danquah that's Got People Talking," *GhanaWeb*, August 14, 2023, https://www.ghanaweb.com/GhanaHomePage/NewsArchive/What-Akufo-Addo-actually-said-about-renaming-UG-after-JB-Danquah-that-s-got-people-talking-1824287.

14. Danquah, "Historical Significance," 3.

15. Danquah, "Historical Significance," 7. He also specifies, "Quite roughly, we may distinguish a charter from a bond in this way. A charter grants rights and liberties from a sovereign or other authority to those in need of them; a bond, on the other hand, binds a person in need to another, who is in a superior position, to secure the need." The Fante "need" in this case is for protection.

16. Shumway, "Palavers and Treaty-Making," 168–69.
17. Shumway, "Palavers and Treaty-Making," 176.
18. Danquah, "Historical Significance," 7.
19. Shumway, "Palavers and Treaty-Making," 173.
20. Shumway, "Palavers and Treaty-Making," 175.
21. Shumway, "Palavers and Treaty-Making," 180.
22. Shumway, "Palavers and Treaty-Making," 179.
23. Danquah, "Historical Significance," 3.
24. J. E. Casely Hayford, *West African Land Question*, 153.
25. For a more detailed explanation of how this system worked as well as British misunderstandings of it, see, for example, Olufemi Omosini's essay "The Gold Coast Land Question."
26. An unsigned editorial in the *Gold Coast Methodist Times* on September 30, 1897—likely written by the paper's editor S.R.B. Attoh Ahuma—captures this broad tenor. Titled "Not In Vain," it states on page 2 of that issue: "Still the Land Bill starts upon an assumption. It takes for granted, without any warrant whatsoever, that the Lands in this Country are Public Lands. This is a delusion and a snare. There is no such thing. Every foot of land has an owner, any law that proceeds on the hypothesis that such is not the case, is doomed to everlasting destruction." A second editorial in the paper, "Quite Unconvincing," was published under the pseudonym "One of *Scholars Like These*" on October 15, 1897. On page 3 of that issue, the unnamed scholar writes, "Reading Governor Maxwell's reply to the speeches delivered by Counsel the feeling one has is, that it is very unsatisfactory. Though an able speech, it is extremely remarkable for the several points passed over in silence."
27. While *The Truth about the West African Land Question* is his major work on this perennially contentious issue, he also published a shorter, more targeted pamphlet in London in 1912 called *Gold Coast Land Tenure and the Forest Bill, 1911: A Review of the Situation*.
28. Omosini, "Gold Coast Land Question," 467.
29. J. E. Casely Hayford, *Land Question*, 55.
30. *Land Question*, 57–58.
31. *Land Question*, 10, italics added.
32. *Land Question*, 10.
33. *Land Question*, 13, 14.
34. The most prominent of these other factors as far as the Lands Bill defeat was concerned was the 1898 Hut Tax War in Sierra Leone. The war was in fact a series of linked efforts to resist British attempts to tax Sierra Leoneans based on the size of their huts, after unilaterally declaring Sierra Leone a protectorate. Twenty-four chiefs signed a treaty protesting the tax before the resistance became violent, but it went unheeded by British authorities. The British were also dealing with escalating tensions in its South African territories, which led ultimately to the Second Boer War in 1899. They could not afford another serious military engagement on the African continent.
35. *Land Question*, 158.
36. A different editorial in the same issue of the *Gold Coast Nation* muses somewhat smugly, "It must have been a revelation to Mr. Belfield [Henry Conway, a

colonial administrator] when he attended the reception of our Natural Rulers in the famous yard of Cape Coast Castle." A similar kind of confidence pervades the *Gold Coast Leader* around the same period, for example, in the editor's (probably Casely Hayford's) breezy invocations of labor-intensive reading that he *might* easily have done but has chosen not to. In an Editorial Notes column on October 12, 1912, he writes, "In South Africa the question [of Black and White in Africa] has been for some years very prominently before the public and is now the most serious problem the South African Government has in hand. We have not the space at our disposal, even if we have the inclination, to trace the growth of the question in South Africa." A response in the same issue to a patronizing open letter by British journalist E. D. Morel likewise declares, "It is not our intention in this article to go over item for item, and chapter by chapter the various questions which Mr. Morel discussed in the letter to his African friend and to challenge question for question Mr. Morel in his views." The editors, in other words, were learned enough that they *could* do this but instead exercised their better judgment in narrowing their polemical focus.

37. *Native Institutions*, 160.

38. *Land Question*, 34. The proposed shift from judicial to executive oversight of land concessions was seen as catastrophic because Casely Hayford and many of his countrymen had strong faith in the fairness of British judges—who in theory worked in concert with African lawyers and chiefs—as opposed to government officials.

39. *Land Question*, 34–35.

40. Taiwo, *How Colonialism Preempted Modernity in Africa*, 203.

41. Mawani, *Across Oceans of Law*, 14.

42. Valverde, "Jurisdiction and Scale," 143, 145.

43. *Native Institutions*, 160.

44. Bennett and Layard, "Legal Geography," 414.

45. Margaret D. Rouse-Jones and Esther M. Appiah offer an efficient summary of the situation in their impressive biography of the Gold Coast lawyer George James Christian, who succeeded Casely Hayford in the Gold Coast Legislative Council. "The Commissioners' Courts of the Ashanti were established in 1901 by the ordinance of the governor of the Gold Coast," they explain, "and not by the Legislative Council of the Gold Coast" (*Returned Exile*, 118). Many Gold Coast lawyers, including Christian, saw the absence of jury trials in Asante as a grave injustice, because "the officer hearing a case [there] could examine, cross-examine and re-examine a witness for the prosecution and defence. The accused would then be asked to make a statement. The effect of this was that the judicial officer acted as the police, judge, jury, counsel for the prosecution and counsel for the defence" (121). The NCBWA's official correspondence provides further testament to Casely Hayford's moral endorsement of this particular British legal norm. The Congress wrote collectively in a 1920 memorandum to the Crown, "It claims the right in all cases for Africans to be defended by Counsel as British citizens, and abhors the method of being tried and convicted without being represented by Counsel" (*NCBWA Correspondence*, 34).

46. Cormack, *Power to Do Justice*, 3.

47. Cormack, *Power to Do Justice*, 4, 7.

48. J. E. Casely Hayford, *West African Leadership*, 24.

49. Cormack, *Power to Do Justice*, 22.

50. This is from Casely Hayford's Presidential Address at the NCBWA's third convention, held in the Gambia in December 1925, printed in *West African Leadership*, 80. He also champions African scientific education in the same speech, observing, "There is no reason why we, as Africans, should not also harness the discoveries of Science to our everyday need and make them productive of Wealth and prosperity within our own borders" (79).

51. J. E. Casely Hayford, *Ethiopia Unbound*, 79.

52. Cormack, *Power to Do Justice*, 5–6.

53. Cormack, *Power to Do Justice*, 10.

54. Benton, *Law and Colonial Cultures*, 10.

55. Benton, *Law and Colonial Cultures*, 2.

56. Benton, *Law and Colonial Cultures*, 5.

57. J. E. Casely Hayford, *Native Institutions*, 160.

58. Benton, *Law and Colonial Cultures*, 8.

59. There is, however, one small mystery surrounding Casely Hayford's time at the Inner Temple. On Tuesday, August 14, 1896, he is noted in its archives as having petitioned for "a dispensation of two terms with permission to be called in Easter Term, he desiring to return to the Gold Coast on account of the health of his mother and private affairs." His petition was not granted, and no reason is provided.

60. Ford, "Law's Territory," 859, 860.

61. Ford, "Law's Territory," 862.

62. Ford, "Law's Territory," 862.

63. Ford, "Law's Territory," 905.

64. Ford, "Law's Territory," 904.

65. *Ethiopia Unbound*, x.

66. Chanock, *Law, Custom and Social Order*, 225.

67. Mamdani, *Define and Rule*, 3.

68. For a rich discussion of Maine's career and the broad shift away from liberalism to what Karuna Mantena calls a "culturalist" imperial ideology in the late nineteenth century, see Mantena, *Alibis of Empire*.

69. Mamdani, *Define and Rule*, 6–7.

70. For one full-fledged working-through of the contrasts and convergences between these two terms, see Françoise Lionnet's essay "Cosmopolitan or Creole Lives?" In it, she writes, "As a proper noun, Creole refers to a well-defined if not exactly static cultural and linguistic identity (on the model of *French* or *English* as proper nouns, which identify both a national culture and its language). As both common noun and adjective, *cosmopolitan*, by contrast, suggests an orientation and an attitude, a habitus and a conscious ethical stance against the limitations of radical territorialism" (27).

71. Lionnet, "Cosmopolitan or Creole Lives?," 27.

72. Griffith, "Some Account," 329. Griffith's explanation for colonization recalls the reasoning behind the Bond of 1844, albeit with a result of regional political siloing that set the stage for Casely Hayford's efforts to forge regional connection in the following decades. "[The Ashanti War of 1873] was really in defence of the coast tribes," Griffith recounts, "and in order to protect these tribes efficiently it was necessary to bestow upon the local government ample and unassailable administrative and judicial

powers. With this aim in view the Gold Coast was severed from Sierra Leone, and, with Lagos joined to it, was by charter dated July 24, 1874, erected into a separate colony now for the first time styled The Gold Coast Colony."

73. Griffith, "Some Account," 326.

74. As political scientist Donald I. Ray describes it, "The 1883 Native Jurisdiction Ordinance (Gold Coast Colony) of the colonial state allowed paramount chiefs, or headchiefs as they were then termed, and their councils to have the option of making bylaws dealing with such local government functions as the building and maintenance of roads, forest conservation, the prevention and abatement of nuisances, the provision of burial grounds, and the regulation of burials. The governor had the ability to disallow bylaws not in keeping with the colonial state's laws and policies." Ray, "Ghana."

75. Addo-Fening, "Colonial Government," 136.

76. An amendment to the Native Jurisdiction Ordinance in 1910 "extended the civil jurisdiction of native Tribunals to include all suits relating to divorce under native customary law, establishment of children born outside marriage and custody of children" (Addo-Fening, "Colonial Government," 141).

77. Gocking, "British Justice and the Native Tribunals," 95.

78. Gocking, "British Justice and the Native Tribunals," 96.

79. Gocking's extended discussion of what this meant under indirect rule—essentially, that native tribunals could be used to generate cash, while incarceration entailed cash outlay—is significant for the continued division of criminal/civil along British/African lines. "Indeed until the 1930s," he writes, "when the better-organized native states were able to introduce regular taxation and establish treasuries, there were major limits as to how much Native Tribunals could function as instrumentals of criminal adjudication." This is despite the fact that "the Ordinance made an important concession to African sensibilities by including 'seduction', 'slander', 'fetishism', and 'witchcraft' as criminal offenses" that could theoretically be tried under customary law ("British Justice and the Native Tribunals," 99, 97).

80. Joseph K. Adjaye offers a compact but detailed account of Prempeh's exile and return in his essay "Agyeman Prempe I and British Colonization of Asante."

81. For a fuller explanation of this position, as part of a full appraisal of Guggisberg's Gold Coast career, see Agbodeka, "Sir Gordon Guggisberg's Contribution," 63.

82. Mamdani, *Define and Rule*, 2.

83. *Land Question*, 67.

84. See "Persona," Law Dictionary, https://thelawdictionary.org/persona/; *Land Question*, 67.

85. *Land Question*, 70.

86. Morel's most famous texts are the investigative tract *Red Rubber: The Story of the Rubber Slave Trade on the Congo* (1906), which makes an early case for humanitarian intervention, and *The Black Man's Burden: The White Man in Africa from the Fifteenth Century to World War I* (1920).

87. *Land Question*, preface, unpaginated.

88. *Land Question*, preface, unpaginated.

89. *Land Question*, 7.

90. *Land Question*, 8.

91. *Land Question*, 20.

92. *Land Question*, 36.
93. *Land Question*, 37.
94. *Land Question*, 37.
95. *Land Question*, 40.
96. *Land Question*, 41.
97. *Land Question*, 41, 43, 46.
98. *Land Question*, 41.
99. *Land Question*, 42.
100. *Land Question*, 45.
101. Kramnick, *Criticism and Truth*, 33.
102. Kramnick, *Criticism and Truth*, 32.
103. Kramnick, *Criticism and Truth*, 40.
104. *Land Question*, 39.
105. *Land Question*, 39.
106. Younis, *On the Scale of the World*, 49, 51.
107. Younis, *On the Scale of the World*, 58.
108. Younis, *On the Scale of the World*, 59.
109. Beginning his study in the 1840s and working up to the middle of the twentieth century, Palen describes his "motley crew of left-wing free traders" as "the leading globalists of their age, in contrast to the ring-wing free-market advocacy more commonly associated with globalism's champions today" (4). Casely Hayford shared this basic idea that free trade should be a bedrock of economic partnership and equality, though his contention in *Land Question* that Gold Coast timber reserves were, "for all practical purposes," inexhaustible has not necessarily stood the test of time (46). The book's criticism of British imperial half-measures has fared better. "Yes," Casely Hayford writes, "when the Government will have provided the Gold Coast with good roads and canals, subsidiary lines of railway to connect trunk lines, and in other ways to overcome the practical question of transport, so as to make it possible for cutters to exploit the timber; areas yet untouched, it may be time enough then, if necessary, to consider the passing of laws for the preservation of Gold Coast timber" (50).
110. As the major example, see Peterson, Hunter, and Newell, *African Print Cultures*.
111. Younis, *On the Scale of the World*, 62.
112. Appiah, *Honor Code*, 16.
113. Younis, *On the Scale of the World*, 58.
114. Danquah, *Akan Doctrine of God*, 121. Danquah is extrapolating here from an Akan proverb, given as "A thing of dishonour and a son of the Akan go ill together," which he also cites in Fante as "*Enyimguase mmfata Okanyi*" (120). This translates literally as "Disgrace does not suit an Akan."
115. Danquah, *Akan Doctrine of God*, 120.
116. Danquah, *Akan Doctrine of God*, 120, 121.
117. Danquah, *Akan Doctrine of God*, 124.
118. Miescher, *Making Men in Ghana*, 154.
119. Miescher, *Making Men in Ghana*, 153. It nonetheless seems worth it to add that whenever I described my work on Casely Hayford to my Fante teacher as I began research for this book, he corrected me by adding the word *opanyin* before his name.

120. *Land Question*, 91.

121. *Land Question*, 91.

122. A younger, respectable man would in Fante be called an *abrantie*, also typically translated as gentleman.

123. Sussman, "Stylistic Virtue," 228. I quote from Sussman's essay here, which is admirably concise and sufficient for my needs in adapting it for use outside its archival context. But Sussman also develops its argument at greater length in his 2021 book *Stylistic Virtue and Victorian Fiction*.

124. Sussman, "Stylistic Virtue," 228, 229.

125. Danquah, *Akan Doctrine of God*, 123.

126. Sussman, "Stylistic Virtue," 245.

127. Sussman, "Stylistic Virtue," 231.

128. Sussman, "Stylistic Virtue," 241.

129. *Land Question*, 48, 49.

130. *Land Question*, 73.

131. *Land Question*, 83.

132. *Land Question*, 84.

133. *Land Question*, 91.

Epilogue: Where in the World Is J. E. Casely Hayford?

1. A full description of the exhibition and its multi-national origins can be found here: "Building Africa," January 11–March 16, 2024, SOAS University of London, https://www.soas.ac.uk/about/event/building-africa.

2. For more on Mfantsipim's founding amid the Gone Fante movement and ARPS activities, see Tenkorang, "Founding of Mfantsipim." The Mfantsipim curriculum is presented in full in a promotional brochure for the school published sometime between 1925 (the start date of a campaign to raise new building funds) and 1930 (the projected date of new building completion).

3. Its annual report from 1928 lists classes offered in Twi, Fante, Ga, and Ewe, as well as the number of staff with proficiency in each. Fante led the pack, unsurprisingly given its institutional pedigree.

4. Samalin, "Introduction," 426.

5. See Rathbone, *Nkrumah and the Chiefs*.

6. For a detailed and scrupulous discussion of the pitfalls of Ghana's hybrid (American- and British-style) constitutional system, see Van Gyampo and Graham, "Constitutionalism and Constitutional Hybridity in Ghana."

7. Prempeh, "Africa's 'Constitutional Revival,'" 474.

8. For a brief overview of scandals within just the current Ghanaian presidential administration, at the time of this epilogue's writing, see Delali Adogla-Bessa, "How Ghana's President Went from Democratic Darling to Anti-protest Overlord," OpenDemocracy, October 27, 2023, https://www.opendemocracy.net/en/how-ghanas-president-went-from-democratic-darling-to-anti-protest-overlord/. The remark about home decor, I should add, does not accidentally use the wrong preposition ("as" rather than "for"). In 2023, Ghana's Minister of Sanitation and Water Resources (and former Member of Parliament) Cecilia Dapaah was arrested for

hiding $1,000,000 and hundreds of thousands of euros in various odd spots around her home, as well as extraordinarily expensive jewelry and handbag collections.

9. Jeffrey Ahlman's work is exemplary on this front, especially his recent *Ghana: A Political and Social History*. In helping students of African history to understand the profound social destabilization wrought by military rule in the 1960s and 1970s, I often turn to former Ghanaian president John Dramani Mahama's memoir *My First Coup d'Etat*, in which Achimota also figures prominently.

10. The Volta River Authority, or VRA, is Ghana's most famous hydroelectric dam and primary source of electricity, built in 1961 to great fanfare.

11. Casely-Hayford's official brand website is here: https://casely-hayford.com. And Charlie Casely-Hayford's reflections on the Casely-Hayford brand across generations can be heard on the following podcast episodes: "Charlie Casely-Hayford on Modern Craft and High-Low Culture," HandCut Radio, June 30, 2021, https://podcasts.apple.com/fr/podcast/charlie-casely-hayford-on-modern-craft-and-high-low/id1458320520?i=1000527323537; and "Charlie Casely-Hayford on Imperfection and Maximalism," Modern House Podcast, July 9, 2020, https://www.themodernhouse.com/journal/charlie-casely-hayford-the-modern-house-podcast/.

12. Lanre Bakare, "V&A East Director to Cycle to 250 London Schools to Encourage Pupil Visits," *Guardian*, June 30, 2021, https://www.theguardian.com/artanddesign/2021/jun/30/v-and-a-east-director-cycle-london-schools-museum-inclusivity-gus-casely-hayford.

WORKS CITED

Ackerman, Bruce. *Revolutionary Constitutions*. Cambridge, MA: Belknap, 2019.
Ackerman, Bruce. *We the People*. Vol. 1, Foundations. Cambridge, MA: Belknap, 1991.
Addo-Fening, R. "Colonial Government, Chiefs, and 'Native' Jurisdiction in the Gold Coast Colony 1822–1928." *Universitas* 10 (1988): 133–51.
Adjaye, Joseph K. "Agyeman Prempe I and British Colonization of Asante: A Reassessment." *International Journal of African Historical Studies* 22.2 (1989): 223–49.
Agbodeka, Francis. "The Fanti Confederacy 1865–69: An Enquiry into the Origins, Nature and Extent of an Early West African Protest Movement." *Transactions of the Historical Society of Ghana* 7.1 (1964): 82–123.
Agbodeka, Francis. "Sir Gordon Guggisberg's Contribution to the Development of the Gold Coast, 1919–27." *Transactions of the Historical Society of Ghana* 13.1 (1972): 51–64.
Ahlman, Jeffrey. *Ghana: A Political and Social History*. London: Zed Books, 2023.
Anderson, Amanda. *The Powers of Distance: Cosmopolitanism and the Cultivation of Detachment*. Princeton, NJ: Princeton University Press, 2001.
Appiah, Kwame Anthony. *Cosmopolitanism: Ethics in a World of Strangers*. New York: Norton, 2007.
Appiah, Kwame Anthony. *The Honor Code*. New York: Norton, 2010.
Aravind, T. T., and Daithí Mac Sítigh. "Constitutionalism in the Periphery: Revisiting the Roots of Self-Rule Movements in Ireland and India." *Northern Ireland Legal Quarterly* 71.2 (2020): 211–37.
Arhin, Kwame. "Rank and Class among the Asante and Fante in the Nineteenth Century." *Africa* 53.1 (1983): 2–22.
Aristotle. *The Athenian Constitution*. Translated by Sir Frederic G. Kenyon. https://classics.mit.edu/Aristotle/athenian_const.1.1.html
Aristotle. *Nichomachean Ethics*. Translated by W. D. Ross. Book 5. https://classics.mit.edu/Aristotle/nicomachaen.5.v.html.
Asante, S.K.B. "The Neglected Aspects of the Activities of the Gold Coast Aborigines Rights Protection Society." *Phylon* 36.1 (1975): 32–45.
Attoh Ahuma, S.R.B. *The Gold Coast Nation and National Consciousness*. London: Routledge, 2006. First published 1911.
Attoh Ahuma, S.R.B. *Memoirs of West African Celebrities: Europe & c., 1700–1850, With Special Reference to the Gold Coast* Liverpool: D. Marples, 1905.
Bakari, Lanre. "V&A East Director to Cycle to 250 London Schools to Encourage Pupil Visits." *Guardian*, June 30, 2021.
Bakhtin, Mikhail. *The Dialogic Imagination: Four Essays*. Translated by Caryl Emerson and Michael Holquist. Austin: University of Texas Press, 1981.
Barber, Karin. *Africa's Hidden Histories: Everyday Literacy and Making the Self*. Bloomington: Indiana University Press, 2006.
Bennett, Luke, and Antonia Layard. "Legal Geography: Becoming Spatial Detectives." *Geography Compass* 9.7 (2015): 406–22.

Benton, Lauren. *Law and Colonial Cultures: Legal Regimes in World History, 1400–1900*. Cambridge: Cambridge University Press, 2001.

Benton, Lauren, and Lisa Ford. *Rage for Order: The British Empire and the Origins of International Law, 1800–1850*. Cambridge, MA: Harvard University Press, 2016.

Blyden, Edward W. "West African Problems." In *West Africa before Europe, and Other Addresses, Delivered in England in 1901 and 1903*. London: C. M. Philips, 1905.

Brizuela-Garcia, Esperanza. "Cosmopolitanism: Why Nineteenth Century Gold Coast Thinkers Matter in the Twenty-First Century." *Ghana Studies* 17 (2014): 203–21.

Burbank, Jane, and Frederick Cooper. *Post-Imperial Possibilities: Eurasia, Eurafrica, Afroasia*. Princeton, NJ: Princeton University Press, 2023.

Casely Hayford, Archie. "Casely Hayford: The Man and His Work." Unpublished, 1935.

Casely-Hayford, Augustus. "A Genealogical History of Cape Coast Stool Families." PhD diss., SOAS University of London, 1992.

Casely-Hayford, Augustus. "Prosopographical Approaches to Fante History." *History in Africa* 18 (1991): 49–66.

Casely-Hayford, Augustus, and Richard Rathbone. "Politics, Families and Freemasonry in the Colonial Gold Coast." In *Peoples and Empires in African History: Essays in Memory of Michael Crowder*, edited by J. F. Ade Ajayi and J. D. Y. Peel, 143–60. London: Longman, 1992.

Casely Hayford, J. E. *Correspondence Relating to the National Congress of British West Africa*. Accra: Gold Coast Government Press, 1920.

Casely Hayford, J. E. *Ethiopia Unbound: A Critical Edition*. Edited by Jeanne-Marie Jackson and Adwoa Opoku-Agyemang. Lansing: Michigan State University Press, 2024.

Casely Hayford, J. E. *Gold Coast Native Institutions: With Thoughts upon a Healthy Imperial Policy for the Gold Coast and Ashanti*. London: Sweet and Maxwell, 1903.

Casely Hayford, J. E. *The Truth about the West African Land Question*. London: C. M. Phillips, 1913.

Casely Hayford, J. E. *United West Africa*. London: F. T. Phillips, 1919.

Casely Hayford, J. E. *West African Leadership*. Edited by Magnus J. Sampson. London: Frank Cass, 1969.

Casely Hayford, J. E. *William Waddy Harris, the West African Reformer: The Man and His Message*. London: C. M. Phillips, 1915.

Chanock, Martin. *Law, Custom and Social Order*. London: Heinemann, 1998.

Coletu, Ebony. *Assembly Codes: The Logistics of Media*. Durham, NC: Duke University Press, 2021.

Coller, Ian. "African Liberalism in the Age of Empire? Hassuna D'Ghies and Liberal Constitutionalism in North Africa, 1822–1835." *Modern Intellectual History* 12.3 (2015): 529–53.

Colley, Linda. *The Gun, the Ship, and the Pen: Warfare, Constitutions, and the Making of the Modern World*. New York: Liveright, 2021.

Collini, Stefan. "The Idea of 'Character' in Victorian Political Thought." *Transactions of the Royal Historical Society* 35 (1985): 29–50.

Collis-Buthelezi, Victoria J. "Under the Aegis of Empire: Cape Town, Victorianism, and Early Twentieth-Century Black Thought." *Callaloo* 39.1 (2016): 115–32.

Constable, Marianne, Leti Volpp, and Bryan Wagner. Introduction to *Looking for Law in All the Wrong Places*. New York: Fordham University Press, 2019.

Cooper, Frederick. "Possibility and Constraint: African Independence in Historical Perspective." *Journal of African History* 49.2 (2008): 167–96.

Cormack, Bradin. *A Power to Do Justice: Jurisdiction, English Literature, and the Rise of Common Law, 1509–1625*. Chicago: University of Chicago Press, 2007.

Cover, Robert. "The Folktales of Justice: Tales of Jurisdiction." In *Narrative, Violence, and the Law: The Essays of Robert Cover*, edited by Martha Minnow, Michael Ryan, and Austin Sarat. Ann Arbor: University of Michigan Press, 1995.

Cromwell, Adelaide M. *An African Victorian Feminist: The Life and Times of Adelaide Smith Casely Hayford, 1848–1960*. New York: Routledge, 2004.

Culler, Jonathan. "Anderson and the Novel." *diacritics* 29.4 (1999): 20–39.

Danquah, J. B. *The Akan Doctrine of God: A Fragment of Gold Coast Ethics and Religion*. New York: Routledge, 2017. First published 1968.

Danquah, J. B. "The Historical Significance of the Bond 1844." *Transactions of the Historical Society of Ghana* 3.1 (1957): 3–29.

Daston, Lorraine, and Peter Galison. *Objectivity*. Princeton, NJ: Princeton University Press (Zone Books), 2010.

De, Rohit. "The Jurisprudence of Decolonization: The Postcolonial Career of D. N. Pritt and the Labor of Insurgent Lawyering." *Humanity* 14.1 (2023): 121–45.

De, Rohit. *A People's Constitution: The Everyday Life of Law in the Indian Republic*. Princeton, NJ: Princeton University Press, 2018.

Desai, Gaurav. *Subject to Colonialism: African Self-Fashioning and the Colonial Library*. Durham, NC: Duke University Press, 2001.

DiGiacomo, Mark. "The Assertion of Coevalness: African Literature and Modernist Studies" in *Modernism/Modernity* 24.2 (2017).

Diouf, Mamadou, and Jinny Prais. "'Casting the Badge of Inferiority Beneath Black People's Feet': Archiving and Reading the African Past, Present, and Future in World History." In *Global Intellectual History*, edited by Samuel Moyn and Andrew Sartori, 205–27. New York: Columbia University Press, 2013.

Du Bois, W.E.B. *Black Reconstruction: An Essay toward a History of the Part Which Black Folk Played in the Attempt to Reconstruct Democracy in America, 1860–1880*. New York: Harcourt, Brace, 1935.

Du Bois, W.E.B. Letter to Archie Casely-Hayford, October 25, 1930. https://credo.library.umass.edu/view/full/mums312-b185-i345.

Du Bois, W.E.B. *The Souls of Black Folk*. New York: Penguin, 1996. First published 1903.

Du Bois, W.E.B. "The Talented Tenth." In *The Negro Problem: A Series of Articles by Representative Negroes of To-day*, 33–75. New York: J. Pott, 1903.

Dworkin, Ronald. *Law's Empire*. Cambridge, MA: Belknap, 1986.

Earle, Jonathon L. "African Intellectual History and Historiography." *Oxford Research Encyclopedia of African History*, November 20, 2018. https://oxfordre.com/africanhistory/display/10.1093/acrefore/9780190277734.001.0001/acrefore-9780190277734-e-305.

Elias, Olawale T. *The Nature of African Customary Law*. Manchester: Manchester University Press, 1956.

Eliot, George. *Daniel Deronda*. Edited by Graham Handley. World's Classics ed. Oxford: Oxford University Press, 1984. First published 1876.

Falola, Toyin. *Nationalism and African Intellectuals*. Rochester, NY: University of Rochester Press, 2002.

Ferguson, George Ekem. *The Papers of George Ekem Ferguson: A Fanti Official of the Government of the Gold Coast, 1890–1897*. Edited by Kwame Arhin. African Social Research Documents vol. 7. Leiden: Afrika-Studiecentrum, 1974.

Fitzmaurice, Andrew. *King Leopold's Ghostwriter: The Creation of Persons and States in the Nineteenth Century*. Princeton, NJ: Princeton University Press, 2021.

Ford, Richard T. "Law's Territory (A History of Jurisdiction)." *Michigan Law Review* 97.4 (1999): 843–930.

Frank, Alex. "Casely-Hayford's Inherited Resistance." *Fader*, March 11, 2011. https://www.thefader.com/2011/03/11/feature-casely-hayfords-inherited-resistance.

Gebeye, Berihun Adugna. *A Theory of African Constitutionalism*. Oxford: Oxford University Press, 2021.

Gee, Sophie. "'Such Opinions Cannot Cohere': Swift's Inwardness." *Republics of Letters* 4.1 (2014): 1–13.

Gershoni, Yekutiel. "Common Goals, Different Ways: The UNIA and the NCBWA in West Africa—1920–1930." *Journal of Third World Studies* 18.2 (2001): 171–85.

Getachew, Adom. "The Problem of Liberal Empire Reconsidered." *small axe* 60 (2019): 167–77.

Getachew, Adom. *Worldmaking After Empire*. Princeton, NJ: Princeton University Press, 2019.

Gewirtz, Paul. "Narrative and Rhetoric in the Law." In *Law's Stories*. New Haven, CT: Yale University Press, 1996.

Gikandi, Simon. *Maps of Englishness*. New York: Columbia University Press, 1996.

Gikandi, Simon. Foreword to *Foundational African Writers: Peter Abrahams, Noni Jabavu, Sibusiso Nyembezi and Es'kia Mphahlele*, edited by Hein Willemse. Johannesburg: Wilts University Press, 2022.

Gocking, Roger. "British Justice and the Native Tribunals of the Southern Gold Coast Colony." *Journal of African History* 34 (1993): 93–113.

Goodlad, Lauren. "Moral Character." In *Historicism and the Human Sciences in Victorian Britain*, edited by Mark Bevir, 128–53. Cambridge: Cambridge University Press, 2017.

Gordon, Ruth. "Growing Constitutions." *University of Pennsylvania Journal of Constitutional Law* 1.3 (1999): 528–82.

Goyal, Yogita. "Africa and the Black Atlantic." *Research in African Literatures* 45.3 (2014): v–xxv.

Greenblatt, Stephen. *Renaissance Self-Fashioning: From More to Shakespeare*. 1980. Reprint, Chicago: University of Chicago Press, 2005.

Griffith, W. Branford. "Some Account of the Various Editions of the Gold Coast Ordinances." *Journal of the Royal African Society* 16.64 (1917): 326–35.

Gualtieri, Elena. "The Essay as Form: Virginia Woolf and the Literary Tradition." *Textual Practice* 12.1 (1998): 49–67.

Haliburton, G. M. "Mark Christian Hayford: A Non-Success Story." *Journal of Religion in Africa* 12.1 (1981): 20–37.

Higney, Robert. *Institutional Character: Collectivity, Individuality, and the Modernist Novel*. Charlottesville: University of Virginia Press, 2022.
Hogue, Arthur R. *Origins of the Common Law*. Bloomington: Indiana University Press, 1966.
Jackson, Jeanne-Marie. *The African Novel of Ideas: Philosophy and Individualism in the Age of Global Writing*. Princeton, NJ: Princeton University Press, 2021.
Jacobsohn, Gary Jeffrey. *Constitutional Identity*. Cambridge, MA: Harvard University Press, 2010.
Johnson, J. W. De Graft. *Towards Nationhood in West Africa: Thoughts of a Young Africa Addressed to Young Britain*. London: Routledge, 2014. First published 1928.
July, Robert. *The Origins of Modern African Thought*. London: Faber and Faber, 1968.
Kimble, David. *A Political History of Ghana: The Rise of Gold Coast Nationalism, 1850–1928*. Oxford: Clarendon, 1963.
Konadu, Kwasi. "Euro-African Commerce and Social Chaos: Akan Societies in the Nineteenth and Twentieth Centuries." *History in Africa* 39 (2009): 265–92.
Konadu, Kwasi. *Our Own Way in This Part of the World*. Durham, NC: Duke University Press, 2019.
Korang, Kwaku Larbi. *Writing Ghana, Imagining Africa*. Rochester, NY: Boydell and Brewer, 2004.
Kramnick, Jonathan. *Criticism and Truth: On Method in Literary Studies*. Chicago: University of Chicago Press, 2023.
Laumann, Dennis Heinz. "Compradore-in-Arms: The Fante Confederation Project (1868–1872)." *Ufahamu: A Journal of African Studies* 21.1–2 (1993): 120–36.
Lennon, Brian. "The Essay, in Theory." *Diacritics* 38.3 (2008): 71–92.
Levine, George. *Dying to Know: Scientific Epistemology and Narrative in Victorian England* Chicago: University of Chicago Press, 2002.
Limberg, Lennart. "The Economy of the Fante Confederation." *Transactions of the Historical Society of Ghana* 11 (1970): 83–103.
Lionnet, Françoise. "Cosmopolitan or Creole Lives? Globalized Oceans and Insular Identities." *Profession* (2011): 23–43.
Loughlin, Martin. "The Concept of Constituent Power." *European Journal of Political Theory* 13.2 (2014): 218–37.
Loughlin, Martin. "The Constitutional Imagination." *Modern Law Review* 78.1 (January 2015): 1–25.
Loughlin, Martin. "Constitutionalism: An Opium for the Lawyers." Interview by Kasia Krzyżanowska. *Review of Democracy* (podcast), March 15, 2023.
Mahama, John Dramani. *My First Coup d'Etat: And Other True Stories from the Lost Decades of Africa*. New York: Bloomsbury, 2012.
Mamdani, Mahmoud. *Define and Rule: Native as Political Identity*. Cambridge, MA: Harvard University Press, 2012.
Mantena, Karuna. *Alibis of Empire: Henry Maine and the Ends of Liberal Imperialism*. Princeton, NJ: Princeton University Press, 2010.
Matera, Marc. "Colonial Subjects: Black Intellectuals and the Development of Colonial Studies in Britain." in the *Journal of British Studies* 49.2 (2010): 288–418.
Mawani, Renisa. *Across Oceans of Law: The Komagata Maru and Jurisdiction in the Time of Empire*. Durham, NC: Duke University Press, 2018.

McConnell, Michael W. "The Forgotten Constitutional Moment." *Constitutional Commentary* 11.115 (1994).
McIlwain, Charles Howard. *Constitutionalism: Ancient and Modern.* Ithaca, NY: Cornell University Press, 1940.
Meyer, Birgit. "Going and Making Public: Pentecostalism as Public Religion in Ghana." In *Christianity and Public Culture in Africa*, edited by Henri Englund, 149–66. Athens: Ohio University Press, 2011.
Michelman, Frank I. "Constitutional Authorship by the People." *Notre Dame Law Review* 74.5 (1999): 1605–29.
Miescher, Stephan F. *Making Men in Ghana.* Bloomington: Indiana University Press, 2005.
Mignolo, Walter. *The Darker Side of Western Modernity: Global Futures, Decolonial Options.* Durham, NC: Duke University Press, 2011.
Moretti, Franco. "Conjectures on World Literature." *New Left Review* 2.1 (2000). https://newleftreview.org/issues/ii1/articles/franco-moretti-conjectures-on-world-literature.
Nagel, Thomas. *The View from Nowhere.* Oxford: Oxford University Press, 1989.
Newell, Stephanie. *Literary Culture in Colonial Ghana.* Bloomington: Indiana University Press, 2002.
Newell, Stephanie. *Newsprint Literature and Local Literary Creativity in West Africa, 1900s–1960s.* Woodbridge: Boydell and Brewer, 2023.
Nkrumah, Kwame. *Ghana: The Autobiography of Kwame Nkrumah.* New York: International Publishers, 1971.
Ofosu-Appiah, L. H. *Joseph Ephraim Casely Hayford: The Man of Vision and Faith.* Accra: Academy of Arts and Sciences, 1975.
Okonkwo, Rita. "Adelaide Casely Hayford: Cultural Nationalist and Feminist." *Phylon* 42.1 (1981): 41–51.
Okonkwo, Rita. *Heroes of West African Nationalism.* Enugu: Delta, 1985.
Okoth-Ogendo, H.W.O. *Constitutions without Constitutionalism: Reflections on an African Political Paradox.* New York: American Council of Learned Societies, 1988.
Omosini, Olufemi. "The Gold Coast Land Question 1894–1900: Some Issues Raised on West Africa's Economic Development." *International Journal of African Historical Studies* 5.3 (1972): 453–69.
Palen, Marc-William. *Pax Economica: Left Wing Visions of a Free Trade World.* Princeton, NJ: Princeton University Press, 2024.
Parker, John. *In My Time of Dying: A History of Death and the Dead in West Africa.* Princeton, NJ: Princeton University Press, 2021.
Parker, Kunal M. "Law 'In' and 'As' History: The Common Law in the American Polity, 1790–1900." *UC Irvine Law Review* 1.3 (2011): 587–609.
Pepitone, Ren. *Brotherhood of Barristers: A Cultural History of the British Legal Profession, 1840–1940.* Cambridge: Cambridge University Press, 2024.
Peterson, Derek R., Emma Hunter, and Stephanie Newell, eds. *African Print Cultures: Newspapers and their Publics in Modern Africa.* Ann Arbor: University of Michigan Press, 2016.
Pitkin, Hanna Fenichel. "The Idea of a Constitution." *Journal of Legal Education* 37.2 (1987): 167–69.

Plaatje, Solomon T. *Native Life in South Africa*. Johannesburg: Ravan Press, 1995. First published 1916.
Pocock, John. "Virtues, Rights, and Manners: A Model for Historians of Political Thought." *Political Theory* 9.3 (1981): 353–68.
Poovey, Mary. *A History of the Modern Fact: Problems of Knowledge in the Sciences of Wealth and Society*. Chicago: University of Chicago Press, 1998.
Prempeh, H. Kwasi. "Africa's 'Constitutionalism Revival': False Start or New Dawn?" *International Journal of Constitutional Law* 5.3 (July 2007): 469–506.
Priestley, Margaret. "Richard Brew: An Eighteenth-Century Trader at Anomabu." *Transactions of the Historical Society of Ghana* 4.1 (1959): 29–46.
Quayson, Ato. *Oxford Street, Accra*. Durham, NC: Duke University Press, 2014.
Rathbone, Richard. *Nkrumah and the Chiefs: Politics of Chieftancy in Ghana 1951–1960*. London: James Currey, 2000.
Ray, Donald I. "Ghana: Traditional Leadership and Rural Local Governance." In *Grassroots Governance?: Chiefs in Africa and the Afro-Caribbean*, edited by Donald I. Ray and P. S. Reddy, 83–122. Calgary: University of Calgary Press, 2003.
Reindorf, Carl Christian. *History of the Gold Coast and Asante, Based on Traditions and Historical Facts*. Basel: Reindorf, 1895.
Rorty, Richard. *Objectivity, Relativism, and Truth*. Cambridge: Cambridge University Press, 1991.
Rouse-Jones, Margaret D., and Esther M. Appiah. *Returned Exile: A Biography of George James Christian of Dominica and the Gold Coast, 1869–1940*. Kingston: University of the West Indies Press, 2016.
Samalin, Zachary. "Introduction: A Map the Size of the Empire." *Criticism* 61.4 (2019): 423–42.
Sarbah, John Mensah. *Fanti Customary Laws*. London: William Clowes and Son, 1904.
Sarbah, John Mensah. *Fanti National Constitution*. London: Frank Cass, 1968.
Sartori, Giovanni. "Constitutionalism: A Preliminary Discussion." *American Political Science Review* 56.4 (1962).
Scott, David. *Conscripts of Modernity*. Durham, NC: Duke University Press, 2004.
Sedley, Stephen. "Cloudy Horizon." *London Review of Books* 45.8 (2023). https://www.lrb.co.uk/the-paper/v45/n08/stephen-sedley/cloudy-horizon.
Shank, D. A. "The Prophet Harris: A Historiographical and Bibliographical Survey." *Journal of Religion in Africa* 14 (1983): 130–60.
Shumway, Rebecca. "Palavers and Treaty-Making in the British Acquisition of the Gold Coast Colony (West Africa)." In *Empire by Treaty: Negotiating European Expansion, 1600–1900*, edited by Saliha Belmessous, 161–85. New York: Oxford University Press, 2014.
Stark, Heidi K. "Nenabozho's Smart Berries: Rethinking Tribal Sovereignty and Accountability." *Michigan State University Law Review* 2 (2013): 339–54.
Stimson, Shannon C. "Constitutionalism and the Rule of Law." In the *Oxford Handbook of Political Theory*, edited by John S. Dryzek, Bonnie Honig, and Anne Phillips, 317–32. Oxford: Oxford University Press, 2008.
Sussman, Matthew. "Stylistic Virtue in Nineteenth-Century Criticism." *Victorian Studies* 56.2 (Winter 2014): 225–49.

Sussman, Matthew. *Stylistic Virtue and Victorian Fiction: Form, Ethics, and the Novel.* Cambridge: Cambridge University Press, 2021.

Taiwo, Olufemi. *How Colonialism Preempted Modernity in Africa.* Bloomington: University of Indiana Press, 2010.

Taylor, Charles. "Buffered and Porous Selves." *Immanent Frame*, September 2, 2008. https://tif.ssrc.org/2008/09/02/buffered-and-porous-selves/

Taylor, Charles. *A Secular Age.* Cambridge, MA: Harvard University Press, 2007.

Taylor, Christopher. *Empire of Neglect: The West Indies in the Wake of British Liberalism* Durham, NC: Duke University Press, 2018.

Tenkorang, S. "The Founding of Mfantsipim, 1905–1908." *Transactions of the Historical Society of Ghana* 15.2 (1974): 165–75.

Tenkorang, S. "John Mensah Sarbah, 1864–1910." *Transactions of the Historical Society of Ghana* 14.1 (June 1973): 65–78.

Tribe, Laurence H. "The Idea of the Constitution: A Metaphor-morphosis." *Journal of Legal Education* 170 (1987): 170–73.

Tully, James. *Strange Multiplicity: Constitutionalism in an Age of Diversity.* Cambridge: Cambridge University Press, 1995.

Valverde, Mariana. "Jurisdiction and Scale: Legal 'Technicalities' as Resources for Theory." *Social and Legal Studies* 18.2 (2009): 139–57.

Van Gyampo, Ransford Edward, and Emmanuel Graham. "Constitutionalism and Constitutional Hybridity in Ghana." *African Review* 6.2 (2014): 138–50.

Waldron, Jeremy. *The Dignity of Legislation.* Cambridge: Cambridge University Press, 1999.

Walters, Joseph Jeffrey. *Guanya Pau: A Story of an African Princess.* Edited by Gareth Griffiths and John Victor Singler. 1891. Peterborough, ON: Broadview, 2004.

Wenzel, Jennifer. "Zones of Occult Instability: The Birth of the Novel in Africa." *NOVEL* 54.3 (2021): 335–61.

Willemse, Hein, ed. *Foundational African Writers: Peter Abrahams, Noni Jabavu, Sibusiso Nyembezi and Es'kia Mphahlele.* Johannesburg: Wilts University Press, 2022.

Wiredu, Kwasi. "Towards Decolonizing African Philosophy and Religion." *African Studies Quarterly* 1.4 (1998): 17–46.

Yankah, Kwesi. *Speaking for the Chief: Okyeame and the Politics of Akan Royal Oratory.* Bloomington: Indiana University Press, 1995.

Younis, Musab. *On the Scale of the World: The Formation of Black Anticolonial Thought.* Oakland: University of California Press, 2022.

Zachernuk, Philip. *Colonial Subjects: An African Intelligentsia and Atlantic Ideas.* Charlottesville: University Press of Virginia, 2000.

INDEX

Note: J. E. Casely Hayford is referred to as "CH" in subentries of this index.

Aborigines' Rights Protection Society (ARPS), 2, 34, 37, 40, 42, 45, 68, 75, 82, 112–15, 131, 142, 143
accuracy. *See* facticity
Achimota College, 6, 24, 127, 141–42
Ackerman, Bruce, 84, 90, 95, 162n13
Adansi, 106
Addo-Fening, R., 126
Ado Literary Club, 22
Aeschylus, *Prometheus Bound*, 87
Aesop, 90
African Company of Merchants, 108
African intellectualism: CH and, 3–6, 8, 15–17, 20–24, 30–40, 83; Fante people and, 8–9, 26, 30–31, 36–37, 48, 52–53, 55, 59, 74, 79, 80, 87, 107, 120, 131, 136; on the Gold Coast, 30–40, 47–56, 58–59, 63, 99, 109, 119, 125, 130, 140; hard work as component of, 20–21; historical context of, 7. *See also* the elite
African Mail (newspaper), 59
African self-governance/self-determination/self-representation: within the British Empire, 3, 35–39, 41, 52–53, 55–58, 70, 79–80, 121, 125–27; CH and, 16, 123; and constitutionalism, 70–71, 74; Fante elite and, 34; Gold Coast and, 30, 33; Legislative Council and, 16, 17, 21, 34; NCBWA and, 68; political ideals of, 3
Agamben, Giorgio, 119
Agbodeka, Francis, 32, 87, 164n68
Aggrey, J.E.K., 142, 150n4
Akan people: British criticism of, 47; and constitutionalism, 72–73; cosmology of, 8; customs and traditions of, 11, 26, 41–44, 129, 136–37; as Ghana's meta-ethnicity, 5; kingship and stool succession of, 9, 158n33; land use by, 28, 112, 123
Amo, William, 45

Anderson, Amanda, 44–45, 47
Anderson, Benedict, 162n10
Anishinaabe people, 71
anona (parrot) clan, 11
Appiah, Esther M., 169n45
Appiah, Kwame Anthony, 136
Arhin, Kwame, 14, 152n42, 158n33
Aristotle, 27, 72, 94, 138, 162n13, 165n86
Armah, Ayi Kwei, 15
Arnold, Matthew, 138
ARPS. *See* Aborigines' Rights Protection Society
Arvind, T. T., 75, 79
Asante people: British relations with, 32, 107, 111; characteristics and customs of, 26, 44, 48–49, 51, 52, 91, 117, 158n33, 169n45; Fante relations with, 32, 39, 41, 58, 65, 108, 111; travel guide to region of, 37
Ateko, Kwao Brakatu, 6, 151n16
Attoh Ahuma, S.R.B., 21, 30, 31, 35, 39, 45–48, 50, 55–56, 74, 168n26; *The Gold Coast Nation and National Consciousness*, 45; *Memoirs of West African Celebrities*, 45–46
Axim, 82, 120, 146, 147, 150n14

Bakhtin, Mikhail, 38, 88
balance: as constitutional ideal, 2, 69, 89–90, 96, 98; *Ethiopia Unbound* and, 90–91; goldilocks method and, 90–91. *See also* moderation
Bannerman, Charles, 63
Belfield, H. Conway, 115, 168n36
Belgian Congo, 131–33
Bennett, Luke, 117
Benton, Lauren, 9, 119–20
Berlin Conference (1884), 97
Big Six (political party leaders), 109
Black intellectualism, 4, 6–7, 21. *See also* African intellectualism

[183]

Black radicalism, 13
Black's Law Dictionary, 129
Black Star Line Organization, 13
Blavatsky, Helena, 6, 83
Blyden, Edward Wilmot, 5, 61, 73, 86, 91
Bolingbroke, Henry St. John, 74
Bond of 1844, 27–28, 107–12, 114–17, 120–23, 126, 128, 140
Brew, James Hutton, 75, 88
Brew, Richard, 8
Britain/British Empire: abolition of slavery within, 108; African criticisms of, 114–15, 121, 127; African grasp of the truth/facts of, 26, 30–31, 40; and African land use, 2, 28, 31, 34, 35, 82–83, 112–13, 121, 123, 131–35, 168n26, 169n38; and African self-governance, 3, 35–39, 41, 52–53, 55–58, 70, 79–80, 121, 125–27; Asante relations with, 32, 107, 111; CH and imperial politics of, 1, 5, 6, 11–18, 30–31, 37–38, 52–55, 115, 136, 140, 169n38; CH's and other Africans' law training in, 2, 22–23, 32, 155n86, 156n87; CH's criticisms of, 26, 30–31, 37–38, 40, 51–53, 55, 172n109; colonization of the Gold Coast by, 125–26, 170n72; and constitutionalism, 71, 74, 75, 80; entry to the Gold Coast, 34–35, 108; and indirect rule, 34, 35, 47, 114, 124, 126, 127, 129, 131, 138; and international law, 9; and jurisdiction in the Gold Coast, 27–28, 32, 107–12, 114–17; liberal-constitutional institutions of, 33; and Sierra Leone, 168n34
British South Africa Company, 167n10
Brizuela-Garcia, Esperanza, 157n10
Building Africa (exhibition), 141
Burbank, Jane, 151n19

Cape Coast Literary and Social Club, 24, 83, 88, 149n3
Casely Hayford, Adelaide (née Smith), 13, 58, 82, 146, 163n40
Casely Hayford, Archie, 6, 13, 25, 58, 83, 91, 96, 145, 150n4, 154n67
Casely-Hayford, Augustus (Gus), 9–10, 73, 77, 87, 123, 146, 151n27
Casely-Hayford, Beattie, 145
Casely-Hayford, Charlie, 146
Casely Hayford, Gladys, 58

Casely Hayford, J. E.: African cultural identity of, 15; and African politics, 2–3, 5–6, 10, 12–13, 15–16, 23, 30–31, 34–35, 39, 48–49, 52–55, 58, 79, 95, 98–99, 101–2, 105–6, 115, 119, 121–40, 143–44 (*see also* imperial sympathies and politics of, *this entry*); Attoh Ahuma's commentary on, 45–46; and Bond of 1844, 115, 117, 120, 122–23; and character, 57–58, 96–98, 129–30; and Christianity, 51, 99–103; clothing of, 57–58, 63; cosmopolitanism of, 6, 33, 58, 89, 122, 125; criticisms of, 10, 14–15, 79; cultural presentation and advocacy of, 14; death and burial of, 24, 96, 150n14; descendants of, 145–46 (*see also* family lineage of, *this entry*); and education, 16, 82, 83, 141–42; elite status of, 3, 8, 15, 17–18, 58, 86, 145, 167n7; fame and reputation of, 3–4, 7, 69, 82–83, 93, 96–99, 149n3 (*see also* legacy of, *this entry*); family lineage of, 8, 10–11, 27, 75–77 (*see also* descendants of, *this entry*); geographies significant in the life of, 5–6; historical understanding evinced by, 31, 36, 39–43, 48–50, 54, 73–75, 81–82, 125–29; honors received by, 13, 24; imperial sympathies and politics of, 1, 5, 6, 11–18, 30–31, 37–38, 52–55, 115, 136, 140, 169n38 (*see also* and African politics, *this entry*); income and finances of, 8–9, 154n67, 155n76; intellectualism of, 3–6, 8, 15–17, 20–24, 30–40, 83; and land use issues, 112–15, 131–35, 169n38; and language, 6, 10–11, 58; and law, 9–11; legacy of, 28–29, 141–47 (*see also* fame and reputation of, *this entry*); legal education of, 2, 22–23, 141, 170n59; legal practice of, 82, 154n67; life advice given by, 25, 91; name of, 6; as newspaper owner/editor, 21, 82, 99, 136, 154n67; and objectivity, 44–45, 61–67; past and present allegiances in the constitutionalism of, 73–78; peers and predecessors of, 3, 149n2; personal tragedies of, 66–67, 83–84; practical and institutional concerns of, 20–23, 39–40, 63, 118–19, 150n15; scholarship on, 3, 7,

12–15, 142–43, 145, 153n45, 154n55; self-fashioning of, 1–2, 8–9, 20, 23–24, 58, 62; significant contributions of, 1–3, 6; and spirituality, 8, 101–2; wives of, 13, 58, 67, 82–83, 150n14, 163n40
Casely Hayford, J. E., writings of: "The Atavistic Tendencies of the Age," 5–6, 128; characteristics of, 7, 12, 16; *Ethiopia Unbound*, 1, 5, 8, 10–11, 20–22, 27, 69–71, 73, 78, 82–94, 96–99, 102–4, 118–19, 123, 130, 138–39, 142–43, 146, 149n1, 165n104; *Gold Coast Land Tenure and the Forest Bill, 1911*, 168n27; *Gold Coast Native Institutions*, 2, 10, 16, 20, 26, 30–32, 34–35, 37, 39–46, 48–49, 51–52, 56, 63–64, 75, 82, 88, 99–100, 115, 117, 130, 143; and land use issues, 168n27; "Progress of the Gold Coast Native," 59; speeches to NCBWA, 16, 68–70, 105; "To a Young Friend," 24–25; *The Truth about the West African Land Question*, 2, 28, 98, 106, 112–13, 115, 128–40, 172n109; *United West Africa*, 24; *William Waddy Harris, the West African Reformer*, 27, 98–104
Casely-Hayford, Joe, 29, 57, 146
Casely-Hayford, Louis, 145–46
Casely-Hayford, Margaret, 146
Casely Hayford, Muriel, 83
Casely-Hayford, Sydney, 146
Casely-Hayford fashion design house, 29, 146
Center for Democratic Development, 144
Chanock, Martin, 124
character: Akan honor culture and, 136–38; Attoh Ahuma and, 45; CH and, 57–58, 96–98, 129–30; constitutionalism linked to, 27, 69–70, 84–98, 103; constitution/presentation of, through writing, 1, 24; of the Educated Native, 56–64; education and the building of, 53–54; *Ethiopia Unbound* and, 83–94, 96–98; facticity/objectivity linked to, 26–27, 41–42, 45; Fante, 11; institutional, 23–24; leadership linked to, 20; novels as means of conveying, 27; objectivity in relation to, 59; of the okyeame, 11; of the *opanyin*, 137–38; political role of, 19–20; racialized conceptions of, 54; Victorian notion of, 53–54; *William Waddy Harris* and, 98–104. *See also* discernment and distinction; morality; self; virtue
charismatic leadership, 27, 84–87, 95, 98, 100, 102, 104
Christian, George James, 169n45
Christianity: CH and, 51, 99–103; conversions to, 100–101, 103; in Ghana, 104; Gold Coast intelligentsia and, 48, 99–100; Harris's impact on African reception of, 100; law in relation to, 9; muscular, 20; Pentecostal, 104. *See also* spirituality
citation, CH's practice of, 130–38
Claridge, William Walton, 110, 111
Clifford, Hugh, 138
Coleridge-Taylor, Samuel, 73, 86
Coletu, Ebony, 167n4
Coller, Ian, 80
Colley, Linda, 69, 74, 83
Collini, Stefan, 54–55
Collis-Buthelezi, Victoria J., 36
colonialism. *See* Britain/British Empire; politics: anticolonial; postcolonialism
common law: CH and, 2; customary law in relation to, 126; imperial law and, 9; logic of, 80–81; and precedent, 17, 75
Concessions Ordinance (1900), 113
Congo, 131–33
constitutionalism: African, 81–82; African self-governance and, 70–71, 74; ancient and modern, 72–73; and authorship of constitutions, 94–95; balance as ideal of, 2, 69, 89–90, 96, 98; Britain and, 71, 74, 75, 80; CH and, 68–82, 89, 93–94, 96–97, 104, 143; character linked to, 27, 69–70, 84–98, 103; constituent power and, 85; defining, 71–72; *Ethiopia Unbound* and, 27, 69–71, 84–94; Fante culture and, 27, 70, 74–82, 87–88; as form of being and action, 68–69; liberal, 3, 33, 102; and modernity, 72–73, 85; NCBWA and, 75–78, 94; Nkrumah's criticism of, 166n122; novels as means of presenting, 69–70, 78, 82–84, 88–90, 92; postcolonialism and, 81, 92, 166n122; restraint as ideal of, 2, 69, 84–85, 88, 89, 92, 98; rule privileged over rulers

constitutionalism (*continued*)
in, 84–85, 93–94; scholarship on, 72;
as spiritual calling, 97–98, 100; and
text, 74, 80, 83
constraint, moral, 54–55. *See also* moderation; restraint
Cooper, Frederick, 35, 151n19
Cormack, Bradin, 106, 118, 119
cosmopolitanism, 6, 33, 58, 89, 92, 122, 125, 137, 142, 170n70
Coventry University, England, 146
Cover, Robert, 8
Creole identity, 125, 170n70
Crisis (journal), 5
Cromwell, Adelaide M., 83, 146
Crummell, Alexander, 50
Cugoano, Ottobah, 45
Culler, Jonathan, 162n10
culture: CH and, 122, 125, 127–29; fixed vs. dynamic quality of, 124–25; jurisdiction as means of shaping, 119–20, 122

Danquah, J. B., 97, 109–11, 114–16, 137, 138–39, 167n13; *The Akan Doctrine of God: A Fragment of Gold Coast Ethics and Religion*, 109, 137; *Akan Laws and Customs and Akim Abuakwa Constitution*, 109
Daston, Lorraine, 47, 62–64
De, Rohit, 64
decolonization, 14, 17, 33, 36, 51
democracy, 85
Derrida, Jacques, 119
Desai, Gaurav, 157n21
Diouf, Mamadou, 4, 49
discernment and distinction, 28, 105, 112–18, 121, 139–40
Dɔnkɔ, Kofi, 153n45
double-consciousness, 61, 160n116
Drah, F. K., 32–33
Du Bois, W.E.B., 4–5, 21, 49–51, 61–62, 73, 86, 153n49, 160n116; *Black Reconstruction*, 50; *The Souls of Black Folk*, 4, 49–50, 91
Dunbar, Paul Laurence, 73, 86
Dutch. *See* Netherlands
Dworkin, Ronald, 94

Earle, Jonathon, 3
economic structuralism, 135–37

Educated Native, 30–31, 52, 56–64, 67, 101, 122, 133
education: and character building, 53–54; CH's interest and investment in, 16, 82, 83, 141–42; definition of, 57; Fante people and, 40, 53; in Ghana, 141; ideal, as presented in *Ethiopia Unbound*, 89, 92. *See also* Educated Native
Egypt, 70
Elias, T. Olawale, 162n22
Eliot, George, 44–46, 51
the elite: of African Americans, 21; CH and, 3, 8, 15, 17–18, 58, 86, 145, 167n7; of the Fante, 9; of Ghana, 14; of the Gold Coast, 11, 20. *See also* African intellectualism
Eminsang, George, 42
English language, 57–58, 160n110
Ethiopia, 141

facticity: Africans' purported grasp of, 26–27, 30–31, 40, 44, 51–52; character linked to, 26–27, 41–42, 45; CH's valorization of, 2, 27, 40–42; historians and, 50–51; ideal of, 40, 43, 60; spirituality in relation to, 101. *See also* objectivity; rationality/reasoning
Fanon, Frantz, 15, 38
Fante Confederation, 27, 30–33, 35–36, 38–40, 42–43, 45, 48, 54, 56, 60, 70, 75–77, 79, 83, 85, 87–88, 156n6, 157n32, 164n68
Fante National Education Fund, 82, 142
Fante people and culture: ancient Greeks compared to, 20, 73, 87, 138–39; Asante relations with, 32, 39, 41, 58, 65, 108, 111; and British jurisdiction, 28, 107–12, 114–17; CH on the characteristics of, 58, 63; CH's lineage and, 8, 10–11, 27; and constitutionalism, 27, 70, 74–82, 87–88; discernment practiced by, 118, 140; ideals of, 152n42; importance of language, text, and speech in, 10–11, 80–82, 87, 110–12; intelligentsia of, 8–9, 26, 30–31, 36–37, 48, 52–53, 55, 59, 74, 79, 80, 87, 107, 120, 131, 136; language of, 58, 142, 160n113; leadership of, 34, 51, 79, 111, 114–15, 140; national character and

political role of, 5–6, 47, 122; prophetic powers imputed to, 8, 49–51; relationship of elite of, to the British elite, 9. *See also* Gold Coast
Ferguson, George Ekem, 14
Ferris, William Henry, 4, 49
First Anglo-Asante War (1823–1831), 107
First Conference of Africans of British West Africa (Accra, 1920), 68
First Universal Race Congress (1911), 4
Fitzmaurice, Andrew, 14, 25
Fomena, 106–7
Ford, Lisa, 9
Ford, Richard T., 122–23
Forest Bill (1911), 82, 112, 140, 168n27
Forster, E. M., *Howards End*, 143
Foucault, Michel, 119
Fourah Bay College, Sierra Leone, 5
Freemasonry, 151n16

Ga language, 142
Galison, Peter, 47, 62–64
Gallagher, Julia, 141
Gambia, 68, 119
Gandhi, Mohandas, 143
Garvey, Marcus, 12–13, 70, 153n49
Gebeye, Berihun Adugna, 81–82
George V, King of the United Kingdom, 76, 78
Getachew, Adom, 36, 150n5
Gewirtz, Paul, 17
Ghana: Akan meta-ethnicity of, 5; architecture and politics in, 141; Christianity in, 104; constitution of, 166n122; Danquah's role in, 97, 115–16, 167n13; education in, 141; the elite of, 14; independence of, 3, 34, 104, 109, 150n4; leadership in, 28; post-independence history of, 143–46. *See also* Gold Coast; Nkrumah, Kwame
Ghana Arts Council, 145
Ghana Broadcasting Corporation, 145
Ghana National Dance Ensemble, 145
Ghartey IV, King, (Robert Johnson Ghartey), 32, 37, 68, 70, 75, 80, 87, 164n68; *Guide to Coomassie*, 37
Gibson, S. J., 114
Gikandi, Simon, 35–36, 77
Gilroy, Paul, 36
global intellectualism, 6

Globe theater, London, 146
Gocking, Roger, 126, 171n79
Gold Coast: African Americans' repatriation to, 13; CH on history and culture of, 26, 118–19; Christianity and, 48, 99–100; colonial status of, 34–35, 108, 125–26, 171n72; and constitutionalism, 75; the elite of, 11; intellectual culture of, 30–40, 47–56, 58–59, 63, 99, 109, 119, 125, 130, 140; legal culture in, 9–11, 16–18, 20, 32–34, 120, 155n76; map of, xiv; spiritual practice in, 66–67. *See also* Fante people and culture; Ghana
Gold Coast Echo (newspaper), 21, 38. See also *Western Echo*
Gold Coast Leader (newspaper), 5, 21, 49, 52, 59–62, 82, 117, 128, 136, 154n67
Gold Coast Methodist Times (newspaper), 35, 37, 45, 46, 51, 74, 80, 121, 168n26
Gold Coast Nation (newspaper), 11, 17–18, 59, 99, 114, 127, 140, 149n3, 169n36
Gold Coast Rifle Volunteer Corps, 32
Gold Coast Youth Conference, 109
goldilocks method, 90–91, 93
Gone Fante movement, 5, 76, 122
Goodlad, Lauren, 53–54
Gordon, Ruth, 81
Goyal, Yogita, 36
Greek culture, 20, 73, 87, 138–39
Greenblatt, Stephen, 8–9
Griffith, William Brandford, 38, 125–26, 170n72
Guggisberg, Gordon, 24, 34, 126–27

Harris, William Wadé, 98–104
Hayford, James (Kwamina Afua), 10
Hayford, Joseph de Graft, 9, 75, 77
Hayford, Mark C., 4, 59, 150n11
Hazzledine, G. D., 134, 140
Hegel, G.W.F., 39, 54
Higney, Robert, 23–24
Hogue, Arthur R., 80
Holt, John, 131
Homer, *Odyssey*, 20
Horton, James Africanus Beale, 31, 40, 149n2, 160n115
Hut Tax War (Sierra Leone, 1898), 168n34
Hutton-Mills, Thomas, 15, 68, 70, 105

India, 70
Inner Temple, London, England, 2, 22–23, 109, 120, 141, 155n86, 156n87, 170n59
institutional character, 23–24
intellectualism. *See* African intellectualism; Black intellectualism; the elite; global intellectualism
International Conference on the Negro (Tuskegee Institute, 1912), 4, 59
Ivory Coast, 100

Jacobsohn, Gary Jeffrey, 81
James, C.L.R., 7, 36
Johnson, J. W. De Graft, 32
Johnson, Samuel, 149n2
jurisdiction, 2, 27–28; Bond of 1844 and, 107–12, 114–17, 120, 126; CH on, 113, 115, 118–19, 123; as conceptual frame in CH's work, 116, 121–22; criminal vs. civil, 107–8, 115, 121–22, 126, 171n79; culture-shaping function of, 119–20; and law, 116–20; moral aspect of, 28, 116–17, 126, 130–38; organic vs. synthetic, 122–23; and the relationship of local and wider perspectives in politics, 106, 115, 117–18, 120, 122
jury trials, 117, 169n45

Kant, Immanuel, 54, 102, 138
Kimble, David, 157n10
Kipling, Rudyard, 12
Konadu, Kwasi, 108, 153n45
Korang, Kwaku Larbi, 9, 14, 23, 30, 33, 62, 107, 167n7
Kramnick, Jonathan, 134–35

Lands Bill (1897), 31, 34, 37, 40, 112–14, 168n26, 168n34
land use, British-African conflict over, 2, 28, 31, 34, 35, 82–83, 112–13, 121, 123, 131–35, 168nn26 and 27, 169n38
language: African debates over, 6; Akuapem, 160n113; CH and, 6, 10–11, 58; English, 57–58, 160n110; Fante, 58, 142, 160n113; Ga, 142; instruction in, 142; Twi, 137, 142. *See also* text and speech
Laumann, Dennis, 32

law: anticolonial, 27; British imperialism and, 9; CH and, 9–11; Christianity in relation to, 9; as conceptual foundation of CH's thought, 1, 7–9, 16–17, 24–25, 65–67, 91–92; critiques of, 17; and foundationalism, 55–56; on the Gold Coast, 9–11, 16–18, 20, 32–34, 112, 155n76; as instrument and source of rationality, 2, 8–9, 80, 91–92, 94; intellectual approach to, 17; jurisdiction and, 116–20; liberal conceptions of, 19; modernity linked to, 9; okyeames and, 10. *See also* common law
Layard, Antonia, 117
leadership: Black, 86–87; CH and, 1–2, 5, 7–8, 15–17, 20–21, 27, 85, 90, 99, 145; character linked to, 20, 85–86; charismatic, 27, 84–87, 95, 98, 100, 102, 104; constitutionalism and, 27; Fante, 34, 51, 79, 111, 114–15, 140; in modern Africa, 1, 5, 7, 15–17, 20, 90; prophetic, 50–51; traits and skills of, 2, 8, 20, 26, 90, 91, 116, 140
legal pluralism, 28
Legislative Council (Gold Coast): and African language education, 6; and African self-governance, 16, 17, 21, 34, 68; CH's career on, 2, 5, 17, 20, 94, 104; CH's critiques of, 37; and civil service salaries, 8; and land jurisdiction, 132–33
Lennon, Brian, 102
Leopold II, King of Belgium, 131
Levine, George, 47, 51–53
liberal conservatism, 74
liberal-constitutionalism, 3, 33, 102
liberalism: Africans and, 80–81, 99; and the law, 19; Morel and, 131–33; in Victorian culture, 53, 55
Liberia, 5, 78, 100, 153n49
Limberg, Lennart, 32, 156n6
Lionnet, Françoise, 125, 170n70
literacy, 57
literature. *See* novels
Lobengula, King of the Ndebele, 167n10
Locke, John, 19
Loughlin, Martin, 71, 85

Macaulay, Herbert, 78
Machiavelli, Niccolò, 19
Maclean, George, 107, 111

Mac Síthigh, Daithí, 75, 79
Magna Carta, 75
Maine, Henry James Sumner, 124
Malta, 70
Mamdani, Mahmoud, 124–26
Mandela, Nelson, 92
Manful, Kuukuwa, 141
Mankessim Constitution, 39, 87
Markham, Edwin, 130
Mawani, Renisa, 116
McIlwain, Charles, 72, 74
Mfantsipim School, 141–42
Michelman, Frank, 94–95
Miescher, Stephan, 137
Mignolo, Walter, 51
Mill, John Stuart, 53
moderation, 69, 96, 165n86. *See also* balance; constraint, moral; goldilocks method; restraint
modernity: African polities and, 130; African spirituality and, 102; Bond of 1844 and, 108, 109, 114–15, 140; CH and, 1, 7, 21, 23, 102; constitutionalism and, 72–73, 85; law linked to, 9; political, 3, 18–19, 21, 33, 38
Mofolo, Thomas, 38
morality: Akan honor culture and, 136–38; citation and, 130–38; constraint as component of, 54–55; distinction making and jurisdiction as components of, 28, 116–17, 126, 130–38; objectivity in relation to, 44, 47, 55. *See also* character; discernment and distinction; virtue
moral jurisdiction, 28
Morel, E. D., 59–60, 130–35, 169n36, 171n86
Moretti, Franco, 79
muscular Christianity, 20

Nagel, Thomas, 27, 41
Nana Amonoo V of Anomabo, 70
National Congress of British West Africa (NCBWA): CH and, 2, 3, 75–78, 94, 98–99, 104–5; and constitutionalism, 75–78, 94; criticisms of, 152n45; demise of, 104; first Conference (Accra, 1920), 68; founding of, 2, 15, 99; fourth Conference (Lagos, 1929), 24; second Conference (Freetown, 1923), 105; third Conference (Bathurst, Gambia, 1925), 16
nationalism, 105, 116, 121, 124, 147
Native Jurisdiction Ordinance (1883), 126, 128–29, 171n74
Natives' Land Act (South Africa, 1913), 142
nativism, 124–25
NCBWA. *See* National Congress of British West Africa
Negro World (newspaper), 153n49
Netherlands, 32, 39, 42, 108
Newell, Stephanie, 7, 57, 160n110
Nigeria, 68, 78, 113–14, 131, 134
Nigerian Daily Telegraph (newspaper), 96
Nkrumah, Kwame, 3, 12, 92, 97, 104, 115, 143–44, 145, 150n4, 152n45, 166n122; Midnight Speech, 15, 150n4
nongovernmental organizations, 144
novels: character as feature of, 27, 69; CH's *Ethiopian Unbound* as first among English-language African, 1, 2, 69; and constitutionalism, 69–70, 78, 82–84, 88–90, 92; and nationhood, 162n10

objectivity: as African virtue, 30–31, 44, 63; CH and, 44–45, 61–67, 131; character in relation to, 59; criticisms of, 44; ideal of, 47, 51, 62; morality in relation to, 44, 47, 55; performance of, 64–67; in politics, 26–27; the self and, 61–64; situated, 27, 30, 41. *See also* facticity; rationality/reasoning
OccupyGhana, 146
Ofosu-Appiah, L. H., 97, 154n55, 165n104
Okoth-Ogendo, H.W.O., 89, 164n77
okyeames (spokesmen), 10–11, 152n36
Oluwa, Chief of Lagos, Nigeria, 78
opanyin (elder, figure of authority, gentleman), 137–38

palavers, 111
Palen, Marc-William, 136, 172n109
Pan-African Conference (1905), 91
Pan-Africanism: CH's contribution to, 3–4, 61, 122; CH's politics vs., 7, 12, 16; first Congress (Paris, 1919), 24, 91; NCBWA and, 104
Parker, Kunal, 55–56
Pater, Walter, 138

Patton, Cornelius H., 59
Pepitone, Ren, 155n86
Peterhouse, Cambridge, England, 2
Pinanko, F. A., 150n11
Pinnock, Beatrice, 67, 83, 150n14
Pitkin, Hanna, 84, 90, 95
Plaatje, Sol, 142
Pocock, John, 19–20, 25
politics: African, 2–3, 5–6, 10, 12–13, 15–16, 23, 32–36, 39, 48–49, 52–56, 58, 79, 95, 98–99, 101–2, 105–12, 115, 117, 119–40, 143–44; anticolonial, 3, 26–27, 30–31, 35–36, 117–18; character/virtue and, 19–20; objectivity/facticity as ideal in, 26–27; practical and institutional concerns of, 20–23; pro-imperial, 1, 5, 6, 11–18, 26–27, 30–31, 35, 52–56, 115, 136, 140; relationship of local and wider perspectives in, 106, 117–18, 120, 122; spirituality and, 97–104. *See also* African self-governance/self-determination/self-representation
Poovey, Mary, 43, 45
Portugal, 108
positivism, 40
postcolonialism: CH as object of critique in, 17, 27; and constitutionalism, 81, 92, 166n122; and the imperial presidency, 143–44; and jurisdiction in the Gold Coast, 107; in scholarship, 7, 28, 35–36
Prais, Jinny, 4, 49
precedent, in legal and political matters, 17, 26, 65, 74–75
Prempeh, H. Kwasi, 81, 104, 143, 144, 166n122
Prempeh I, King of the Asante, 127
Proctor, Adelaide Anne, 46
Provincial Council of Chiefs, 34

race: character in relation to, 54; double-consciousness and, 61; and economic critique, 136; global consciousness of, 4–6, 105–6, 119; and self-criticism, 60
Rancière, Jacques, 119
Rathbone, Richard, 143
rationality/reasoning: as African trait, 8, 52, 81; CH's advocacy and use of, 2, 6, 14, 16, 40–41, 65, 89–92, 96, 102, 112–14, 118–19; citational practices as instance of, 130–38; goldilocks method of, 90–91, 93; law as instrument and source of, 2, 8–9, 80, 91–92, 94; as leadership trait, 90. *See also* facticity; objectivity
Ray, Donald I., 171n74
Reindorf, Carl Christian, 106, 149n2, 157n10
restraint: as constitutional ideal, 2, 84–85, 88, 89, 92, 98; *Ethiopia Unbound* and, 89; as Fante virtue, 81; as leadership trait, 91. *See also* constraint, moral
Rhodes, Cecil, 167n10
Rhodesia, 167n10
Riehl, Wilhelm, 44
Rorty, Richard, 47
Rouse-Jones, Margaret D., 169n45
Royal Trading Company, 108
Rudd Concession (1888), 167n10
Ruskin, John, 138, 139

Samalin, Zachary, 143
Sampson, Magnus J., 118
Sarbah, John Mensah, 10, 18, 30, 31, 38, 42, 44, 51, 55–57, 61, 80, 83, 109, 142, 149n2, 157n10; *Fanti Customary Laws*, 16, 31, 42–45, 57, 64, 78; *Fanti National Constitution*, 78, 88
Schmitt, Carl, 85
Scott, David, 7, 30, 33
Scramble for Africa, 97
Sedley, Stephen, 71
Seeley, John Robert, 18
Sekyi, Kobina, 34
self: CH and, 8–9, 20, 23–24, 58, 62; constitutionalism and, 69–70; constitution/presentation of, through writing, 1–2, 64–65; objective perception of, 61–64. *See also* character
self-determination. *See* African self-governance/self-determination/self-representation
Shakespeare, William, 7, 90
Shank, David, 100, 103
Shelley, Percy Bysshe, *Prometheus Unbound*, 87
Shumway, Rebecca, 110–11, 115

Sierra Leone, 5, 13, 58, 68, 82, 91, 98, 113, 119, 168n34, 170n72
Skinner, Quentin, 25
Smith, Adelaide. *See* Casely Hayford, Adelaide
South Africa, 38, 77, 141, 142, 168n34, 169n36
speech. *See* text and speech
spirituality: CH and, 8, 101–2; disenchantment of Western culture with, 102; facticity in relation to, 101; Gold Coast practices of, 66–67; leadership and, 87; and modernity, 102; politics and, 97–104. *See also* Christianity
stare decisis, 75
Stark, Heidi Kiiwetinepinesiik, 71
Stimson, Shannon, 164n77
Sussman, Matthew, 138–39

Taiwo, Olufemi, 39, 72, 76, 79, 85–86, 103, 116
talented tenth, 21
Taylor, Charles, 102
Taylor, Chris, 36, 37
Tenkorang, S., 34
Tennyson, Alfred, Lord, 51, 53
text and speech: analysis and critique of, 3, 7; Bond of 1844 and, 109–12; CH's valorization of, 73; constitutionalism and, 74, 80, 83; importance of, in Gold Coast/Ghanaian culture, 2, 10–11, 14, 73–74, 80–82, 87, 109–12; self-presentation in, 1–2, 64–65. *See also* language
theosophy, 6, 83, 151n16
Third Anglo-Asante War (1873–1874), 170n72
Times of West Africa (newspaper), 109
Tribe, Laurence, 88, 95
Tully, James, 72
Tuskegee Institute, 21, 59
Twi language, 137, 142

UNIA. *See* Universal Negro Improvement Association
United Gold Coast Convention Party, 109
Universal Negro Improvement Association (UNIA), 13, 70, 153n49
University College London, 109
University of Ghana, 143, 167n13
utilitarianism, 138, 139

V&A East museum, London, 146
Valverde, Mariana, 116
Victoria, Queen of the United Kingdom, 35, 107
Victorian culture, 6, 23, 31, 36, 44–45, 47, 51, 53
virtue: Akan culture and, 137; Aristotelian ethics based on, 138–39; CH and, 20, 139; law and, 18–20; stylistic, 138–39. *See also* character; morality
Volta River Authority, 145

Waldron, Jeremy, 17, 18
Walters, Joseph Jeffrey, *Guanya Pau*, 149n1
Washington, Booker T., 4–5, 21, 59, 73, 86
Weber, Max, 85, 86, 87, 95
Wedgwood, Josiah, 132, 133, 135
Wenzel, Jennifer, 38
Wesleyan Boys High School, 142
West African Herald (newspaper), 63
West African Mail (magazine), 131, 132, 134, 139–40
West Africa Times (newspaper), 109
Western Echo (newspaper), 63. See also *Gold Coast Echo*
Wheatley, Phillis, 45
William Clowes and Sons, 42
Wiredu, Kwasi, 8, 151n24

Yankah, Kwesi, *Speaking for the Chief*, 10
Younis, Musab, 135–37, 150n5

Zachernuk, Philip S., 33

A NOTE ON THE TYPE

———◆———

THIS BOOK has been composed in Miller, a Scotch Roman typeface designed by Matthew Carter and first released by Font Bureau in 1997. It resembles Monticello, the typeface developed for The Papers of Thomas Jefferson in the 1940s by C. H. Griffith and P. J. Conkwright and reinterpreted in digital form by Carter in 2003.

Pleasant Jefferson ("P. J.") Conkwright (1905–1986) was Typographer at Princeton University Press from 1939 to 1970. He was an acclaimed book designer and AIGA Medalist.

The ornament used throughout this book was designed by Pierre Simon Fournier (1712–1768) and was a favorite of Conkwright's, used in his design of the *Princeton University Library Chronicle*.

GPSR Authorized Representative: Easy Access System Europe - Mustamäe tee
50, 10621 Tallinn, Estonia, gpsr.requests@easproject.com

www.ingramcontent.com/pod-product-compliance
Lightning Source LLC
Chambersburg PA
CBHW020924230426
43666CB00008B/1555